The Being of Analogy

New Metaphysics

Series Editors: Graham Harman and Bruno Latour

The world is due for a resurgence of original speculative metaphysics. The New Metaphysics series aims to provide a safe house for such thinking amidst the demoralizing caution and prudence of professional academic philosophy. We do not aim to bridge the analytic-continental divide, since we are equally impatient with nail-filing analytic critique and the continental reverence for dusty textual monuments. We favor instead the spirit of the intellectual gambler, and wish to discover and promote authors who meet this description. Like an emergent recording company, what we seek are traces of a new metaphysical 'sound' from any nation of the world. The editors are open to translations of neglected metaphysical classics, and will consider secondary works of especial force and daring. But our main interest is to stimulate the birth of disturbing masterpieces of twenty-first century philosophy.

Noah Roderick
The Being of Analogy

OPEN HUMANITIES PRESS

London 2016

First edition published by Open Humanities Press 2016

Freely available online at http://openhumanitiespress.org/books/the-being-of-analogy

Copyright © 2016 Noah Roderick

This is an open access book, licensed under a Creative Commons By Attribution Share Alike license. Under this license, authors allow anyone to download, reuse, reprint, modify, distribute, and/or copy this book so long as the authors and source are cited and resulting derivative works are licensed under the same or similar license. No permission is required from the authors or the publisher. Statutory fair use and other rights are in no way affected by the above. Read more about the license at creativecommons.org/licenses/by-sa/3.0

Design by Katherine Gillieson
Cover Illustration by Tammy Lu

The cover illustration is copyright Tammy Lu 2016, used under a
Creative Commons By Attribution license (CC-BY).

PRINT ISBN 978-1-78542-022-1
PDF ISBN 978-1-78542-023-8

OPEN HUMANITIES PRESS

Open Humanities Press is an international, scholar-led open access publishing collective whose mission is to make leading works of contemporary critical thought freely available worldwide.

Contents

Acknowledgements   9

List of Figures   11

Introduction   13

1. Sunt Lacrimae Rerum   29
2. Tricksy Things   72
3. Similarity and Reality   110
4. Empiricism and the Problem of Similarity   121
5. Grammar and Emergence   164
6. The Dynamic Lives of Languages and Genres   196
7. Form and Knowledge   214
8. Marxian Amaterialism   227
9. Know. Fish. Happy.   245

Endnotes   255

For Dad.

Akana shai ankeres ande k'o vast kado lil.

Acknowledgements

The more you understand your debts to others, the harder it is to articulate them. With that terrible paradox in mind, I want to thank Charish. Above all. All of my love.

Thanks to Mom and Susannah for persevering and inspiring. Thanks to my great friends for their support, feedback, and encouragement: Chris Al-Aswad (R.I.P.), Lilly Anderson, Ricia Chansky, Eric Lamore, Chris Lackey, Gino Liu, Paul Morris, Travis Olson, and Ericka Wills.

I'm forever grateful to Ron Strickland and Chris Breu for teaching me how to read, and to Kate Beutel and Holly Baumgartner for supporting me with time and infinite patience. Many thanks also go to Sigi Jöttkandt and the reviewers at Open Humanities Press for the transformative feedback and for bringing this book to press.

And finally, this book would not have been possible had Graham Harman not taken a chance on me. I thank him for the revolutionary ideas he brought to the world, for the comma he brought to page 137 of my manuscript, and for everything in between.

List of Figures

Figure 1: The Koch snowflake

Figure 2: The Kouroi statues, Kleobis and Biton

Figure 3: The Riace bronzes

Introduction
The Midday Stars

Einstein's great mystique lies in his intellectually humble beginnings and in his unorthodox thinking. Every eighth grade science student has heard about his inability to speak until the age of four (though this is almost certainly untrue). They know about how his most important ideas were developed while he was a frustrated patent office worker, and about how he dreamt up his theory of relativity while watching trains pass each other. Einstein's exuberance, his funky hair, and his ability to translate startling visuals into beautiful mathematics made him a counter-culture hero. All of it seemed to come naturally to Einstein, a quirk of personality. Not so for Hideki Yukawa. He titled his memoir *Tabibito*, "The Traveler." Yet, it is full of mentions of his distaste for leaving the sanctuary of his home and routine. The book's subtitle might well have been *An Unexpected Journey*. Yukawa had to work hard to become an unorthodox thinker. Since it was not part of his personality, it had to become his philosophy.

In the years following the Russo-Japanese War, in the spirit of Meiji curiosity about the nation's rivals, Russian literature was all the rage in Japan. Because of his crippling shyness and his lack of interest in all of the things boys at the time were supposed to be interested in, Yukawa's classmates took to calling him "Iwan-chan," after Tolstoy's *Ivan the Fool*.[1] In Tolstoy's fairytale, the Devil sends three imps to destroy Ivan, a simple farmer, and his two brothers, one a soldier and the other a merchant. The imps sent to Ivan's two brothers successfully ruin them by using the soldier's ambition and the merchant's greed. Ivan, being a fool with no other desire than to work the land, frustrates all three imps. Each imp in turn becomes exhausted, and Ivan catches them. The first imp offers Ivan anything he wants, and so Ivan asks the imp for something to cure his stomachache. The imp duly provides three roots, one of which Ivan takes and the others he saves. When the second imp, the soldier's imp, is caught, he offers Ivan the ability to turn straw into soldiers. Ivan agrees to this because he'd like the soldiers to sing for him. When the merchant brother's imp is caught, he offers Ivan the ability to turn leaves into gold pieces. Ivan agrees to this because he believes the gold pieces would be pretty things for the peasant children to play with. Through a series of events, Ivan becomes king of his realm, but having no ambition to increase the wealth or the power of his kingdom, all of the wise people flee, leaving a kingdom of fools who have no use for currency or soldiers. Eventually, the Devil himself attempts to ruin Ivan, but he too fails because Ivan and his kingdom of fools refuse to recognize instruments of power as anything but objects for enjoyment.

Yukawa didn't himself relate any of the details of Tolstoy's story, and seems to have taken the "Iwan-chan" nickname at face-value, but his philosophy of scientific invention very much involves Ivan's foolish intuition of objects preceding the assigned meaning of those objects. When he was six years old, his grandfather, a teacher of Chinese classics, began teaching him the *sodoku* method of reading *kanji*. In the *sodoku* method, the student learns the Japanese pronunciation of Chinese characters before ever learning anything about the meanings of those characters. By contrast, in alphabetical learning, a student already has access to the connection between the sound of a word and its meaning. The job is to analyze the word's phonemes so that they fit into the general scheme of a language's orthography. Exceptions to the 1:1 phoneme-grapheme ratio are either unobserved or analyzed later on. In analytic languages, such as Chinese, where the phoneme-morpheme ratio is already close to 1:1, students analyze the morpheme-grapheme (plus radical) relationship. Thus, there is comparatively little analysis in *sodoku* learning. One can only guess at patterns from an infinitude of singularities, and this alarmed the young Yukawa:

> [A]ll of these books were like walls without doors. Each *kanji* held a secret world of its own; many *kanji* made a line and

several lines made a page. Then that page became a frightening wall to me as a boy.[2]

But in 1922, when Yukawa was eighteen, Albert Einstein made a well-publicized visit to Japan, and for a brief time "quantum theory" became a buzzword. Yukawa was drawn to the subject because the words "quantum" and "theory" seemed to bear such an arbitrary relationship to each other. Like the kanji, the two signs came together out of a pure infinity of other signs, and so could only be experienced aesthetically, with all of the terrifying pleasure of the Burkean sublime.

It was around this time that particle physics was beginning to face down its own infinity problem that would drive the science from that point forward. James Clerk Maxwell predicted in the nineteenth century that the behavior of electrical and magnetic forces could be calculated in the same mathematical terms, giving rise to the concept of a combined electromagnetic force, with light behaving as a wavelike structure in the form of electromagnetic radiation. Ludwig Boltzmann further argued that energy levels of such radiation occurred in discrete rather than continuous levels, which Max Planck, at the turn of the twentieth century developed into quantum theory, giving rise to the concept of the dual wave-particle nature of light. Einstein then, in 1905, described the behavior of photons, or individual quantum particles of light, suggesting the concrete connection between energy and matter. In that same year, Einstein proposed his Theory of Special Relativity, which set uniform parameters around distance, movement, and speed, thereby marrying the dimension of space to that of time. In 1923, Louis De Broglie further joined Special Relativity to quantum mechanics, predicting that other fundamental particles, specifically electrons, also share the wave-duality property. Just a few years later, Paul Dirac mathematically formalized the interactions between electrons and photons within the context of quantum mechanics, giving rise to the field of quantum electrodynamics (QED).

The problem was that the energy state of an electron determines its position at a given instant. So, if an electron emits or absorbs a photon, it jumps from one quantum state to another. Now you see it…Now you don't. That bit is conceptually hard to understand from a classical physics point of view, but it can be described mathematically by those who know what they're doing. But an electron can emit and reabsorb a photon within its own electromagnetic field, meaning that the possibilities of the precise energy state from one quantum rung to another add up to infinity.[3] The further you try to reach into this moment, the more virtual particle interactions you see, such as the photon dissolving into a virtual electron-positron pair, with that electron emitting a virtual photon. This process can repeat itself *ad infinitum*, so that the moment becomes like a fractal. And the further down this fractalized rabbit hole you go, the more impossibly large the mass (*qua* energy) becomes. Of course, the possibility of infinite mass at such a high resolution diverges completely from the observed mass of the electron at lower resolutions.[4] This problem of infinity in QED would eventually be resolved (though not solved) relatively independently by three theoretical physicists: Julian Schwinger, Richard Feynman, and Yukawa's long time friend and colleague, Sin-Itiro Tomonaga. They did it through a process that would come to be known as *renormalization*, which makes predictions about the electron's interactions with its electromagnetic field from lower resolutions, and thus lower energy levels.

Renormalization allows for the observable behavior of electron-field interaction to set the parameters for the mathematical prediction of the interaction, using probability amplitudes to predict the positions of the electron's trajectory. Although renormalization turns out to work with astounding accuracy, Feynman himself felt it was a temporary fix, claiming that it was "brushing infinity under the rug."[5] Anyway, you have to admire the gall of Feynman for talking about his own Nobel Prize-winning idea in this way! Although he recognized their use in choreographing the unobservable, Yukawa was also deeply uncomfortable with probability amplitudes, which he claimed had become "almighty or something absolute to most theoretical physicists…"[6] This echoes Einstein's admonishment that "God does not play dice," with regards to quantum mechanics in general. Whereas Einstein's problem seems to have been that uncertainty threw up an epistemological roadblock on the universe, Yukawa's unease was with the homogenizing effects of explaining the world through probability. Yukawa's complaint was aesthetical as well as epistemic. His attitude to imagined concepts was vitalistic, and so although probability worked perfectly well, he worried that it limited the possibility of whole, concrete ideas that could accompany unobservable phenomena in the universe.

Yukawa's own Nobel Prize-winning idea was to imagine a particle whose very existence was ephemeral, a particle that was at once pure concept and manifest phenomenon. It was an idea that would liberate the explanation of nuclear forces from QED, with the ultimate goal of eventually uniting all of the fundamental forces into a "finite quantum field theory."[7] Thus, in an early, unpublished paper, Yukawa predicts, "The problems of the atomic nucleus [...] are so intimately related with the problems of the relativistic formulation of quantum mechanics that when they are solved, if they ever be solved at all, they will be solved together."[8] The story of particle physics in general is a story of the uneven unfolding of analogies, arguments for uniformity which necessarily precede the analysis of those uniformities into singular concepts, always with the hope that the new concepts will find their way back to an underlying uniformity.

By 1911, Ernest Rutherford had explained the stability of atomic electrons with the idea of an atomic nucleus, a small but heavy center of positive charge that kept the atomic electrons in orbit. Rutherford's atomic model worked as an analogy to the solar system, and it suggested an explanation both for the behavior of electrons and for the decay of nuclear particles that had been observed. However, it quickly became apparent that if electrons orbited the nucleus in the same way planets orbit the sun, the very fast-moving electrons would lose steam and be sucked into the massive nucleus in an instant. After the atom-solar system analogy had been analyzed, the remainder was a coherent picture of the nucleus (its size and constituent particles), and a question of how electrodynamics and quantum mechanics could be integrated to explain the separate force that governs electron behavior. The latter question would be addressed by QED, but the question remained that if the constituents of the atom are not all governed equally by the same force, how can the positively charged protons hold themselves together in such a tight formation without repelling each other? Prior to Yukawa's meson theory, physicists trying to answer this question stuck to first principles: matter consisted of an underlying symmetry between electrons (their positron counterparts) and protons. Even when Rutherford predicted the neutron in 1920 (it was finally discovered by

James Chadwick in 1932) to understand the mass of the nucleus, it was thought to consist of an electron and a proton, which explained why it was slightly more massive than a proton.[9] This formulation of the neutron led Heisenberg to suggest an analogy between nuclear binding and molecular binding, in which a neutron and a proton shared an electron. The molecular model also explained observed beta-decay (later to be incorporated into the weak nuclear force), which occurred when that shared electron escaped.[10]

Enrico Fermi carried the electron exchange idea further, proposing that a neutron decayed into a proton and an electron-neutrino pair, which would mean that the same force responsible for slow nuclear exchange (weak force) would also bind the nucleons.[11] However, when Soviet physicists Igor Tamm and Dmitri Iwanenko put the Fermi-field to the test, they concluded that it could not account for both the range and the strength of the binding force together.[12] A few decades later, Abdus Salam, Sheldon Glashow J.C. Ward, and Steven Weinberg would demonstrate that Fermi's weak force is essentially related to the electromagnetic force, now known together as the electroweak force.[13] After Tam and Iwanenko's 1934 results, it was clear that the strong nuclear binding force was fundamentally different. Instead of synthesizing QED with the nuclear binding force, Yukawa was liberated to create an analogy between the two.

Whereas the electromagnetic field is structured by the exchange of photons, Yukawa imagined a similar field existing between nucleons, in which a heavy particle rather than a photon is exchanged. Yukawa determined from its strength and short range that the particle would have to be at least 200 times more massive than an electron.[14] Yukawa first called the heavy particles U-quanta, but they would later be regarded as part of a whole class of hadronic particles called *mesons*. A nucleon can, in a very short amount of time, jump from proton state to neutron state, or vice-versa, depending on the charge of the meson. In classical physics, this process would violate the law of energy conservation; however, in quantum physics, if a particle has a sufficiently short existence, it can take energy from its surroundings briefly enough to leave the energy of the entire system unchanged.[15] Yukawa had not only demonstrated that there was a strong nuclear force that was fundamentally different from the other known forces, but he also showed that in order to probe deeper into the nature of reality, the atomistic thinking that supposed observable processes had to be shaped by a combination of a few irreducible elements would not do. The meson was not just a new particle; it was a new *kind* of particle, which, as Brown and Rechenberg claim, "opens the door to a world of high-energy processes involving the creation and annihilation of new and in many cases ephemeral substances (mesons, leptons, strange and charmed particles, quarks, gluons, intermediate vector bosons, etc.), a world of astonishing variety and novelty."[16] Yukawa later related his discovery to the childhood experience of hitting his head on a gravestone. On the ground, stunned, he noticed how staggeringly differentiated the world around him was: "As I lay on my back, the sunbeams that shone through the leaves of the cherry trees hit my eyes, and I gasped: they were like countless stars—the midday stars!"[17]

Yukawa's postulation of the meson was enough of a breakthrough in particle physics to earn him a Nobel prize, and it's true that without his bold intuitive leap, any real understanding of the strong nuclear force would have been years in the waiting. But as Brown and Rechenberg pointed out, Yukawa also brought a necessary promiscuity to the conservative ontology of particle physics. Physics, being a closer neighbor to mathematics and philosophy than some of the other natural sciences, tends to be a very philosophical discipline. Almost all of the canonical physicists of the twentieth century had something to say about metaphysics, and because physics seems to get at nature in its most fundamental form, the public empowers physicists to speak about reality, ethics, religion, etc. And in turn, contemporary philosophy clings to physics, waiting anxiously to make meaning out of every new development. This is true not only in analytic philosophy where one might expect a lot of physiophilia, but increasingly in continental philosophy as well (even as physicists so rarely return the love). And so it is odd that Yukawa's name is never more than a footnote in popular science writing, and is completely absent from physiophile philosophy, even though the most prominent figures in the early intersection of physics and philosophy (most notably, Oppenheimer) were quick to acknowledge Yukawa's great scientific and philosophical contributions. I can only speculate that the omission of Yukawa, and that of the enormous contributions of his colleagues in the Kyoto Group, is part of an entrenched Eurocentrism that masks itself in scientific universality. Nevertheless,

Yukawa's challenge to the ontological conservativism in physics was absolutely transformative.

I have thus far presented Yukawa's great analogy as a sort of heroic act of a solitary genus, but of course Yukawa would have no truck with this. He was deeply immersed in existing philosophical traditions, such as Taoism,[18] vitalism, and Mitsuo Taketani's three-stage epistemology of systems.[19] Taketani was a core member of that first generation of Japanese particle physicists, along with Yukawa, Tomonaga, and Shoichi Sakata. Taketani, a Marxist who would eventually be arrested for his antimilitarist activities in 1938,[20] developed his three-stage theory, in part, from Hegel's triune dialectical structure, but applied it to scientific phenomenology, which itself would become a dominant methodology with the rise of cloud chambers and particle accelerators. Scientific phenomenology poses new problems by juxtaposing the events observed in a system with the theoretical model of the system. Any inconsistencies between theory and observation are either methodological problems or theoretical problems. If the problem were the latter, then an opening would have been created for new knowledge. But Taketani argued for a third, *substantialistic* stage between the *essential* (theoretical) and the *phenomenal*.[21] The substantialistic opened up the possibility for the inconsistencies between the essential and the phenomenal to be explained not by a better understanding of the relations in the system but by the objects (or relata) in the system. This meant that the postulation of new kinds of objects would not be an absolute last resort. Yukawa's new particle became a sort of proving ground for Taketani's method, despite extreme resistance in the West to admitting new particles. The philosophy of science in the West was still very much devoted to the principle of Occam's Razor, meaning that the introduction of complexity was in direct opposition to rationality. Thus, the interaction of nucleons would have to be reduced to the interactions of known, elementary particles, and it was therefore preferable to alter the properties of a known particle (as Dirac tried to do with the positron) rather than admit something new altogether.

Yukawa's answer to Occam's Razor was Zhuangzi's parable of the happy fishes. Yukawa was well known for his talent with calligraphy, and instead of asking for an autograph, admirers would frequently request a sample of his calligraphy. When asked, he would produce three characters: *Know*

Fish Happy.²² The three characters represented the Zhuangzi story, which itself encapsulated Yukawa's view of knowledge. In the story, Zhuangzi walks onto a bridge, looks down at the fishes below, and is delighted that they have come to the surface to enjoy themselves. Zhuangzi's interlocutor, Huizi, ever the wet blanket, objects that Zhuangzi cannot possibly know if the fishes are enjoying themselves because he is not himself a fish. Zhuangzi counters that if that were the case, how could Huizi know for sure that Zhuangzi didn't know, since Huizi is not Zhuangzi? Zhuangzi continued, "When you asked me how I knew what a fish enjoyed, you admitted that you know already whether or not I knew, on the bridge, that the fish were enjoying themselves."²³ The point, in Yukawa's view, was that rationality does not necessarily beget reason. The only way in which meaningfully new knowledge emerges—knowledge worthy of rational investigation—is by way of aesthetics and intuition. If, at this point, you're detecting the presence of Henri Bergson as well as Zhuangzi, you're not far off. Yukawa was an admirer of Bergson, and his own ontology could be described as being vitalistic. For Yukawa, aesthetic experience was the creation of new being, and so it was by definition more productive to begin with aesthetic experience (for example, analogy-making) than to start with the rational analysis of a problem, using existing principles. The product of the aesthetic experience had the capacity to affect those principles, and the object of the experience might be affecting the object the principles were describing.

I'm aware that the reader, at the moment, may be perceiving some cheap TED Talk anecdote to be followed by a banal exhortation to "think outside the box," to "visualize excellence," etc. But no one could accuse those in the West who dismissed Yukawa early on, such as Dirac and Bohr, of being conventional or dogmatic thinkers. Everybody in those heady days of *l'entre-deux-guerres* physics was thinking outside the box, as it were. It's just that Yukawa was more likely to ascribe being to the box. As I'll discuss in detail later on, Enlightenment science, at its birth, was not so much about the ascendency of human reason or the replacement of superstition with logical reduction; it was about the legerdemain replacement of the *matter-form* pair with the *matter-force* pair. In other words, a cosmology was better described by the interactions between material elements than by the forms of those material elements. The epistemic benefits of such a metaphysical shift are obvious (calculus and thermodynamics, to name just two). But the downside of the force-matter pair is the very ontological conservativism that early particle physics had run into—that is, ascribing reality only to the most elemental objects. Yukawa's work didn't reverse the dominant matter-force pair by any means, but it did open up a cosmology in which non-elemental objects would be granted just as much reality as those which were (sometimes erroneously, e.g. the proton) considered elementals. As Yukawa had it, the search for essence should not always be directed to the interactions between the most basic materials of a system.[24] It was this rejection of atomistic fundamentalism that contributed to a renewed search for new particles and which helped shape the destiny of twentieth century physics.

Again, Yukawa's metaphysics tended towards the vitalistic, which, at a certain point, runs up against the object-oriented metaphysics for which I'll be arguing in this book. However, the particular convergence of being, aesthetic experience, and epistemic generativity at the heart of Yukawa's philosophy is the launching point for my own investigation into emergence (movement), identity, similarity, and the analogical production of knowledge. The idea of analogy as a useful cognitive tool has had a lot of champions over the years. And indeed, some cognitive scientists and artificial intelligence specialists have come to think of analogy not just as an occasional departure from analytical processing but as the basic mechanism for all thinking. But one has to go as far back as Giambattista Vico or even St. Thomas Aquinas to find any serious consideration of the relationship between analogy and being. No doubt, this is in large part due to the subtraction of knowledge from being that propelled Modernity forward. But it's also the legacy of the excluded middle in Western thought, as well as the ejection of similarity from reality, which itself was a part of a larger relegation of aesthetics to the uniquely insular human subject. I join other thinkers in object-oriented philosophy, such as Graham Harman and Timothy Morton, in their efforts to place aesthetics at the center of philosophical realism. My contribution here is to extend that effort to the realm of the epistemic, which I would argue is an under-explored area in object-oriented philosophy, owing perhaps to OOP's turn from postmodern philosophies in which reality could only be ascertained on the discursive stratum. Language is, in fact, well represented in this investigation; however, the referential function of language and the dyadism of the sign are treated as strictly secondary to the beings of grammars and genres, which are considered as objects with affective capacities just like any other object. Grammars and genres will be examined for their effects on the organization and production of knowledge, as well as for their own self-organizing capacities, which I argue demonstrate the dynamic reality of emergent similarity.

There is an undeniable sense of *kairos* about the relatively recent arrival of object-oriented philosophy. The *anthropocene* is steadily making its way into the lexicons of the pundit's table and the dinner table, and with it the uncanny feeling that our closest relatives may in fact be pigeons, synanthropic creatures evolved to live on the edges of cliffs, and yet are found almost nowhere outside of the simulacra cliffs of our cities. We haven't just colonized nature with agriculture, cement, and trash; there is no parallel movement between the nature and the artifice by which nature has been colonized. The agriculture, the cement, the trash, the Ziggy Stardust wigs (not to be confused with trash), the seedbank on Spitsbergen—all of it is moving, affecting, and being affected alongside Namibian fairy circles, giant redwoods, and diminutive tidal pools on the Antrim coast of Ireland. Without the ontological gulf between the natural and the artificial, there are only objects. All of this would suggest, as many in object-oriented philosophy advocate, a *flat ontology*: a reality in which, as Harman contends, all objects are "equally *objects*."[25] I hold this to be the case as well, and while I don't advocate an identifiably hierarchal ontology, I don't think a flat ontology is sufficient either. As Bill Clinton famously said, "It depends on what the definition of 'is' is." It seems to me that the 'is' in the existential copula, *there is*, is more of a linguistic accident than it is a reflection of reality (and, as I'll discuss, the construction is not even a linguistic universal). I argue that there is no self-same relationship between things and their predicates, and in this sense, reality is non-propositional. Objects not only have their own beings, but they have their own modes of being. Objects, I contend, share in their own predication. Being therefore belongs to similarity rather than to sameness. New objects do not emerge as syntheses of self-same properties, and likewise, truly new knowledge is not called out of synthesis of self-same predicates that name the world as it really is, but instead emerges out of a productive distortion of predicates, something we recognize as analogy.

Layout and Thesis

"*Sunt lacrimae rerum*" may be the most disputed phrase in the history of literary criticism, and it is the title of my first chapter. It comes out of the first part of Virgil's *Aeneid*, and it gets translated in a thousand ways, but mostly it comes down to some variation of either: "There are tears *for* things" or "There are tears *of* things." The phrase is followed, by the way, with "*et mentem mortalia tangunt,*" for which a not-so-poetic translation might be "and the mind is touched by mortal things," though we could also have it as "and the mind is *moved* by mortal things." Having been washed ashore in North Africa, Aeneas with his band makes his way to Carthage where he awaits an audience with Dido, Carthage's queen and Aeneas's future lover. There he looks upon murals of the Trojan War and begins to cry. This is both a cry of lamentation and of consolation, since both the Trojans' suffering and their fame are visibly present in the world. There is a strange symmetry here. The suffering of the Trojans is realized in these things—these murals—and also in the tears, which are things too. There are tears *in* things, tears *for* things (mortal things *move* the mind), and tears *are* things. The tears and the murals cease to serve merely as signs or representations of something else. They are things in the world with their own affective powers. The first chapter, then, is an introduction to a metaphysics that follows along those lines. The core issues my first two chapters address are those of interobjective and intraobjective relationships. My argument relies upon a reconsideration of the *form-matter* pairing in which matter is not a metaphysical primitive. From a metaphysical primitive materialism, the interaction of matter instantiates a state of content, and then form is epiphenomenal of that state. I argue instead that the interaction of matter is relative to form, and that, as you can guess, the object is the metaphysical primitive. When objects interact, their material relations are asymmetrical but their formal relations are symmetrical. (I'm aware that this is beginning to sound like a bit of esotericism, but please bear with me.) Symmetry, I contend, is not invariance or sameness but similarity, and similarity is an emergent state that occurs when objects interact with other objects. Thus, while the material interaction between objects is asymmetrical, their formal interaction is one of conformity, which I take to mean both imitation and translation. It is out of this conforming/imitating/translating that entirely new objects emerge. But even as objects conform when they interact, they do not necessarily disappear. They may endure beyond their relations with other objects. They do this because despite their asymmetrical material interactions with others and their translation of others' forms, their own forms from interaction to interaction are self-similar, even though their relative material make-up might change entirely. An object, therefore, relates to itself from event to event in a state of symmetry. It is the state of symmetry that enables an object to have an enduring identity for others. So, a further correlate to this argument—one that will be important when I get to language and knowledge—is that identity is not at all a product of representation.

In order to make all of this stick, I have to demonstrate both that symmetry is similarity (and not invariance) and that similarity is part of reality. The latter task forms the basis of my third and fourth chapters, "Similarity and Reality" and "Empiricism and the Problem of Similarity." In those chapters, I examine premodern metaphysical treatments of analogy and similarity, focusing primarily on those of Aristotle and Thomas Aquinas. I then look at the ways in which modern empiricism and its offshoots have ejected similarity from reality. What I find is that similarity in twentieth century philosophy was caught in a pincer movement between, on the one hand, the neonominalist programs of W.V.O. Quine, Nelson Goodman, and Wilfrid Sellars, and on the other with the Deleuzean program of radical empiricism. I find that while Deleuze has unnecessarily tangled up identity and similarity with representation, the neonominalists have mistakenly thrown similarity out of reality as part of their rejection of classes and categories from reality. With regards to the neonominalists, I argue that categories, insofar as they are necessary for analytic thought, must themselves begin with a prelinguistic grasping of relationships of similarity, which is itself an aesthetic phenomenon. And as per the Deleuzean program, I argue for a Sophistic rather than a Platonistic understanding of similarity, one founded on the idea of imitation (mimesis) as an emergent relationship between objects instead of a relationship between idea and object.

In the following two chapters, entitled "Grammar and Emergence" and "The Dynamic Lives of Languages and Genres," I turn my attention more directly to analogy, language, and knowledge. Here, I examine the evolution of human language, tying together what I see as the two most persuasive approaches to the problem: Alison Wray's *formulaic language* and George Lakoff's *generative semantics*. Generative semantics is correct insofar as it argues that grammatico-epistemic categories emerge from analogies of lived experience. I contend, however, that given cognitive categories of embodied human experience alone are not enough to explain the complexity and dynamism of human grammars. Wray's formulaic language program, on the other hand, opens up a space for phonological and morpho-syntactical objects to play their own role in the emergence of a grammar as a complex system (complex systems being objects too). I then apply the same logic to the evolution of communication genres, which themselves are crucial to the development and performance of specialized knowledges.

The next chapter, "Form and Knowledge," takes an archeological approach to the modern epistemology of form. Related to the replacement of the *form-matter* pair with the *force-matter* pair is what I refer to as the "included exclusion" of *design* in modern science. My contention here is that as our understanding of processes such as cognition and evolution are increasingly informed by metaphors and models of autopoetic systems, we will have to rethink our long-held oppositional relationship between randomness (as equiprobability) and design, which in turn requires that we rethink form in its relationship to material processes.

I end by meditating on the possible implications of rethinking similarity and form in terms of Marx's critical materialism. The chapter is called "Marxian Amaterialism," and in it I argue that the *material transformation* in the labor process that creates value and capital (the latter as the subject of that process) is, in fact, better understood as a *formal translation* of objects, since with respect to the labor process Marx is really talking about *socialized* matter, which occupies a relative rather than absolute position in reality. This, I argue, is a more productive basis for theorizing the exploitation of immaterial labor and the *commons* (and here I focus on grammars and genres as particularly important objects of the commons), as thinkers such as Paolo Virno, Antonio Negri, and Michael Hardt have done.

The titular focus of this book is analogy, and it may not yet be entirely clear to the reader as to why so much time and text is spent on matter, form, emergence, and objects, and less clear still what this book is doing in a metaphysics series in the first place. After all, analogy is supposed to be concerned with knowing, and metaphysics is supposed to be concerned with being. First, analogies exist prior to representation. They are aesthetic experiences and objects in their own right. Second, though it is no doubt far less compendious and skillfully written than Deleuze's *Difference and Repetition*, the goal of my project is to suggest something along the lines of what Deleuze was arguing for in that book with respect to the concept of difference. Whereas Deleuze devised a way of thinking about difference for itself, I am hoping to open up a way of thinking about similarity for itself.

Deleuze argued that in post-Aristotelian metaphysics, there is an implicit distinction between difference and otherness, and that any analysis of the difference between two terms is always predicated on a third term, which is common to the differentiated terms, meaning that difference is merely difference-in-reference-to. For example, the difference between a horse and a rabbit is only meaningful insofar as they are both mammals or animals or whatever common domain you have in mind. Something like this can be said about making analogies between seemingly similar things. Similarity always seems to be predicated on either a geometrical term (i.e. proportion) or on a quality that exists prior to the objects entered into the analogy. In fact, while the third term in an analytical claim is usually implicit, the third term in an analogical claim is very often named, or at least alluded to. Here's one: My rabbit is like a *miniature* horse. Proportion, in this case, is a universal that exists prior to the terms *rabbit* and *horse*. What is understood is that my rabbit and a horse would be the same if they were not different with respect to the universal domain of scale. We see analogy as epistemically useful only insofar as it helps us to name those self-same domains in which difference (and, therefore, analysis) is possible. Thus, with an analogical claim such as, 'The atom is like a miniature solar system,' it is understood that the atom and the solar system would be the same if they were not different in scale. From there, we can multiply the domains by which to analyze the atom-solar system relationship to the point where the initial analogy appears downright naïve, misguided, and idealistic: the atom and the solar system would be the same if they were not different in scale and orbital force and position/momentum, and so on. In this way of thinking, reality is always located beneath the apparent similarity. This is particularly the case in epistemic regimes tied to materialism, in which reality resides entirely apart from the surface of things.

We moderns can congratulate ourselves on being such deep thinkers. This is mostly a good thing. But the trouble is that we have forgotten how to think deeply about the superficial. Yes, that sounds like it's straight out of a *Heidegger for Dummies* book, but it is true, and it's a sentiment that has yielded some incredible philosophical gains for phenomenologists and object-oriented ontologists alike. Surfaces are productive. Even the most supervenient materialists would not deny that experiencing a superficial similarity between ideas of solar systems and atoms is epistemically productive of something. Acknowledging this does not mean an endorsement of the idea that solar systems and atoms themselves are created from the same formal mold. (In fact, sameness itself has no place in my cosmology, whether that be at the formal or the material level.) The experience of superficial similarity (i.e. analogy) is neither an indicator of some deeper commonality nor a mere illusion; it is the effect of objects translating or conforming to the forms of other objects. And wherever there is translation or conformation, there are new objects entirely. There is emergence. In the case of analogy, these objects happen to be ideas of categories. It is in an analogy, no matter how humble or how grand, that we may suspend the distinction between knowing and being.

Chapter 1
Sunt Lacrimae Rerum

It seems astounding whenever a new object is identified by the eye alone. Take, for example, the discovery by Belgian surgeons in 2013 of a new ligament in the knee. That basic human anatomy still has secrets to yield is impressive enough, but the fact that this ligament is perfectly visible to the naked eye is oddly reassuring, consoling even. We take it for granted that the eye's best days are behind it. Perhaps its best days were already behind it when Alhazen finally put the extromission theory of vision to rest in the 10th century. But the 20th century was an especially difficult one for the eye. As Martin Jay points out, continental (particularly French) philosophy rallied itself around "antiocularcentrism,"[26] from Foucault's poking at the clinician's beady eye to the feminist and postcolonialist denudation of the European male gaze. And the discovery of things in science since the 20th century has become less and less distinguishable from the *fabrication* of the discovery of things, which is to say that before things like exoplanets or oncogenes are discovered, they are effigurated onto a screen or onto an organism (e.g. a lab mouse). The things discovered in this way are not just plucked from their ecologies like some Victorian naturalist netting an island bird to be taxidermied and then sketched into a book *al vif*. The exoplanet and the oncogene are already sketches *al vif*; they are already, as Bruno Latour says, "inscriptions," clasps in a referential chain, "artificial, indirect, and multilayered."[27] When the exoplanet and oncogene are discovered, they are created as information, and the eye is only somewhat instrumental in selecting that information from the surrounding pixelar or cellular noise.

From the standpoint of mind-matter dualism, it is easy to understand how mathematical equations or scientific descriptions are moments of creation—they are explanations or descriptions of phenomena, and therefore belong to language, and so to human genius. From the dualistic standpoint, creating equations and descriptions are new acts, just like a car crash is a new act. The difference is in potentials. Perhaps some Cartesian-flavored evil demon could know, and therefore *be*, the limit of how the car crash could happen, but we do not have access to the demon's limits, or we would be the demon's demon. However, in the case of equations, even if a particular equation happens to be wrong, we do have access to its limits, which look something like $1 \notin 1$.

Similarly, if you want to argue that a particular crater on the moon is volcanic, you have to match up everything that predicates "volcanic" with the descriptions of everything you have observed about the crater. The equation and the description are particular permutations of the same mode of being in mathematics and language.[28] The car crash is more novel because the elements of the car crash (for simplicity, we'll say the elements are just the cars) have entered into new modes of being: the car is crashed. It is a crashed car. The situation can once again be described by matching up the "crashed" qualities of the crashed car to the predicates of "crashed." Except, except! Before the event of the car crash, there was no sense in which "crashed" predicated the car. So, the car itself has a totally different kind of potential than the description of the car crash has. There is an ontological barrier between the two that is untraversable to all but the demon. So much for dualism.

I have already taken up Hideki Yukawa's argument that analogical identification and the creation of new things in the world are similar in being. In Yukawa's rejection of the atomistic view of nature, he argued that nothing newly created could be reduced to a combination of the predicates of a source analogue with the qualities of a target analogue. The man behind our understanding of the strong nuclear force was arguing that form must once again take its place as a metaphysical primitive alongside force and matter. For Yukawa, there was no ontological distinction between the thing and the analogical identification of the thing, just as we can see now that there is no ontological gulf between the exoplanet and the pixilated effiguration of the exoplanet on the screen. They are separate objects, but they are *equally* objects. The creation of new forms everywhere breaks the tethers of matter, just as new forms of knowledge by analogy break the tethers of epistemic domains. A new form is in excess of its component parts, and so when forms act as matter for a new form, their own potentials are not exhausted by the creation of the new form.

If a new form has a surplus of potential that is in excess of all the potentials of its combined parts, then we must decide where that surplus of potential resides. Does it reside in the act of creation or in the being of the thing created? It seems obvious to place surplus in the mechanisms of change in, for example, evolution. Biological evolution is traditionally understood to be powered by spontaneous, random mutation. Spontaneous mutation here takes the place of the Thomistic God, in that it is pure *act* without potential and without predication. Granted, there is potential in the subject (e.g. the monomers of nucleic acids) of spontaneous mutation, and furthermore, the description of spontaneous mutation can be predicated of a few different domains (depurination, tautomerism etc.), but the act itself appears to be in excess of any subject it takes. But on the other hand, there are qualities in evolution that are occasionally predictable, if only by degrees. For instance, according to the Foster rule, an island might nurture growth or diminution of an animal species in physical size, depending upon the abundance of resources and/or predators. If we apply "evolution" elsewhere—let's say in language—we can say that a creole will most likely have fewer syntagmatic redundancies than either its superstrate or substrate languages. Thus, what we understand of evolution, as it is already applied to subjects such as biology or language, is not deep enough ontologically to explain the emergence of new forms.

The attempt to nuance the idea of creativity in evolutionary theory was the starting point for Henri Bergson's vitalist project. Bergson objected in particular to Herbert Spencer's development of a philosophy and ethics of natural evolution, arguing that creativity does not move according to the causality of natural law.[29] Similarly, the convergence in the later part of the 20th century of complexity science on sociobiology has inspired philosophy based not in arboreal, Darwinian evolution, but in the evolution of complex systems wherein the ground onto which agents are supposed to adapt also gives way to the agents that inhabit it in a feedback loop. Whereas the "ought" of liberalism in Spencer's philosophy was deduced from the "is" of arboreal evolution and thermodynamics, the sometimes neoliberal "ought" in philosophies of complexity is deduced from the "is" of fractal mathematics, information theory, and the science of emergent systems. However, for every "is/ought" pairing, there is an "is not/"ought not" pairing, an apophasis that makes the truth of the philosophy unavoidable. For Spencerism, influenced as it is by Malthus, the creative force of evolution is limited by the terrestrial stage on which living actors propagate. The internal and external resources that the living actors have with which to create themselves are absolutely finite, and so maximum creativity happens between the two fixed points of collective ascendency and intraspecific competition. Any attempt to steer life towards one or the other of those points, such as the state mitigating the consequences of an economic or agricultural failure, sends life into a condition of heat death and homogeneity.

In philosophies of complexity, the terrestrial stage is no longer a limit for the creative force of life. In fact, life and the terrestrial stage move together at the same speed, so as to be indistinguishable from one another. So, while evolutionary theories of the 19th century took their mechanics from the uniformitarianist geological movement of Sutton, Lyell and others, the terrestrial stage was stable enough relative to life so as to set identifiable limits on biological movement. In the age of the anthropocene, the terrestrial stage is both the product and producer of biological and cultural movement. Geological history has been folded well into very recent cultural history, which includes the Industrial Revolution and the detonation of the atomic bomb, both events leaving a more or less permanent mark in the geological record.

Self-similarity is the ultimate "is/ought" of philosophies of complexity. I will argue later on in this chapter self-similarity is, in fact, the structure of formal identity in objects; however, in philosophies of complexity, self-similarity is the structure of change. Self-similarity can be represented in very simple mathematical terms by the Koch curve: "For each line segment, replace its middle third by two sides of a triangle, each of length 1/3 of the original segment."[30] Multiply this process several times, and you have a shape that looks like an edge of a snowflake. Multiply it enough times, and you'll get something that looks like a smooth curve. But zoom back in closely enough, and you'll find a series of open triangles of exactly the same size (see Figure 1).

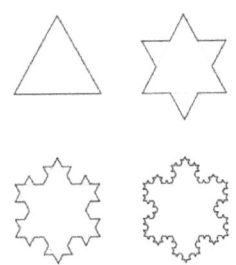

Figure 1: The Koch Snowflake

Coastlines are perhaps the most recognizable examples of Koch self-similarity, though they form imperfect Koch curves.[31] All of the little bulges and coves that you see at ground level on a rocky beach can be seen in a satellite picture of that same region at a much bigger scale. Such self-similarity is also recognizable in tree branches, lightning strikes, circulatory systems, airport designs, and graphic representations of social networks. Philosophers of complexity, such as Adrian Bejan and J. Peder Zane,[32] indeed go so far as to argue for a quasi-theology (*sans* the theos) of design in nature based on self-similarity. Herein lies the 'is not'/'ought not' in philosophies of complexity. Whereas in Spencerism, a cultural artifice such as the state could potentially curdle the creative force of life, the principal "is not" in complexity is that there ever would be cultural, biological, and astronomical movements that interact with one another in fundamentally *different* ways. Again, their speeds and trajectories are essentially the same, so that one never clabbers up enough to serve as a terrestrial stage for another.

It is also the lack of any terrestrial stage whatsoever that distinguishes complexity from critical materialist philosophies. Marx famously compared the workings of ideology to a *camera obscura* in which history and technology appear to be products of human ideas. He insisted instead that "men, developing their material production and their material intercourse, alter, along with this their real existence, their thinking and products of their thinking."[33] And in using this wonderfully evocative comparison, Marx also inspires another simile: human existence as a multi-story house. In this house, we might put astronomical movements at the basement, biological movements on the first floor, material culture on the mezzanine, and ideation on the second floor. Philosophers of complexity, however, much prefer ranch-style accommodations. Whereas artificial interference with evolutionary creation is the "ought not" of Spencerism, the mere divide between artifice and nature is the "ought not" of complexity.

Dialectical materialism refuted the notion that the creative movement of history was powered by a human intellect insulated from its own arrangement of material products. And if the interaction of human intellects was a distorted reflection of the arrangement of material production, then language was the lens that created the distortion. Language was the thing that could naturalize the interaction of human intellects, and thus the arrangement of material power in society. And it was through language that such arrangements could be critiqued and *denaturalized*. In order therefore to maintain the "epi-" in the epistemological power of language, questions of the ontology of language had to be minimized. Even Heidegger, that Swabian champion of ontology, seemed to have preserved language's special epistemological power in his thoughts about the supremacy of German-language philosophy.[34] But what became increasingly apparent in the twentieth century, as language was being materialized in new ways through the proliferation of communication technologies, was that although language might or might not be the stuff of knowledge, information was surely the stuff of language. Furthermore, as Claude Shannon's Information Theory showed, information itself is composed of stuff, the dimensions of which can be quantified mathematically in terms of "channel capacity."[35] As information can be quantified, it can be internally divided by its properties, access to which can be economically valuated in dimensions of size, speed, and content. And as information becomes a more central object of production and consumption in the capitalist economy, language loses its mediating position between the human subject and objects of nature, as well as the position between the social subject and objects of technology, such that the entire quadrupole implodes.

For Bruno Latour, that very quadrupole (the human subject/objects-of-nature and the social subject/objects-of-technology) was the sustaining illusion of Modernity.[36] It's not just that we have realized that the subject has no authority over language, and cannot therefore play arbiter to an extralinguistic reality, as postmodernists would have it; rather, there is no real gap between the subject and external reality for language to mismediate in the first place. Again, we find ourselves in our own synanthropic zoo, right next to the pigeons, for whom there is no nature outside the ledges of our cities. The processes that go into selecting information from redundant noise during data compression are essentially the same whether we communicate to, through, or without machines. And as Mark C. Taylor argues: "Noise… is never absolute; rather noise and information are bound in a relation in which each is simultaneously parasite and host for the other."[37] External reality, nature, noise: these are no longer subtractions from the subject, the organism, and information; the latter enfold former, and vice-versa.

If noise and information, nature and the organism, reality and the subject are not different in substance, we eventually discover that their difference lies in scale. The water around swimming fish is noise, but the water tunnel that emerges from a group of fishes individually responding to variations in hydrodynamic resistance is information. In other words, the water tunnel and the water around the individual fish exist simultaneously, but the former lies upscale from the latter. Here, the distinction between complexity and compositionality must be reaffirmed. The term *compositionality* is probably most commonly deployed in linguistics, wherein a finite number of substantively different elements and functions within a domain (e.g. language) are combined in order to create a potentially infinite number of identifiable or meaningful things (e.g. sentences) inside of that domain. Likewise, in complexity, multiple elements (usually referred to as *actors*[38] or *agents*) come together, albeit not to dissolve into one another. What is different in complexity is that the actors are performing the same function simultaneously. The water is responding to the resistance of the fish, and the fish is selecting that resistance information from the noise of space through its lateral mechanosensory system (another complex network), and positioning itself to minimize the water's resistance.[39] The water's resistance is, of course, conditioned by the fish's movement so that the fish's response to the water's resistance is already a part of the other fishes' movements. Once again, self-similarity supposedly structures the mechanics of the complex system.

Another important difference between compositionality and complexity is that complex systems are not cut off by domains. When substance is replaced by scale, domains become just a matter of perspective. Thus, the electrical signals of a fish's lateral mechanosensory system are no more or less fundamental than the water molecules in their adaptive function within the water tunnel system. From the supervenient, compositionalist point of view, the mechanosensory signals can be described in the domain *electrodynamics*, unless we want to extend the description to QED. The actions of the water molecules can be explained in the domain *hydrodynamics*, unless we want to extend the description to magnetohydrodynamics, which would ultimately lead us back to QED. As Salam, Glashow, and Weinberg showed, the electromagnetic interaction is, at more fundamental energy levels, the same as the weak nuclear force; and furthermore, if the principle of supersymmetry[40] turns out to be correct, the strong nuclear interaction would be included in this too.[41] But how many more layers of domain can we peel away before we find ourselves back at the simple mechanics of self-similarity or at some more fundamental force better described by metaphysics?

As I've pointed out, one of the main complaints that philosophers of complexity have with the modern subject and its compositional reality is that there is supposed to exist some sort of *cordon sanitaire* between the mind and the world. And indeed, beyond philosophies of complexity, the early 21st century has seen the emergence of philosophies devoted specifically to critiquing the Kantian legacy of "correlationism" in Western philosophy.[42] Speculative Realism, as it is called, is an umbrella term for a number of fairly diverse recent philosophies, which nonetheless share a commitment to a reality, access to which neither excludes non-humans nor privileges human subjects. As we can see in the allegory of Achilles and the tortoise, the condition of Achilles-the-subject being stuck in the representation of distance between him and the tortoise on the racetrack rendered Achilles-the-object immobile. But closer to the speculative realist's complaint about correlationism, Achilles couldn't catch up to the tortoise because the tortoise didn't have the same kind of reality that Achilles had. The tortoise's reality was simply an abstract limit of Achilles's place in space. One can neither touch nor overtake an abstract limit. Another way to describe the race, then would be to grant Achilles, the track, and the tortoise the same reality by arguing that they share a relational existence. Thus, it is not so much for Achilles to overtake the tortoise because the point past the tortoise is not a spatial limit for Achilles to reach by pulling together an infinitesimal number of successive points in between himself and the tortoise. Rather, Achilles would emerge together with the track and the tortoise as a different being than the being that was Achilles, the track, and the tortoise at the starting line. This gets Achilles the victory, but it's a pyrrhic victory, since it can no longer be said that Achilles and his athletic prowess—the confident Achilles at the starting line—caused the victory. Neither his athletic prowess nor the victory existed independently of the tortoise and the piece of track just ahead of the tortoise.

If a firm commitment to realism outside of the human subject means that we must put the assemblage of actors at the center of identity and movement, then what is the nature of these assemblages? Philosophies of complexity make claims about what the assemblages look like but are perhaps too beholden to the physical sciences to make any metaphysical claims about the assemblages themselves. Harman argues persuasively that there exist at least two opposing camps on this matter.[43] In the one camp, we have Latour's metaphysics of actors and events, as well as Isabelle Stengers' *cosmopolitics*, both of which are much inspired by Alfred North Whitehead's process metaphysics. In the other camp, we have Deleuze and Guattari—and more recently, Manuel DeLanda and Iain Hamilton Grant—all of whom can trace an intellectual lineage to Bergson's metaphysics of becoming, and ultimately to Spinoza's monism. The question at the heart of it all is that of whether or not there is a substance or a force that underpins the existence of the assemblages. Furthermore, depending upon whether or not there is an underlying substance, how does change happen?

Asymmetry houses movement: Latour's asymmetry as a state of affairs

A surprising treatment of this pair of questions, which sets up the assemblage debate nicely, comes from Leo Tolstoy. *War and Peace* was by no means the first work of historical fiction, but its status in the Western canon is such that the novel is nearly synonymous with the genre. But *War and Peace* rejects the very historiography of the traditional historical novel. Historical fiction is nothing if not an argument that history is composed of "internal homologies."[44] That is to say, the narratives of the fictional characters that the reader follows are local manifestations of the great events and actors of a specific period. Yet at every turn in *War and Peace*, Tolstoy works to dismantle this argument. Indeed, in one historiographical interlude, he draws upon the image of Achilles and the Tortoise to argue that any search for rational laws of movement in history necessarily involves the fragmentation of moments and human wills into "arbitrary, discrete units,"[45] which obscures the real, continuous movement of history. Tolstoy has no truck with either Carlyle's heroic thesis or Hegel's dialectical movement. He argues instead that history is "that unconscious, collective swarm life [*roevaya zhiizn*] of mankind,"[46] which "uses each minute of a king's life for its own ends."[47] Thus, Napoleon's disastrous 1812 adventure into Russia is not a story of hubris, because hubris implies a monopoly of the will. As characters, both Napoleon and Alexander are hollow. But more importantly, neither the emperor nor the tsar have very much in the way of agency. On the battlefields of Austerlitz and Borodino, their agency is deferred to their generals, which in turn is deferred to their battalion commanders, and then to the soldiers, and then to the topography of the land, which the generals mistakenly thought they had account of in the first place.

Not only is agency diffused, it is diffused locally. For instance, when Pierre discovers through his Masonic associations that the numerological value of *l'empereur Napoléon* is 666, he tries to connect himself to Napoleon's power as the Antichrist. Pierre fudges his own name several times before finally getting the desired result of 666 for himself, after which he determines that he is predestined to assassinate the emperor.[48] This is clearly a fool's errand, and it demonstrates that the closer one places oneself next to a distant abstraction of power, the faster the proliferation of hollowness becomes.

For Tolstoy, therefore, there is indeed an abstract substance that makes up the stuff of assemblages, and it is the will. Tolstoy has displaced the power of an abstract thing like history, and moved it to the apertures between the multitude of wills. Moreover, as we see in Pierre's Antichrist episode, non-localized charisma is not a fundamental unit of currency in the economy of power. Power, movement, and change, in Tolstoy's vision, emerge out of local, concrete connections of will. By hollowing out the person of Napoleon (particularly in battle scenes), Tolstoy wasn't denying him his lion's share of historical power that someone like Carlyle would recognize; rather, since Tolstoy had already posited history as an inchoate power, he was dividing Napoleon's agency as an individual from Napoleon's agency as, what Latour calls, a "figuration."[49] A figuration, for Latour, is not the signifier to the signified, the image to the object, nor the Antichrist to the bored Corsican man sitting on a log, waiting to cross the Niemen River. Instead, a figuration is all of the actors acting upon each other to generate some effect: for instance, the Antichrist, including that bored Corsican fellow (as well as the log, if you wish). Latour might tell the gentle Pierre that his mistake in fudging the numerology was forgetting that "no one knows how many people are simultaneously at work in any given individual," and, "conversely, no one knows how much individuality there can be in cloud of statistical data points."[50] After all, the Masons who calculated Napoleon's identity themselves fudged his name from the orthographically correct *l'empereur Napoléon* to *le empereur Napoléon* in order to get their 666.[51] Even what seemed like an analytical correspondence between Napoleon and the Antichrist—a fact that must always have been—required a number of actors to effect it into existence.

We have established that for both Tolstoy and Latour, identity and change occur locally. As we have seen in Tolstoy's historiography, there is no such thing as a history that has its own identity and laws which exist prior to and independently of actual, local interaction. Similarly, Latour has moved the idea of the social both from its a priori existence and from its human (or animal) domain:

> The presence of the social has to be demonstrated each time anew; it can never be simply postulated. If it has no vehicle to travel, it won't move an inch, it will leave no trace, it won't be recorded in any sort of document. Even to detect Polonius behind the arras that became his shroud, the Prince of Denmark needed to hear the squeak of a rat.[52]

Within the social interaction of Hamlet and the figure he thought to be Claudius, there was another social interaction between Hamlet and something (or someone) that made the sound of a rat squeak. As it turns out, within every effect that is created between one actor and another, there are other things acting upon each other. Those things, if they are not part of the identity of the original action (e.g. Hamlet killing Polonius)—that is to say, if they are without a figurative existence—are called *actants*.[53] Borrowing from Whitehead, Latour displaces change itself by *concrescence*, which is a changed state of affairs between actors.[54] This would appear to be unsatisfying because concrescence only seems to describe the effect of change, and change is supposed to include both effect *and* cause. In fact, within concrescence there is both effect and cause; it is just that the two are not in a 1:1 ratio. Thus, there is no cause in the sense of "a compulsory movement…that permits one to sum up an even in order to explain its emergence."[55] If that were the case, Latour goes on, "one would not be faced with an event, with a difference, but only with the simple activation of a potential that was there all along."[56] An effect, or a state of concrescence, simultaneously houses multiple causes. This asymmetry of cause and effect is necessary in order for actors to act upon each other in new ways (and, of course, to create new actors). If there were a 1:1 ratio of causes to effects, the logic goes, the universe would have already spent its potential in an instant. This is very much like the argument for asymmetry in physics. If the 1:1 ratio of matter to antimatter had not been broken (perhaps by antimatter particles decaying at a slightly faster rate), we would all be a smooth sheet of nothing.

Deleuze's Evental Asymmetry

Latour's universe is, therefore, an asymmetrical assemblage of mediators without an intermediary force. Deleuze's universe too is composed of asymmetries. Indeed, he is perhaps *the* philosopher of asymmetry. In the Deleuzean universe, three major asymmetries are apparent: Time-Movement, Intensity-Extensity, and Content-Effect. But whereas the stuff of newness in Latour's world emerges without an intermediary force but from the excess of causes to effects, newness for Deleuze emerges from the intermediary of desire, which both flows through and exceeds the relationship between affects.

Time and movement are asymmetrical in the Deleuzean universe. Time is an oscillation between deterritorialization and reterritorialization, a highly uneven process of change that depends not upon an abstract frame, but upon differently intense interactions between things. For example, Deleuze talks about a stick-tool as a deterritorialized branch.[57] As a reterritorialized stick-tool, the branch may be a part of much larger assemblages than it was a part of on the tree, meaning that deterritorialization and reterritorialization is not just an equal exchange of being. The same is true at much larger scales, which is why capitalist time moves faster than feudalist time, given the sheer amount of energies and materials that are moved under the capitalist regime. Thus when it comes to the creation of newness, movement exceeds time.

Asymmetry is also built into things themselves in terms of the difference between their actual qualities (extensity) and their sensations (intensity). The difference between the two may be equated to Locke's distinction between the primary and secondary characteristics of a thing in which primary characteristics are objective, and secondary characteristics are sensible. Deleuze decries "our tendency to consider intensive quality as a badly grounded empirical concept, an impure mixture of a sensible quality and extensity, or even of a physical quality and an extensive quality."[58] Intensity, for Deleuze, should no longer be considered a pale shadow of extensity, a near illusion of a mind that is insulated from the world. For although intensities arise out of extensities and extension, they are at once more variable and more durable than extensities.[59] In other words, you can slice up an apple into as many volumes you want, but doing so doesn't make the apple slices any less red. The red of the apple is experienced as pure difference, beyond even the static quality of redness. Intensity, being pure difference, is the virtual realm in which affects transform potentiality into actual becoming. Affect, as Brian Massumi explains, "is in the gap between content and effect."[60] In other words, affect is what throws the effect-a-thing-has-on-something-else in a different direction from the thing's content. Affect multiplies effect, giving it an asymmetrical relationship to content.

We like to think of things coming together and combining based on their contents. So, a lemonade shake-up is sour because of the lemons in it. A lemonade shake-up is sweet because of the sugar in it. A lemonade shake-up is wet because of the water in it. If this were the end of the story, then, in principle, all lemonade shake-ups of equal proportions would be the same, would have the same affective capacities. This author, however, is enough of a carnival food savant to recognize the error in this logic. It would also mean, for instance, that the sugar has exhausted its content in sweetening the shake-up. This says nothing about the fact that I have just dispatched a bag of freshly fried, sugar covered mini-donuts, and that upon feeling the bits of undissolved sugar from the shake-up in between my molars, I begin to wonder if synthetically grown pancreas replacements will be available in my lifetime. Thus, the sweet content and the texture content of the sugar are far exceeded by the event in which I contemplate the long-term consequences of the poor choices I have made at the Heritage Days festival in Macomb, Illinois. My regrets, which are followed by my musings on 21st century medical technology, are not a chain of mental causes and effects set off by a chain of physical causes and effects. They are, in Deleuzean ontology, the same in their relation to an assemblage that includes the particular sensation of grittiness that occurs between the undissolved sugar and my molars. The sugar has been deterritorialized from the nectarous gulp of shake-up in my mouth, and then reterritorialized into a machine that includes my relationship with medical technology.

Described in terms of a Latourian concrescence, my lemonade shake-up situation is a social state of affairs. The sociality in the relationships between the sugar as a component in the shake-up, the sugar between my molars, and my worries did not pre-exist those relationships, but was only made apparent because, for instance, the sugar in my molars could exist as more than one causal actor within the single effect of grittiness. The sugar was an actor in the network that registered the sensation of grittiness and also an actor in the network that registered the sensation of anxiety, and so on. Again, the social state emerged from the excess of interactions that a thing (sugar, molar, nerves, etc.) could have with adjacent actors. A non-social relationship would be one in which the thing-itself and the thing-as-actor were 1:1 respectively, whereas the social relationship is a product of that ratio being $1:n$, in which n is >1.

However, in Deleuzean terms, the lemonade shake-up situation is not a state of affairs, but a moving event. Neither the virtual capacity of the sugar to affect the molars nor the molars' virtual capacity to affect the sugar preexist the other. They emerge together in a "double capture,"[61] with neither combining with, absorbing, nor canceling out the other, but with both becoming a new thing, a new thing that does not bear a relationship of "descent and filiation" to the former capacities of the things involved.[62] The reason that the two complementary capacities in this double capture do not cancel each other out or combine to create a static thing is that there is an intermediary force that brings them together in space and moves time through them. This intermediary force is *desire*.

To be clear, Deleuze and Guattari do not claim that desire is a transcendent force acting from the outside on every occasion in the universe: "Desire has nothing to do with a natural or spontaneous determination; there is no desire but assembling, assembled desire."[63] What Deleuze and Guattari have in mind is closer to the immanent force of the Spinozist God; however, they have found Spinoza standing on his head. The first proposition of Spinoza's *Ethics* is "A substance is prior in nature to its affections."[64] Actualization, for Deleuze and Guattari, passes first not through substance and form but through virtual capacities, and so desire cannot be said to occupy the same place for Deleuze and Guattari that God does for Spinoza. As they argue, "Desire is never an *undifferentiated* instinctual energy, but itself results from a highly developed, engineered setup rich in interactions…"[65] Desire is not undifferentiated because the intensities inherent in the capacities of things are themselves "susceptible to *more or less*,"[66] and are therefore emergent and highly differentiated. The sugar between my molars may be more or less gritty, depending not only on the number and size of sugar granules present but also on the condition of my molars, whether my jaw moved back and forth or side to side, etc. The potential interfaces between sugar and molar and, therefore, the intensity of desire in the interstices, are absolutely singular.

Because the intensive character of the desire between capacities is the same as the capacities themselves with respect to the event/assemblage, it is reasonable to ask how it can be that "desire is the real *agent* merging each time with the variables of an assemblage."[67] In other words, as Graham

Harman has demanded of process metaphysics in general, how is there surplus desire enough to draw assemblages to other assemblages?[68] How can desire continue to do the work of *agencer* [assembling] when it has been nominalized into an *agencement* [assemblage]? In order for movement/change to occur within Deleuze's univocal universe, in order for various inflections of the One to keep from converging upon one another and becoming the same, we need to inject a sort of symmetry, in which affect and desire appear as opposite pairs, with one part of the pair constantly projecting the other away from itself.

In Deleuze's "double-capture," we see a symmetry of emergent affects between things in an assemblage that are themselves asymmetrical to the actual forms of those things, which is why relational quantity supervenes on formal quality. And because the attraction between things (desire) flows between emergent affect and emergent affect—rather than from static form to static form—there is a further asymmetry within assemblage-things themselves, even when the same geometric forms assemble recursively in increasing scales. So, if we return to Koch curved coastlines or snowflakes, we can see that angular shapes assemble into smoother, more rounded shapes than their constituent parts. However, those up-scaled, rounded shapes do not assemble into a larger system that has stable spherical symmetry, but bulge outwards in different directions, forming an n-fold symmetry[69] that rotates in an increasing "poly-rhythm" in order for symmetry to become apparent.[70] Here again is why relative speed is so central to the Deleuzean universe. As an assemblage increases in quantity of relations, and then in the quantity of folds (or bulges, if you like), the relative distance between folds decreases, which increases the speed with which an assemblage can interact with other assemblages.[71] The proliferation of surfaces within a system brings greater dynamism. This is why, for Deleuze, entropy is only "local," and not characteristic of the "general" evolution of systems.[72] It's also why flexible, circular tires are such an astonishing improvement on those old *Flintstones* models.

And yet, such an increase in surfaces in which assemblages can affect each other at greater relative speeds should not be seen, according to Deleuze and Guattari, as overcoming a pre-existing lack between assemblages, since "Desire does not lack anything…"[73] Deleuze and

Guattari border on antinomy when they argue that even lack itself, with the intensive images of fantasy or distortion it produces, is evidence of a productive *something* ("an 'essence of lack'") rather than an antithetical *nothing*.[74] Surfaces never stare out into the void, but emerge as double affects which are staring at each other. Here we finally return to the question of surplus desire. Why would these double affects not exhaust their desires on themselves, like an expanding (but ultimately finite) two-dimensional jigsaw puzzle inside of a single present?

For Deleuze, there are no presents inside of presents, only presents coexisting on the one plane of immanence. Some presents bear a relational quality of pastness to one another, just as the virtual and actual are related, but these are not ordinal relationships. In other words, it's not as if $n+1$ contains n within it. A pastness only relates to a presentness as another present. An assemblage, therefore, as a present thisness, is part of a single, totally denumerable infinity. There could be, in the Deleuzean universe, a natural number correspondence to every assemblage that ever was and ever will be. Of course, Deleuze would object to such talk of "ever was and ever will be," since the whole-of-things is not the same as the all-of-things. Yet this objection doesn't quite work in a state of pure immanence. The problem with the claim that the Whole ≠ All in immanence is that even the denumeration of haecceities (assemblages) can be included as however many haecceities you want. There is no Russellian predicative jump,[75] so even if the All is never completed as an All in the midst of your counting of all those haecceities, you're still stuck with the same infinity. Deleuze is fine with this, by the way. Or at least he should be. Because, despite the whole Whole ≠ All problem, the outcome is the same: if there is only the single infinity of all assemblages, then it can't be said that reality has an identity because there is no symmetrical or negative entity (e.g. a Void) with which it can emerge as an identity.

Symmetry houses identity

What I've been arguing in this tour of the metaphysics of movement is that change depends upon asymmetrical relationships, whereas formal identity, which holds surplus for movement, is based in symmetry. Again in very practical terms, we may point to the asymmetrical processes of particle decay, which was necessary for the emergence of the material universe, as well as diversity therein. In both Latour and Deleuze, change is dependent upon there being an asymmetry between the content of things and their potential to be changed. The latter always exceeds the former because the possibility to effect change and to be changed lies away from the content of things themselves; it is instead located in the relations between things. So, we can develop a kind of axiom, one that will hardly be earthshaking to anyone: change requires asymmetry, and asymmetry requires surplus. The real point of contention is just what the stuff of that surplus is in the first place. With Deleuze, the potential for change, which is located in the virtual realm, is characterized by the swarm of desire around the content of a thing. Though again, there are some real questions about how a surplus of desire is possible. Going back to the matter/antimatter asymmetry, we cannot say that the surplus required for the asymmetrical decay in antimatter is located in an even difference between the rates of decay between particles and antiparticles. In other words, there is no surplus of speed in the lives of antiparticles. According to the principle of charge conjunction-parity violation (CP violation), the preference for being in the particle state (as opposed to the antiparticle state) does not appear to happen in the process of decay itself. In this instance, then, surplus is a state of affairs without a firm cause (Point: Latour). It is not immediately clear what the underlying cause of this surplus is; nor is it even clear that observed CP violation in particles, such as kaons,[76] is part of the same process that led to the initial imbalance of matter over antimatter in the short time after the Big Bang.

Deleuze maintains that identity is less real than difference for the same reason (we might assume) that intensive qualities are more real than extensive qualities. Deleuzean reality is in the *this*, *this* and *this*. Intensive qualities belong to the *this* rather than the *what*. The *what* is identifiable and potentially measurable and therefore extensive. And although physicists don't usually trouble themselves with the intensive/extensive problem (though wave function collapse is implicitly such a problem), they tend to be in agreement with Deleuze that identity is essentially a subtractive phenomenon. The difference is that physicists see this as a good thing. Elementary particles, such as electrons, are not only elementary because they don't appear to be made up of any other stuff besides themselves; they are elementary because they are identical in every identifiable way. Here we're talking about spin type, charge and mass. Electrons don't have other qualities that we associate with identity, such as odor or stripes, for obvious reasons. Ah, you say, but if all other identifiers fail, surely there is at least haecceity. And it's true that when we're talking about fermions in particular (electrons are fermions), there is the Pauli Exclusion Principle, which says that no two fermions can occupy the same quantum state.[77] In other words, if one electron is pretty excited, the other electron has to very excited or just somewhat excited (i.e. in a different orbit). No two can occupy the same energy state. You should be able to say that *this* electron is occupying this state and *that* electron is occupying that state, but you'd be wrong. In quantum mechanics, you can't track a single particle because they don't move continuously; they move by quanta. And so you would have no idea whether you were identifying this electron or that electron. Just don't ever get pulled into a game of Three Card Monte with these particles—they'll rob you blind.

From a monadistic point of view, this particular problem of haecceity is merely an issue of access. Just because we can't distinguish this electron from that electron, it does not mean that haecceity does not exist between the particles themselves. You don't have to be a panpsychist to see that this is a perfectly reasonable metaphysical position. But even here, we might be assuming too much about the physical state of affairs. Consider John Wheeler's weird guess about electrons. Perhaps the most poetic physicist of the quantum canon—he's responsible for concepts like *quantum foam* and *wormhole*—Wheeler speculated that there aren't multiple totally identical electrons, but a single, self-identical electron racing back and forth from here to the end of time.[78] At every moment, there exist a large but finite number of recordings of these travels, which we can't help but think of as multiple but identical electrons. As for those electron-like things—positrons—whose only distinguishing attribute is their positive charge, they are simply the one electron making a return trip, which is why they look backwards. Wheeler's idea is captivating but, for the moment, it is empirically damned because we seem to have more matter than antimatter in the universe. Nonetheless, the one-electron universe is plausible enough to demonstrate that a Parmenidean picture of reality can be suggested by explanations of the physical world alone, and without reference to any metaphysical system per se.

Ontic structural realists[79] have seized upon the electron identity problem in particular in order to assert a metaphysics of identity that progressively empties the universe of objects without sliding back into monism. OSR is broadly characterized by its preoccupation with the relationship between relata and relation. Defenders of OSR, such as French and Ladyman, see objects only as necessary heuristic things, since we supposedly lack the semantic tools to conceive of relations without relata. They argue that "there are mind-independent modal relations between phenomena (both possible and actual), but these relations are not supervenient on the properties of unobservable objects and the external relations between them, rather this structure is ontologically basic."[80] Note well that what is being advanced here is not just process metaphysics by another name. It is not just that the residuum of a thing after its relations with others is null—there was never a thing in the first place. And of course, when relata are subtracted from relation, there is no need to worry about something like haecceity. Instead of being mere tools of cognitive economy or apophenia, patterns in nature are, for OSR, more real than their singular constituents. Thus a field is more real than its electrons (since a field is already a set of structures), whereas an electron is a thing with properties. If properties, the logic goes, are the effects of interfacing with other properties of things, then that which is constant about the interfacing is all that's really there. The field is the interface is the structure, and it can be described without any "ontological residuum."[81] Basically, OSR does indeed hold that things are nothing more than bundles of properties, but unlike the empiricists, OSR doesn't stop there: properties are subtractions from structures, and structures are mathematical, which means they are identical in any context.

One of the ways in which the OSR position can be achieved is by conflating symmetry with invariance. The appealing thing about conflating symmetry with invariance is that invariance is described by mathematical relationships, whereas symmetry begins either from relations between objects or between the constituent parts of an object or from the orientational possibilities[82] of an object. In other words, invariance is concerned with relation and symmetry is concerned with relata. In physics, the rules of conservation are built into both symmetry and invariance. Take, for instance, the continuous symmetry of space. We know that space is the same in all directions because of the conservation of momentum. Back to electrons. When two electrons with either the same or different momentums collide, the total momentum of both electrons does not change, even if the post-collision electrons walk away with different momentums from the ones they met with. Momentum as a property has changed location (has undergone spatial translation), but it has remained the same as far as space is concerned. The specific quantity of momentum in this situation is *invariant*. Invariance, then, is the thing in this situation that is described mathematically.[83] To sum it up, the rule is conservation; the thing is symmetrical; the properties are invariant.

But fine. It's rather easy to see something like momentum as the property of a system, and then a little way down the scale, a property of a system's constituent particles. But how do you justify stopping with the invariance of a system when the momentum values of the system's constituent particles may or may not have varied betwixt themselves? You do this by turning to another symmetry, namely permutation symmetry (variously, *the indistinguishability postulate* or *permutation invariance*). Permutation symmetry is a way of identifying the possible states of a local system consisting of multiple indistinguishable elements. Depending upon whether you are dealing with a particular kind of boson or with a particular kind of fermion,[84] the number of possible permutations of a given number of elements is invariant. Intuition might tell you that permutation symmetry can be traced to the identity of the particles involved (in that they have no individual identities). In OSR, on the other hand, permutation symmetry (being itself a mathematical structure) is ontologically prior to the non-individuality of the elements. However, as Christian Wüthrich admits, a simple ontological pledge to mathematics itself doesn't necessarily guarantee that you won't be left with either a surplus or a deficit of identity:

> The mathematical structure of equations often does of course grasp the structure of what is postulated by the theory to physically exist, but it should be noted that the mathematics of a theory alone can be very similar for completely dissimilar 'stuff,' while theories trading in more or less the same physical

existents may be formulated in terms of rather different mathematics.[85]

The ontological pledge, then, is to sets themselves. Permutation symmetry is part of group theory, which is in turn supported by set theory. Finally, of course, sets are ontologically primary in mathematics. OSR privileges mathematical structure not because mathematical operations can be used to make novel predictions about the physical world; there can be serious disparities between predictions and explanations in the physical world. Rather, it is because sets are ontically productive. When you're dealing with entities that are inaccessible by direct observation, it makes sense not to reduce your ontology down to fundamental things, like Democritean atoms, because thing-based philosophies are so easily trampled in the march of science. Committing to fundamental elements and forces is just about as tricky as putting God in the gaps. But even committing to certain structural divisions, such as that of force and matter, could leave you on the wrong side of reality if, for instance, supersymmetry turns out to be correct. On the other hand, the distinct advantage of having a fundamental thing in your ontology is that you can bootstrap your way up to a cosmos. The nice part about sets is that, if you choose to do so, you could see them as mere structures, but they can also bootstrap like fundamental things do. But whereas fundamental things bootstrap by combining purely arithmetically, sets build upon each other by recursion.

A recursive system doesn't add things onto a foundation. It doesn't build from a background to a surface. This is going to sound grievously Heideggerian, but you can say that rather than adding, a recursive system *withins* at the surface of a structure or at the identity of the set.

Symmetry is not self-sameness and, therefore, identity is not subtractive

I've been talking a lot about symmetry and how it is treated in relation to objects and structures as well as to identity and non-identity. But I haven't really made any metaphysical claims about symmetry itself. Let's remedy that.

For such an important concept, our inherited notions of what symmetry is are surprisingly pretty vague. Aquinas, for instance, leaves us with a pretty dismal, negative definition of symmetry—as in symmetry is not similarity. From a primitive aesthetic standpoint, we can talk about harmony in proportion, which can be mathematized. Geometrical objects can be defined by their symmetrical movements under which they are invariant (rotation, glide reflection, etc.). Number groups can be defined by the sets of permutations by which they are invariant. If invariance is the key to symmetry, then we could safely say that symmetry is the same as sameness or isotropy. But what about the symmetry of equivalents? Opposites are not the same, but they can be equivalent. It's true that a system of opposites can be described by invariance, but the system itself doesn't necessarily determine what the opposite equivalents are. For instance, every color in a palate might have an opposite color (e.g. Black/White or Red/Blue), but the system itself does not determine those equivalents, unless we give the system some sort of geometrical referent or numerical value like a color wheel or an energy spectrum. It's the same problem you get with a set of all sets—a domain must be chosen if the values of the set's elements are to be known.

But perhaps Thomas is wrong on this one. I want to suggest that symmetry really does have something to do with similarity. Again, OSR makes a firm connection between a subtractive identity of structures, symmetry and sets. Furthermore, sets bootstrap by recursion rather than by arithmetic. And indeed, I think recursion points to something crucial about symmetry itself. But I'm going to argue that the train from recursion to symmetry leads to a surplussive identity of objects rather than to subtractive identity of structures.

According to Leibniz's principle of the Identity of Indiscernibles, an object is the same as itself. Stated differently, no two objects can have the same properties and still be considered different objects. Again, unless you subscribe to Wheeler's cosmology, elementary particles like electrons present a serious challenge to Leibniz's principle. The other way out, which is furnished by OSR, is that identity is a local symmetrical structure, and objects in that structure are at best invariant location points of the structure. In geometrical terms, identity is defined by movement, in that identity is non-movement or a zero-point transformation. The great phenomenological mathematician Hermann Weyl gives us roughly the same geometrical definition of identity, but with a little nuance:

> A mapping of S of space associates with every space point p a point p' as its image. A special such mapping is the identity I carrying every point p to itself.[86]

That's just kind of a weird way to put it. Suddenly, this negatively defined property has an almost positive quality. Identity is a sort of vortex or suture *carrying* symmetrical points into themselves. This positive definition of identity is a good place to start if you want to make the argument that identity is surplussive. Thus, if zero is the place where you want to start talking identity, then there is more to say about identity than simple sameness. Frege, for instance, shows us that zero is a particular kind of thing that is not identical with itself.[87] Zero is pure separation. It's not so much that zero is the opposite equivalent of one; zero is rather that which allows for the separation of one from nothing, one from the other. As an empty set, zero (here we're talking about zero as void) is an element present in every set. Multiplicity, therefore, is not the repetition of the same; it is the repetition of the non-same.[88] This actually comes back to Leibniz's indiscernibles: as objects (albeit of the mathematical flavor), sets that have the same elements are equal, so a set with no elements is non-equal, and is therefore unique. So, at the downward level of any set object, identity is not sameness.

Let's reverse course and go up to infinity. Our intuition is once more tempted to define the thing negatively. It's right there in the *in-* prefix. And indeed, before the 19th century, infinity was treated as the undifferentiated non-finite. But anybody who has ever played the "Jinx" game as a child knows that infinity is not self-same. When two kids happen to say the same word at the same time (e.g. "burrito"), each is obliged to yell: "Jinx! You owe me a Coke!" before the other can yell it. If they both manage to yell it out at the same time, they'll try again. Of course, no one wins here either, so:

> Jinx! You owe me a Coke!
> Jinx! You owe me a Coke INFINITY!
> Jinx! You owe me a Coke INFINITY plus ONE!
> Jinx! You owe me a Coke INFINITY plus INFINITY!

Jinx! You owe me a Coke INFINITY plus
INFINITY plus ONE!

Somehow, the manipulation of infinity is supposed to settle the uncanny feeling of having the same thought at the same time as someone else, to restore individuality and propriety to the thought: "*I really thought to say 'burrito' first. You just copied off me. However, I will allow you to rent my thought. Leasing fees shall be tendered in a single unit of Coke or the cash value thereof.*" Scary internalization of capitalist logic aside, what these children know is that infinity is an upward limit of the finite, but not an upward limit of itself.

And it is here that we can see a positive definition of infinity in which the existence of infinity precedes the succession of finite numbers.[89] One simple definition is furnished by Richard Dedekind in his description of an infinite system:[90] "A system S is said to be *infinite* when it is similar to a proper part of itself."[91] Unconvinced that he's dealing with anything but abstract forms, Dedekind gets no more concrete than the thoughts in his own head:

> Proof. My own realm of thoughts, i.e., the totality S of all things, which can be objects of my thought, is infinite. For if s signifies an element of S, then is the thought s', that s can be object of my thought, itself an element of S. If we regard this as transform $\varphi(s)$ of the element s then has the transformation φ of S, thus determined, the property that the transform S' is part of S; and S' is certainly proper part of S, because there are elements in S (e.g. my own ego) which are different from such thought s' and therefore are not contained in S'. Finally, a, b, that if a, b are different elements of S, their transforms a', b' are also different, that therefore the transformation φ is a distinct (similar) transformation. Hence S is infinite, which was to be proved.[92]

Okay. It's not so simple. But it's worth understanding the centrality of *similarity* and not sameness in the existence of the infinite. The relationship between an object of thought (s) and the thought image of the object of thought (s') is one of similarity, meaning that s' does not cancel out s as the same, nor does S' cancel out S. Rather, both s and s' belong to the thought system S as multiple, ordered elements, that as long as they function as successive images, can go up to infinity and still belong to *S*. Any system that doesn't have this attribute of self-similarity is finite. Therefore, it is the finite which is defined negatively.

If we leave Dedekind's head and proceed to Georg Cantor's more general idea of infinite successions of ordinals, we can see the same sort of recursive process. If we take the series 1, 2, 3, 4... and push it all the way up to infinity, we can play the "Jinx" game:

1, 2, 3, 4....ω

ω + 1, ω + 2, ω + 3... ω + ω

(ω + ω) + 1, (ω + ω) + 2... (ω + ω) + ω[93]

It's as though each ω and each combination of ω becomes a new zero. But again, zero is the repetition of the non-same. And here, the new "zeros" are repetitions of the similar. The old zero and the new "zeros" are alike in that they repeat, and neither is self-same. And since the set definition of each finite number includes the non-self-same zero (empty set), we can say that nowhere in numbers is identity self-same. What we can say about the relationship between the old zero and the new "zeros" of infinity is that they share the attribute of endurance.

Symmetry hides and identity endures.

Against the metaphysics of complexity theory,[94] I contend that self-similarity has as much to do with the enduring identity of an object as it does with movement from form to form. Endurance is repetition without sameness. Endurance is what recursion looks like with a sufficient amount of movement. Similarity, I contend, is a state of affairs that emerges between multiple objects in contact or within an

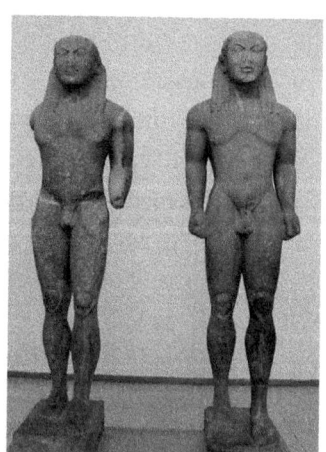

Figure 2: The Kouroi Statues, Kleobis and Biton

object in contact with itself as it endures contact with others. Recall once more the Koch curve snowflake. Again, the operation consists of adding triangles of 1/3 the size of an original triangle to the sides of that original triangle. After the first operation, you will have a six-pointed object. And after n operations, the six-pointed object remains, but you might encounter the six points as bulges instead. The matter of the snowflake—the number of surfaces—has changed, has multiplied. The form of the snowflake has also changed, but it has also endured. The surface perimeter between the snowflake at moment$_1$ and moment$_n$ is proportionate (specifically $(4/3)^n$), but the relationship between the form of the snowflake at moments 1 and n is one of similarity. The snowflake at moment$_1$ and moment$_n$ can also be said to be structurally invariant in that at both moments it is six-fold symmetrical, and furthermore, some two-dimensional properties (height, width) of the snowflake between moments may be the same. But since the surface perimeter has increased dramatically, the total form of the object is certainly not-self same. On the other hand, it's also quite obvious that the snowflake is not asymmetrical to itself. Despite the material changes the snowflake has undergone, it is symmetrical from moment to moment in its self-similarity. It is this more profound kind of symmetry—the symmetry of enduring self-similarity—that houses the surplus of identity for objects. If this kind of symmetry cannot be described in terms of structural invariance, then it is perhaps an aesthetic phenomenon.

Indeed, aesthetics might offer an understanding of surplus that we can more easily speculate upon. Consider the 6th century B.C. *Kouroi* sculptures, *Kleobis* and *Biton*, against the 5th century B.C. *Riace Warrior* bronzes (see Figures 2. and 3.).

Figure 3: The Riace Bronzes

In order to achieve the *contrapposto* effect of movement and tension in the latter, a certain amount of lateral symmetry had to be given up.

Deleuze warns us that when we talk about "productive dissymmetry" in art and nature, we should not be misled by "the negative expression, 'lack of symmetry,'" since, again, 'lack' is "positivity itself."[95] Deleuze might well share the immediate impression that most of us would have if we looked at the *Kouroi* sculptures and the *Riace* bronzes side-by-side: the *Riace* are more lifelike. For many of us, that would simply mean that the *Riace* figures effect a more truthful imitation of the male human body. For Deleuze, on the other hand, it might be a more truthful imitation of life itself, in so far as the *Riace* figures contrast to the *Kouroi*, who never really depart from a point of immobile symmetry in the first place. (Let it be acknowledged that 'lifelike' wouldn't really be in Deleuze's lexicon anyway.)

Departing from either the common view or the Deleuzean view, the art historian E.H. Gombrich spent a career arguing that the intentional creation of *more* life-like representations is like building your ship while you're already at sea; all you can do is make repairs to the ship you're already on. That is to say that no cultural tradition has ever decided that they were not already creating lifelike representations and that they would begin doing so presently. As to the evolution of Greek sculpture from the Archaic period to the Classical period, Gombrich doubts that a sudden preoccupation with naturalism would have instigated such an astonishing technical coup. We may argue as to whether or not nature is itself a cultural construct, but surely *naturalism* is one, and artists have been in the business of naturalism since the get-go. Gombrich argues instead that contrapposto in sculpture was actually a move away from representing universals in nature; it was about injecting the particularity of narrative into representation.[96] The movement we perceive in figures like the *Riace* is not the *automatos* of life itself, but movement inside of a particular event. The particular event does not antecede the figure that is represented, but rather the figure becomes joined to whatever or whoever else is present to witness the event. When we witness the *Kouroi*, we are supposed to be witnessing them as they are in their manifest symmetry; we are supposed to be witnessing the entirety of their being, and we are joined to them by nothing. The *Kouroi*, in other words, endure beyond the event of our witnessing them or any other event. But with the *Riace*, we are with them, witnessing an event. Thus, Deleuze is correct in the sense that we should not speak of a 'lack' of symmetry in reference to asymmetry. Symmetry in the *Riace* figures is instead *hidden* in a way that it is not hidden in the *Kouroi* in the same way that the symmetry of fundamental forces may have been hidden as the universe cooled after the Big Bang. Symmetry, it turns out, has a way of being there without being present.

The surplus of identity exists in a state of symmetry, a state that hides away from events in which asymmetrical movement occurs. So far, we have been talking about the enduring identities of objects in terms of how the forms of objects remain symmetrical to themselves. But objects also relate to each other (and thus have identities to relate) beyond their forms. So, how does formal identity relate to objective identity? Identity is a funny thing because it connotes both separateness from others and endurance of the self.[97] Picture a Prilosec sitting in a pillbox with an ibuprofen, a paroxetine, and a calcium supplement. Placed together in the pillbox, this is a scene of asymmetry: one pill is large, round and grey; another is a red and white capsule; the other is small, pink and oblong. The Prilosec is oblong and purple. It first of all has the quality of purpleness that your senses find in a particular light, background, and contrast to the other pills in the box. This may change slightly as you shift perspective or as the pillbox is jostled. These sense impressions are asymmetrical to each other. And then there is the purpleness of the pill that is self-similar outside of any particular sensual experience of the pill. The purpleness is self-similar and not self-same because its purpleness is not the manifestation of some abstract and eternal purple; it is a repetition of purpleness from moment to moment that integrates particular sensual changes. Nor is this repetition of purpleness an expression of pure difference in the Deleuzean sense, since it is a repetition of the object's own purpleness. Since it endures as itself beyond sensual events, this purpleness is symmetrical. In so far as the pill's sensual qualities are concerned, this purpleness is similar to itself in a way that that sensual qualities are not to each other.

In his philosophy of the fourfold object, Graham Harman might draw a distinction between, for instance, the purple of the pill in the sensual encounter, and the purple of the pill that endures beyond such events: *sensual qualities* and *real qualities*. Harman associates real qualities with Husserl's notion of *eidos*, which is a lexical cousin to both *idea* and *separate*.

Real or eidetic qualities are those that mark an object as what it is and what it is not.[98] Contrary to Husserl's eidetic traits, Harman's real qualities do not depend upon semantic investment or non-linguistic human intuitions of extension, movement, etc. Nor are real qualities fully accessible to the senses or to the intellect. As Harman explains, "A proton or volcano must have a variety of distinct properties, but these remain just as withdrawn from us as the proton and volcano themselves."[99] Since real qualities do not depend upon concepts or intuitions to exist (i.e. a subject), they must be held together by the object itself. This is what Harman terms the *real object*, and like the real qualities, it withdraws from access. The real object has a similar kind of relationship with the sensual object (which holds together sensual qualities) that real qualities have with sensual qualities. Real qualities can change from moment to moment as the real object enters asymmetrical events of contact with others, but the real object may endure beyond those events. For instance, the art museum in Toledo, Ohio can be robbed of a few paintings, and it may add some paintings in a temporary exhibition, but the Toledo Museum of Art endures.

In Aristotelian terms, we may say that the real object is the *form* of its real qualities. The real qualities, in relation to the form, are matter. If we think about real qualities as a kind of matter, then we run into a problem, since, at least for Aristotle, form is predicated of matter.[100] Thus, if the matter of a form is replaced by other matter (e.g. paintings in the Toledo Museum of Art), then the original form should perish as well. Good Aristotelian that he was, St. Thomas Aquinas faced this very problem when he tried to argue that the soul was the form of the body, with the body in turn being the matter. The problem was that the body is corruptible. Aquinas was quite taken with the problem of the cannibal, which was originally posed by St. Augustine. It goes something like this. If a cannibal spent all of his life eating the bodies of other people, it stands to reason that the cannibal's body would be sustained and replaced by the bodies of others. So at Resurrection, wouldn't the souls of the victims have to attach themselves to the body of the cannibal? This is the kind of thing that sets Catholic Christianity apart from other monotheisms, because it is a very pagan problem in need of a solution that will inevitably be a pagan-monotheistic synthesis. Aquinas's answer is both that matter is variable and that it need not be localized to be a part of the identity of a form. The cannibal problem is a colorful thought experiment with which I suspect Aquinas had a lot of morbid fun because he brings it up in a few different works. (You can almost hear the muted chuckles echoing out of a University of Paris lecture hall, the baby Dominican monks wondering if it's okay to laugh along.) The original, perhaps more serious problem, however, was how the soul could be the form of the body in the first place, since the soul was incorruptible, and the body was quite corruptible. St. Thomas's answer was that had it not been for original sin, the body too would be incorruptible.[101] Original sin was accidental (in the metaphysical sense), and the form endures beyond the accident. In this way, too, having your body devoured by a cannibal is also accidental, and so as long as the soul-form endures, you shouldn't have a problem at the Resurrection. It's not that the soul travels alone, separate from the body; it's that the soul is both non-local and individuated by the body. Therefore, the body is the variegated real qualities of the soul, and these qualities interact with each other asymmetrically. For example, one of my arms may be eaten by the cannibal while the other remains attached to my shoulder. However, both arms interact similarly with my soul. The corporeal real qualities interact with the soul similarly and not samely because the soul is not a perfect, self-same idea that exists without the body. The soul, for Aquinas, only exists in a degree of perfection from God's perfection, a degree that we only have a sense of by analogy. The soul is self-similar all the way through, and, in so far as it is the form of its real qualities, we can say the same about the real object.

Objects are identified as sensual objects, but the sensual object is not the basis of the fourfold object's being, since being itself is not contingent upon its interactions with others. The sensual object is the object's form for others, and thus it is its formal identity. The sensual object is projected by the sensual qualities which the sensual object, in turn, holds together. But the sensual object is capable of enduring self-similarly from moment to moment, whereas the sensual qualities may be asymmetrical to each other from moment to moment. The sensual object can endure self-similarly from moment to moment for another object because it is held together from moment to moment by the real qualities, even if those real qualities may themselves be moved, added, or subtracted. Aristotle says that the form of something is both its essence and its primary substance,[102] but this says nothing about formal identity—that is, how an object is individuated for other objects. It turns out that the sensual object is a form in a way similar to that in which the real object is a form. It's just that the sensual object is the form for others. So, when we talk about *form* with regards to the interactions between objects, we must be talking about the sensual object.

Similarity as an emergent state of affairs between forms in contact

When we think about the sensual object as form, and how it interacts with others, it is hard to come up with a better illustration than Marcel Duchamp's *Fountain*. It's an overused example, but it is so for a good reason. Duchamp's piece, along with Magritte's *Ceci n'est pas une pipe*, epitomizes the modernists' fascination with the impossibility of representation. They are pure presentations of objects, just as Joyce's *Ulysses* is a pure presentation of a day in the life. Magritte's work achieves this through an almost calligramic text, whereas *Fountain* does it through the undecidability between form and function. Under the idealist understanding of art that had taken hold in Modernity, individual works of art, as manifestations of the pure idea of art, should serve no function at all. The individual work is pure form. Such an understanding worked hand-in-glove with, and in contradistinction to, the increasing tendencies of capitalism to instrumentalize every aspect of life. And then Duchamp gives us a urinal. A mass-produced thing designed for the most private, banal, and forgettable moments in a man's day. The more banal the function of an object is, the more functional it seems to become. And the more functional an object becomes, the less we would seem to interact with it as form (hence the familiar opposition of form to function). But along with collapsing of the representation-presentation binary, Duchamp also dissolves the opposition between form and function. The urinal, which, quite plainly, reeks of function, is presented as a pure form. Duchamp is not attacking the idealization of art by showing that anything could be art; rather, he is demonstrating that when we take the idea of pure form to its extreme, we actually find it difficult to escape function. *Fountain* is a urinal presented to function for an aesthetic experience. It is difficult, in other words, to imagine that all objects (particularly manufactured objects) exist in any other way than that for which we intend them to exist. The formal identity of objects would therefore seem to spring from a one-sided relationship.

If we enter the question of identity into Aristotle's matrix of intrinsic and extrinsic causes, we can say that either the septic function of the urinal or the artistic function of *Fountain* is the object's *final cause*. The *final cause* as well as the *efficient cause* (the means by which the thing is assembled) are extrinsic. Thus, the *efficient cause* resides with the urinal's maker(s), and the *final cause* is with the urinal's user(s) and what it is used for. That leaves the intrinsic causes, which are the urinal's *material cause* and its *formal cause*. It seems that when you start asking about the form of something, you can overshoot the mark in at least two ways: you can either go intrinsic and end up at the thing's material components, or you can go extrinsic and arrive at the idea of the thing's purpose (as *Fountain* demonstrates). Either way, you're engaging in intellectual speculation and intention. But I would argue that the *formal cause*, like the *final cause*, is also extrinsic; it's just that the form is extrinsic for the senses rather than for the intellect. Aquinas says of the *formal cause* that it effects a thing "either as its intrinsic form, and this is called its species, or as the extrinsic form to whose likeness it is made..."[103] Aquinas then points out Plato's mistake in thinking that the extrinsic form is primary, since, for Plato, it was made as the image of an idea. Aquinas, like Aristotle (and *contra* Plato), believes in the primacy of species over genus. And yet, I argue that extrinsic form does have something to do with likeness or similarity, but it is an emergent rather than a created similarity.

Again, when any object encounters another, the sensual qualities of the encountered object may shift from moment to moment, but the sensual object that holds the sensual qualities together endures self-similarly. For example, when one takes a bite of an apple, one still senses that she is holding the same apple as before the bite. The apple's appearance is not totally the same as before the bite, but it's not perceived as a different thing after the bite either. It maintains a similar form for the one who took the bite. Furthermore, in her interaction with the apple, the biter grasped the form of the apple by conforming her hand and mouth to the size, shape, and texture of the apple, thus making part of her form—the form that the apple encountered—similar to the form of the apple. Once again, we find similarity as an emergent state of affairs rather than as the realization of a transcendent unity of signs.

Let's return to the urinal in Duchamp's piece. Again, the idea is that we take the form of the urinal for its *final cause* (its septic function). We might retreat from that assumption and talk about its form in terms of the shape and texture of the urinal's porcelain matter. This too would seem to be a category mistake since we could create an infinite list of such features without ever getting to the metaphysics of form. In which case, we might as well abandon form altogether for pure materiality. But as facile as it might seem to think about form as shape, texture, etc., we need not go any further than that to get as close as we can possibly get to an understanding of the form of the thing. The form of an object is what it is in its sensuous encounter with another object. But, at least in the case of the urinal, we need not talk about features like shape and texture to the exclusion of function. We can speculate upon what an object like a urinal is for (its *final cause*) because a human male's relationship to it is functionally aesthetic, or ergonomical.[104] A man can interact with the urinal ergonomically because there emerges a likeness between its shape and his shape. The urinal (unlike Duchamp's *Fountain*) rests vertically. The man stands vertically with it. The urinal has a gentle, oblong shape that bows out at its base. A man's lower torso is also an oblong shape that bows and vees at its base. The emergent similarity we see in form does not, however, extend to the material interaction between man and urinal, which is obviously asymmetrical. And, importantly, the man's shape is not always similar to that of the urinal (he sits and lies down at other moments). In his interactions with the urinal, the man must *conform* to that object. And, at the very minimum, the urinal must conform by resting vertically rather than horizontally. (Even if the urinal did not make the choice to do so, the urinal has the potential to rest other than vertically.) But even in conforming to the urinal, the man does not become the same as the urinal. Nor do the urinal and the man lose themselves in the moment to become some sort of torso-urinal machine, as Deleuze might have it. The man's shape becomes similar to the urinal's shape because his shape translates the shape of the urinal. The man's torso takes on what it grasps as the essence of the urinal and translates that grasping into its own form.

The ergonomics of a urinal is a useful way of talking about how sensuous encounters between objects work, but the point is not that objects are always designed for one particular kind of interaction with one particular kind of object. Rather, in order for one object to interact with another, it must establish some similarity between its form and the form of the other object; it must translate the other object's form into its form. This has nothing to do with the necessity of two objects existing within the *same* spatial and temporal dimensions, as are the prerequisites for Kant's *analogies of experience*. (Space and time, as we will discuss later, radiate from objects themselves.) My thinking here is very much informed by Timothy Morton's arguments about "Causality as Sampling,"[105] in which, for instance, an MP3 recorder does not record the whole of a frog's croak, but instead translates the form of the croak into its own form as an MP3 recorder.

I think Morton is spot-on in his notion of causality; however, the metaphor "sampling," along with the MP3 device, suggests something digital. I prefer to describe such an interaction as being ontologically analog. The idea behind digital recording is that the sound is converted into pure information that can be reproduced in exactly the same way over and over again in different media (even though the recording itself starts off as analog). In analog recording, the translation process is much more apparent: the sound as air or an electrical current pattern is translated into an electrical signal, which is then translated mechanically to the recording medium, such as a vinyl record. The variations in the form of the vinyl record are similar to the variations in the form of the electrical signal, which are similar to the variations in the form of air pressure or electric current that are being recorded. My technical knowledge in this area is extremely limited, as is my ability to discern the difference between analog and digital recordings. But those audio brahmans who do claim the ability to grasp the distinction describe the sound of analog as being less precise or less clean but more complete. What I think is meant by this distinction is that the form of the musical piece is more graspable as a whole, coherent object, even if there is an overlay of distortion (e.g. crackling) on the record. Indeed, the overlay of distortion may add to the experience. For one, there is the felt authenticity of the old, a sense that the record is an enduring object that brings its own world and history to presence. The record, in other words, has been cooking long enough to be soft and warm. But on a more basic level, the overlay of distortion suggests a ghostly presence. It's the kind of ghost that appears with a sheet draped over it. The ghost under the sheet could take on many forms,[106] and perhaps it is not even living in our time, but if the ghost were to appear as a fully detailed human, its potential would be somewhat limited. That fact that its form for us is merely an analog protrusion through another medium adds a terrifying element of the uncanny. This, apparently, is the magic of analog vinyl recordings: instead of getting super hi-fi samples of tom-tom snaps in, let's say, Led Zeppelin's "Moby Dick," the recording session itself protrudes through the vinyl grooves so that you could almost run your fingers over the cast of John Bonham's corybantine beats and cold vodka sweats and Los Angeles, 1969.

Identity and the aesthetics of completeness

The form of the object is what is grasped as the object's identity by another object, but it is only graspable in translation. Since this is always a particular interobjective translation, I argue that the form of the object is the same as the sensual object in Harman's *ontography*.[107] But if the form of an object for others is neither its real qualities nor the real object itself, is there a further symmetry that underpins the object's formal identity? Again, the mechanism by which the real object endures is withdrawal, but into what does it withdraw? One of Harman's key disagreements with Heidegger is when the latter talks about "earth," and the idea that there is a general Being into which things withdraw. Harman rightly dismisses this argument as "a half-cooked form of monism."[108] And yet, a retreat into some larger lump of Being is exactly what constant withdrawal seems to look like: a retreat into either the Deleuzean furnace of flux or a cold cavern of nothingness. It seems to me, then, that what an object does when it withdraws is that it conceals the starting point by which it can be grasped. Think of an object with rotational symmetry, such as a drop of water. Clearly the drop of water had a beginning, but its symmetry obscures that beginning from view. There is no entry point from which you can peel away all of the water molecules inside of the drop to find the one molecule that started it all. You can explain its formation by talking about the behavior of water molecules in general, but finding the beginning point of this particular drop of what would be considerably more difficult.

Internal symmetry (self-similarity) explains how objects can have a surplus identity that endures beyond particular experiences, but against what else does the object have identity? Either objects have identities for the beings of other objects, or they have an identity for non-being itself, such as we see in Alain Badiou's notion of the Void. Badiou doesn't just draw upon set theory; verily, set theory is Badiou's ontology. Specifically, Badiou's ontology is a non-Platonic (and therefore post-Cantorian) Zemelo-Frankelian set theory in which a multiplicity of multiplicities cannot present itself as a structure. This is because the structure of a presentation is not part of the original presentation; it is another presentation altogether. The presentation and the structure are two non-related types. There is not a set of sets, then, and so there can be neither one All or nor cardinalization of everything. The flip side of this is that there can be larger and smaller infinities.[109] Within Badiou's 'inconsistent multiplicity' of structure and presentation, we get a Void ($\emptyset$).[110] With multiple infinities, we have the possibility of unthinking two infinities of the same cardinality, which means the two infinities would have the same identity; they would be an identifiable One among other ones.

As for Harman, he too has "no concept of 'universe'" or a One of ones.[111] He's not thinking of self-member sets but of a superobject that would contain all other objects. Harman is able to set his cosmological limit without mathematics to guarantee it, and without the need to fold back on univocity. The advantage of not needing mathematics or the One as a guarantor of his cosmological fabric is, as we shall see, that non-local movement becomes possible. Harman's superobject limit is possible because no object can be the real object of another RO. So far, this is consistent with Badiou as well because every set is necessarily incomplete; a set's predication is always in excess of the set itself. But for Harman, objects are complete until they are destroyed. Could we then imagine a superobject containing all other objects that is complete by virtue of the fact that is holds the possibility of being destroyed? Not really, because there must exist another complete object *for* which the other object is destroyed. Something is either complete or destroyed for something else.

Think about a dinette set. The complete dinette set consists of a table and four chairs. If I took away one of the chairs, the chair I took away would still be a complete chair; yet the dinette set would no longer be complete, and so would be, as far as I were concerned (i.e. for the me-object) destroyed. As for the chair, I could simply move it to another room and continue using it as a chair, or I could take a sledge hammer to it and destroy it as a chair. What actually happens to the chair doesn't matter as far as the event of the dinette set's destruction is concerned. Thus, we have an asymmetry. Even if both the chair and the dinette set get destroyed, they do not get destroyed together. It's this asymmetry that provides the opportunity for movement or change. No two objects can be completed or destroyed together.[112] And so, all objects cannot converge into the same unchanging thing or non-thing.

On the other-other hand, two complete objects can interact with each other without one complete object subsuming the completeness of the other. Suppose I parked a fifth chair at the dinette table. For the me-object, the fifth chair doesn't necessarily make the original dinette set more complete, and taking it away won't necessarily leave the original dinette set incomplete (or destroyed). It is in this relationship of non-necessity that we see the potential of real objects to withdraw. When multiple objects can interact without completing or destroying each other, we get a symmetry that makes identity possible. Of course, the act of identifying, as we know it, requires some kind of consciousness unique to what we call animals, and the act of associating a particular sign with a thing is unique to fewer animals than it is to simple identification alone. But the basic conditions of mutual completeness which are necessary for identification lie in the objectness of things, not in the consciousness of things.

But let's return to the fifth chair. Although we have a state of mutual completeness between the fifth chair and the dinette set (and thus, we have identity), we may also have a new object that does not interfere with the mutual completeness of either the fifth chair or the dinette set. This depends upon the new object's relations with other complete objects. As Harman argues, "If certain components are arranged in such a manner as to give rise to a thing that exceeds them, in such a way that it can withstand certain changes in these components, then they have entered a genuine relationship with each other as real objects rather than merely stroking one another's sensual facades."[113] So, perhaps the me-object doesn't perceive the dinette set + the fifth chair as a new object. But the floor-object beneath groans a little under the weight of an additional chair. Here, $DsCh_5$ (or the molecule Dinettium Pentachairide, if you like) doesn't need the me-object to notice it or proclaim it as a new object; the floor-object can do that well enough. Maybe all that happens to the floor-object is that it groans under the additional weight, or maybe as Chairs 1 and 4 get pushed aside to make way for Chair 5, the floor gets scuffed a bit. Both of these effects can certainly be considered as a mere "stroking" of "sensual facades." The floor-object doesn't stop being an object because of the groan or the scuff. In which case, $DsCh_5$ should not be considered as a new object. What if, however, the groan is an index of $DsCh_5$'s potential to break the floor-object and fall through? We may first of all say that in such an event, the floor-object is destroyed. The question then is whether the floor-object's destruction came from the dinette set plus the fifth chair, or if it came from the object, $DsCh_5$. We shouldn't, of course, forget the Deleuzean lesson that the event had just as much to do with the floor's capacity to break (its affect). But if we bracket the notion that the floor-breaking event was nothing more than the positive production of a new assemblage, we could say that it was the complete object $DsCh_5$, and not the dinette set plus the fifth chair that played a key role in the breakage event. In which case, the groan was a moment of identification between the mutual completenesses of the floor-object and $DsCh_5$, whereas the scuff was just a moment of identification between the mutual completenesses of the floor-object and the fifth chair, both of which had their separate relationships with the dinette set.

None of this is to say that assemblages are initiated into objecthood by some blood-in-blood-out ritual. A complete object need not have the innate potential to destroy another object in order for it to be complete. Indeed, the destructive power of $DsCh_5$ didn't emanate from itself alone. (I neglected to tell you that the floor was riddled with termites.) A complete object is simply something that's been up to something. That is to say that it has affected and has been affect as an object. Some objects get up to quite a lot; others, not so much. A heart surgeon would not be much of a heart surgeon if all she's ever been up to is heart surgery. Ghastly bedside manner at the very least.

Even a robot heart surgeon is up to not doing surgery between surgeries. The careful reader will now reward herself with a little indignant vexation at that last point, for haven't we found ourselves back at the predicative jump, where the robot surgeon is exceeded by the there-is-a-robot surgeon, which cannot belong to the robot surgeon?

Objects share in their own predication

It's worth reminding ourselves that Badiou's version of the predicative jump is non-Platonic, and is therefore in this respect non-Pythagorean. That is to say that a number like 4, for instance, does not precede specific instances of 4. Furthermore, the number 4 does not exist in reference to an absolute limit of a complete set of all numbers, nor is 4 limited downwards by a count of its smallest elements (e.g. 1). As to the upward limit, set theory tells us that an infinity itself is a presentation of a set that is not itself. And, as for the downward limit, even the smallest considerable element contains within it something that is not itself: the empty set or the Void (Ø). The empty set is a non-one or a no-thing, and so it has nothing in common with the set in which it exists as a subset. This means that the smallest conceivable element already exists as a multiplicity rather than as a unity. Movement in Badiou's universe depends upon this asymmetry of the parts of a set to the set's elements (the former exceeding the latter). The Void itself is "unpresentable,"[114] but there are two ways in which Ø can be thought.

Some time before the rock star Prince decided that he was too original even to be a mononym, set theory designated the Scandinavian Ø for the empty or null set, which Badiou takes as his Void. Ø is above all a proper name, rather than a "property, a species, or a common name."[115] So, Prince was not so original, but of course, neither is Ø. Ø is not unlike the Greek ὁ ὤν (*ho ōn*), which is a nominalization of the verb εἶναι (*einai*). Ὁ ὤν occupies an unnamable place between "the being" and "the one who is," which is a pure presentation of being. But, instead of a pure presentation of being, as God is, Ø is a pure presentation of non-being by which being must be situated. Thus, while Ø obviously has lexical value as a noun in *metaontological* discourse, its ontological value is purely predicative. Ø's real being is an elided copula in the existential copular clause, "There is one." Mathematics is useful as an ontological language because, like Russian, it elides the present-tense copula,[116] thereby offering negative proof that the copula is beyond any representation as a form-class word (i.e. a logos); it is purely an operation. As a pure operation, this elided existential copula, then bears no relation to the elements of which it is an operation. Remember too that Ø, as a subset (a part), has no common elements with the set to which it belongs, and this is how we get more parts than elements.

Badiou insists unapologetically that "If philosophy—which is the disposition for designating exactly where the joint questions of being and of what-happens are at stake—was born in Greece, it is because it is there that ontology established, with the first *deductive* mathematics, the necessary form of its discourse."[117] That is to say that the Greeks formalized the operation of succession so that movement was the same in logic as it was in language. The creation of the new (the new that points to the infinite) by repetition of the same operation is central to Badiou's notion of movement. It's the idea that the new is possible only because the elements that are named as *new* are excluded from the operation itself. So, a simple succession of the new takes on the following repetitive form, beginning with the name of Ø:

$$\emptyset, S(\emptyset), S(S(\emptyset)), S(S(S(\emptyset)))\ldots$$

which gets denumerated as

$$\emptyset, S(\emptyset), S(S(\emptyset)), S(S(S(\emptyset)))\ldots^{118}$$
$$0 \quad 1 \quad\quad 2 \quad\quad\quad 3\ldots$$

Each successive number is new insofar as it names the operations of that which it succeeds. To return to the language of copulas, "$S(\emptyset)$" becomes the "there is" of "one" in the existential clause "There is one." So on and so forth.

In the post-postmodern philosophical climate in which we find ourselves, I hesitate to ask just how universal this elided copula of mathematical logic that the Greeks discovered really is. Had the Greeks discovered something universal, or had they discovered something about their own language? Or both? The question of its ontological universality aside, the existential copula is not necessarily universal across human languages. Certainly, Heidegger made a lot of hay out of the German existential *es gibt* [there is/ is given], which demonstrated that such a copula is not semantically void.[119]

It is indeed quite common that copulas get grammaticalized from stative verbs, such as "lie," "sit," and "stand." Even as recently as 1979, Guugu Yimidhirr (a northeastern Australian language) was undergoing such a process, with "lie" [*wu*-] becoming universalized as a copula among younger speakers, much to the chagrin of the elders.[120] In still other languages, such as Arabana (another Australian language), the object itself determines the existential copula. Different stative verbs are used depending upon whether the object is extended vertically, horizontally, or if its extension appears to be neither.[121] English speakers can imagine themselves saying something like "There lies Abraham Lincoln," whereas "There stands Abraham Lincoln" might only make sense in front of a statue (in other words, something that we know is not actually Abraham Lincoln). But both are deictic constructions, which means that both "lies" and "stands" have much more to do with "there" (and for whom there is a 'there') than they do with Abraham Lincoln. Cantonese speakers get a little closer to the Arabana situation with their complex and beautiful system of noun classifiers. As McWhorter points out, for instance, an object is usually not spoken of without being chaperoned by classifiers whose descriptive powers vary in their opacity. Thus, "table" exists as something like a "flatty of table."[122] English occasionally has something similar in its classifiers for multiples, which are most often nothing other than a statement of multiplicity (i.e. a "pair" of scissors), but are sometimes more qualitative, as in the case of animal multiplicities (including the perennial fan favorite: a *murder* of crows). I'm not making any claim that classifier nouns in Cantonese or English are traces of a pre-Babelian state of human language in which object-dependent existential copulas were universal, however. Nor am I making the claim that Arabana speakers have a special insight into the ontology of objects because their existentials oblige them to notice something specific about the object before tacking any other modifiers onto the hitherto noun-object. The point is just that it's actually very easy to imagine a way of thinking in which the count-as-one, as Badiou puts it, is not the point where pure quantity distinguishes itself from quality. As such, mathematics may not actually be a pure ontological operation, but an epistemological tradition that has chosen to impose the distinction between quantity and quality upon its practices. In fact, Badiou is quite right to name set theory mathematics as an *event*, with its practitioners being faithful to the multiplicity of things which includes a language group that uses non-object-dependent existentials. Things might have been otherwise.

This too is not to reassert the primacy of qualities in the description of being. That's always ultimately a shaky move, since qualities themselves can always take on an eidetic existence, either in terms of their sheer quantity (even if they are not countable) or in terms of qualities in contact, which is why Deleuze embraced the idea the affective intensity was a matter of quantity.

Beyond questions of quantity and quality, we can go back into the object itself. This is what Harman does in his slightly enigmatic notion that the whole of an object is "*less* than the sum of its parts."[123] To say that an object is the sum of its parts is to say that it is a consistent multiplicity, an arrangement of fundamental units. To say that an object is more than the sum of its parts is to say that it is its interactions with others. On the other hand, to say that an object is less than the sum of its parts is to posit an internal distinction between the object as a count-as-one and its qualities. Because the distinction is internal to the object, we can also treat ourselves to an external indistinction, where, just as in the Arabana existential copula, the object shares in its own predication. The object interacts with itself, which, again, means that an object is something that's been up to something.

I like to say that an object "has been up to something" because it's cute. Because it reminds me of rabbits, who get up to mischief more stealthily than any creature I know. If I hear nothing right now, I'm sure to find a ripped up patch of carpet later. That's the thing about something getting up to something: the getting-up-to is always out of view from the one making the accusation, if only just so or just now. When we speak of an object sharing in its own predication and being up-to-something that's out of view, we are, of course, talking about some version of Heideggerian facticity. But bunnies are much more pleasant to think about than Heidegger. That should be clear even to philosophers. Also, rabbits are historically tricksy creatures. They are shapeshifters who are "very fond of rumpots, crackpots, and how are you, Mr. Wilson?"[124] They live simultaneously inside and not inside of hats. They are objects both local and not.

Chapter 2
Tricksy Things

Objects have been up to something. Nowhere is this truer than in the case of non-traditional objects like complex systems and what Tim Morton has termed *hyperobjects*. Like rabbits, they are tricksy things. They are tricksy because they do not present themselves within the normal spatio-temporal wrappings we have come to expect of our objects. We tend to conceive of traditional objects as bundles of qualities or data, and we're able to do that because such objects appear to have definite and limited extensions in time and space. And if it is a requirement of an object that it be extended from an absolute time and an absolute space, then it makes sense that other qualities, such as red or round, would exist separately and prior to objects, even if those qualities exist only as discrete data given to the senses. From there, it is easy to assume that reality is structured predicatively. That is to say that the existence of objects is predicated upon qualities which are prior to and more real than the objects themselves, and that objects are just different combinations of the same predicative relationship with their qualities: The ball *is* five inches in diameter, and the ball *is* round, and the ball *is* red. A non-traditional object—if you have the imagination for such a thing—is so confounding because it escapes the predicative structure we impose on other objects. A non-traditional object might not extend in absolute space and absolute time in such a way that it can be bundled up to qualities we can sense with our eyes or any other apparatus as being somewhere or some way. A non-traditional object, such as an internet, a city, or a climate phenomenon, might bring with it its own space and time. The identity of such objects as objects, in turn, raises some interesting questions about the relationship between objects and their predicates in general, and so it is on the identification of non-traditional objects that this chapter will focus.

There is a profound connection between the notion that objects share in their own predication and the possibility for non-locality. The most obvious way to think about this is through the relativity of time and space to an object, the idea that the former two emerge as properties of the latter, rather than the other way around.[125] The connection between self-predication and non-locality can also be seen in the metaphysics of presence, particularly in Heidegger's tool-analysis, which has done so much to inspire Harman's philosophy. And despite the language of functionality around the tool analysis, presence, as we shall see, is an aesthetic phenomenon. As it goes, we rely upon the existence of so many objects of which we're not aware until they stop functioning as they had been doing. Harman is fond of the very simple image of the floor, which might only become present to us as something if there is an earthquake, and the floor gives out.[126] The floor's being is obviously not born in the earthquake, but rather the earthquake alerts us to the fact that the floor has been up to something. But floors seem pretty local.

This works in non-local cases as well. My iPod, which is a relic of portable media player antiquity, crashed a while ago, and I lost all of the music I had stored in it over the years, most of which I hadn't bothered to back up. This included my Radiohead albums, so I've just been listening to a compilation of hits on YouTube. Here, I have the familiar experience that one has when listening to a hits compilation, namely the uncanny sensation one gets when one goes through an unfamiliar song transition. In this case, when "Paranoid Android" crashes to a halt, the next thing I hear is the andante piano of "Karma Police" instead of the whirly first chords of "Subterranean Homesick Alien." My head starts playing "Subterranean" before the album does, and in this case, the album doesn't play it at all. My conditioned response, from an easy empiricist standpoint, is caused by what appears as a process of transition. It could also be said that there are a number of neurological processes involved as well, which function in similar ways to my conditioned responses to other regularities I experience in the world. Here, we can see how incredibly easy it is to go from the notion that all knowledge is process, to the notion that all interaction is process, to the notion that all being is process. The alternative is that the process of transition between the two songs is an object that has presented itself by being broken by the hits compilation. Is it possible that the song transition had been up to something before it was presented in all of its many splendid brokenness? The abrupt turn that the course of *OK Computer* takes between "Paranoid Android" and "Subterranean" is one of a few that contribute to a sense of caprice or even bipolarity in the album's narrative. It could also just be a memorable point in my daily jog, the 11:06 mark which occurs roughly at the moment when I pass the house with the cruck-frame façade. None of this proves that the transition or the perception of the transition aren't just bundles of processes, but it does tell us that the transition is more than just the final notes of one track, a short silence, and the first notes of the next track. On the hits compilation, we have the final notes of "Paranoid Android" and a short silence, but that doesn't mean that we have 2/3's of the transition. That would sound ridiculous even to the most supervenient among us. On the other hand, it can't be said that the transition wasn't there at all because the last notes of "Paranoid Android" and the short silence did index the transition. The transition was there, but it was broken in a way that can't be named in terms of regular units of time, amplitude, etc. Its brokenness, and therefore, its presence, is aesthetic. So, we can say three things about what the aesthetic presence of this transition-object is not:

1. It is not completely present.
2. It is not completely absent.
3. What is present of the transition-object cannot be regularized into units of 1s (whatever the anterior of 1 might be) which would be predicated on their relationship to 0.

If we cannot say that the object is completely[127] present or absent, and if there is not even a location for all of the parts of it that are either present or absent, and if the object has been up to something, then we're dealing with an object that exists non-locally.

Again, in his *Realist Magic*, Timothy Morton offers the wonderfully evocative image of "Causality as Sampling,"[128] which includes the croak of a frog being *sampled* by a passing mosquito as a "fluctuation in the air," and then by another frog as a hormonal signal, and then as a disturbance at the edge of a spider's web, and then as an inscription into an MP3 recorder's memory, and then as a sound in a human's ear.[129] The obvious way of describing such events is to say that a wave of kinetic energy compresses mediating particles together while leaving spaces of rarefaction in between the compressions. This process of alternating compression and rarefaction passes through different media, such as the near-limpid tympanic membrane, but it's essentially a single, linear repetition of cause and effect. But Morton calls this sort of conventional description "clunk causality," which he claims is "fetishistic reification"[130] because it presupposes that linear time precedes objects as the blank canvas onto which reality is painted. Instead, Morton notices something very profound about the simple fact that ears hear *as* ears, and digital recorders hear *as* digital recorders, and so on and so forth. To put it less-than-simply, "The ears otomorphize; the recorder recorder-morphizes."[131] This is aesthetic causality. The ears and the digital recorder have already been up to something. They already have a hidden symmetry and an identity when they encounter the frog's croak, and so they identify the croak in their own ways, which means the croak, if it moves, is part of all sorts of asymmetries. Or, in Morton's terms, "Causality is…distributed."[132] This is true of both space and of time, hence the expansion of the idea of non-locality beyond the examples we already have in the quantum world (i.e. entanglement).[133]

The objects Morton has in mind are what he calls "hyperobjects," and they are characterized by *viscosity, non-locality, temporal undulation, phasing*, and *interobjectivity*. The most prominent example of such an object in Morton's thinking is global warming. Global warming is viscous, in that it sticks to other objects and creates stickiness, such as the Atlantic Ocean swelling over Miami's shoreline. Global warming is obviously non-local, and it exists in the future as much as it exists in the present. All of those things are easy enough to imagine about global warming, but the claim that global warming is an object at all—and not a process—claws at the intuition just a bit more. It's the attribute of *phasing* that reveals global warming's objectness. Phasing refers to all of the possible states of a system, and it can be illustrated in the butterfly-shaped Lorenz Attractor model,[134] which was first used to describe the dynamics of weather. Phase space is a kind of space, but not one we are attuned to seeing, given our three-dimensional constraints. However, as Morton argues, "A high enough dimensional being could see global warming itself as a static object."[135] He pushes this even further, claiming that any "process is simply an object seen from a standpoint that is 1+n dimensions lower than that object's dimensionality."[136] Imagine being able to see a drop of water, a puff of vapor, and a snowflake as a single object, and you'll get some idea for what kind of magnificent weirdness we're dealing with. A hyperobject is an object whose underlying symmetry is so obviously withdrawn that we have to trade in our binocular vision for some sort of time-lapsed x-ray panorama just to get a concept of its identity.

Non-traditional objects cannot be identified by synthetic thinking

If global warming is indeed an object, then it is surely one of the most important objects we can think of. For Morton, global warming seems to be paradigmatic of objects that are non-local, phased, etc., but he never says it is the only such object. The Internet would be an obvious example of another one of these extraordinary objects. But how are we to identify new objects of this type as they come along?

Certainly, we can take things that have already been identified as processes, and then begin to think about how they behave as objects, as Morton has done with global warming. But not all unconventional objects are identified as processes first. For instance, although the Internet is not a typical object in the sense that a train or a can of snuff may be, it actually stretches the intuition more to think about the Internet as a process than it does to think about it as an object.[137] Why do we "go surfing" on the Internet for information instead of "internetting" for information? We could speculate that this is because when the Internet first took off for the general public, the vast majority of users were purely consumers of information and not producers. They were taking from something that was already there, something that was up to something. There are, no doubt, a few senior citizens whose first encounter with the Internet came relatively late, when they were introduced to Facebook or Skype. Their first experience of the

Internet, therefore, would have been of both consumption and production of information. What if these elders had been the first to get there? What sort of metaphors would they have circulated to identify the phenomenon? There's a good chance that those metaphors would have evoked processes instead of objects. Had the Internet been more give-and-take when it reached the public, we might have thought of it as a game or indeed as a second life. But as it is, we integrated this totally new type of experience into our intuitions by analogies to objects like spider webs and highways. This is why it's hard to think of the internet as a process, and why it's so hard to think of global warming as an object, even though we can make pretty persuasive ontological arguments for both being objects or both being processes.

The point is that if we want to think of a way of identifying unconventional objects that, like global warming, could have great interest and/or consequence for us, we can't simply look for previously identified processes and then analyze them as objects. To do so would be to remain tethered to synthetic thinking—that is to say, thinking of objects only in relation to given and naturalized domains of objects. Synthetic thinking works perfectly well to make explanations and predictions from given phenomena, but it is seriously limited when it comes to identifying new phenomena altogether. For instance, when I ask what the next event on the scale of global warming might be, I'm asking for an analogy, not for a phenomenon that could be analyzed from the domain *global warming*.

But if I did ask it as an analytical question, I might come up with a couple of domains at first: *physical qualities* and *social qualities*. In the domain *physical qualities,* I could come up with a near-exhaustive list of elements, such as droughts, melting ice caps, rising sea levels, and so on. I could further analyze those elements as subsets and start loading those subsets with elements. I could do the same with the domain *social qualities*, such as population movements, economic instability, etc. If I wanted to find the next global warming analytically, I could not start with the thing itself. I would have to choose from one of its subset domains. So, I would need to decide that I'm looking for the next global warming as either a physical or social phenomenon (or whichever domains take the primary domain as predicate).

Let's say I decide on the domain *social qualities*. From there, I would need to decide upon which elements in the domain are the most important to look for in my next global warming (let's call it GW_2). Fine. I've decided to look for population movements and sectarian conflict. As soon as I have identified another phenomenon (GW_2) that contains the identical elements—population movements and sectarian conflict—I will have to climb back up the analytical ladder and see if GW_2 is not just another element of global warming. If it is not just another element of global warming, then it has to be an element of something more primary than global warming, of which global warming is also an element. Perhaps I decide that GW_2, along with global warming, belongs to a more primary domain that has already been identified, such as capitalism. From there I just need to climb back down the analytical ladder and deduce the elements of GW_2 from capitalism, at which point I haven't really identified a new phenomenon at all, but only a new element or quality of capitalism.

If, however, I decide that GW_2 (which shares elements of global warming) belongs to something more primary than global warming but that it doesn't belong to a more primary domain that I have already identified, such as capitalism, then there must be something totally unknown out there to which both GW_2 and global warming belong. Badiou describes this type of situation in terms of the difference between *nomination* and *signification*. He explains:

> A signification is always distributed through the language of a situation, the language of established and transmitted knowledges. A nomination, on the other hand, emerges from the very inability of signification to *fix* an event, to decide upon its occurrence at the moment when this event [...] is on the edge of its disappearance. A nomination is a 'poetic' invention, a new signifier, which affixes to language that for which nothing can prepare it. A nomination, once the event that sustains it is gone forever, remains, in the void of signification.[138]

Here's another way of getting at it, furnished by Bob Dylan:

> *You raise up your head*
> *And you ask, "Is this where it is?"*
> *And somebody points to you and says*

> "It's his"
> And you say, "What's mine?"
> And somebody else says, "Where what is?"
> And you say, "Oh my God
> Am I here all alone?"[139]

In the event of the nomination, something is happening, but you don't know what it is (do you, Mr. Jones?). You might have identified the multiplicity of elements or qualities (e.g. the elements of global warming and GW_2) but the multiplicity itself (i.e. the domain) is unnamed and unready to circulate as a signifier in a system of knowledge.

Similar to Foucault's *empirico-transcendental doublet*, once named, this new multiplicity-thing bestows significance on its elements; it becomes a subject of knowledge just like other previously identified domains, such as global warming or capitalism. In other words, we could make new explanations and predictions from the new domain, just as we can now study capitalism and global warming for their effects. Whereas new knowledge (explanations and predictions) is predicated from the nominated domain, the domain itself is predicated from the multiplicity of the "there is" (back to the singleton of the Void).

To name a revolution

Understandably, one of Badiou's favorite examples of a true event of a nomination is the French Revolution. "Of the French Revolution as an event," he writes:

> [I]t must be said that it both presents the infinite multiple of the sequence of facts situated between 1789 and 1794, and, *moreover*, that it presents itself as an immanent résumé and one-mark of its own multiple. The Revolution, even if it is interpreted as being such by historical retroaction, is no less, in itself, supernumerary to the sole numbering of the terms of its site, despite it presenting such a numbering.[140]

(No exegetic Dylan quotation to follow.)

The novelty of the Revolution emerges from an undecidability between the Revolution as the thing composed of all of its elements or its matter (the storming of the Bastille, the *sans-culottes*, etc.) and the Revolution as a form "supernumerary" to its own composition.

It's a Buridan's Ass kind of situation. The thing is new because it is in a metastable state between its nomination and its signification. If the Revolution is simply boiled down to the interactions of its stuff, then there is no reservoir of being for it to be a novel event, and thus the stuff of the Revolution will belong to an already-identified domain. If, on the other hand, the Revolution were just a name given by people who wanted a revolution, it would be a sign without substance, a desire mortgaged on the future. In Buridan's thought experiment, the ass, who can't choose between the piles of hay on either side of the road on which it is standing, starves to death. Badiou's Revolution is a little more fortunate than the ass because, at some point, something—a revolutionary subject—recognizes it, adopts it, and feeds it, *becomes* its caretaker. This is called an *interpretive intervention*. The interpretive intervention "consists…in identifying that there has been some undecidability, and in deciding its belonging to a situation."[141] To put it another way, if the ass hadn't been standing in the middle of the road in a state of indecision, its future caretaker would not have been able to see it.

Thus, Badiou's event, as a metastable phenomenon identifiable by an asymmetry of its matter (its elements) and a self-similar symmetry of its form (a single multiplicity of its elements), is consistent with the general identity of objects that I have argued for. But the problem of how exactly the phenomenon/event/object is identified by another remains. Metastable symmetry explains how a thing can endure enough to be capable of being identified by another, but in the terms of Badiou's example, how does the revolutionary subject identify the Revolution so that it can remain faithful to the Revolution? Once again, it is not always enough to identify the parts of a process and then analyze it into an object or an event.

First of all, what evidence do we have that something like an *interpretive intervention* in the French Revolution was projected upon the eventual site, France? Here, we're not talking about the site *France* as a thing contained by its hexagonal boundaries, but about "that historical situation that we call France."[142] In other words, the site of the event is itself a named multiple; it is the clutching roots that grow from the stony rubbish of an event. Indeed, if we compare England as the site of the English Revolution to France as the site of the French Revolution, it is all the more easy to see the latter as a named multiple, for despite the concerted efforts of the Bourbons to consolidate France as a political, linguistic and religious entity, it always struggled to achieve the island sense of identity that the English had enjoyed since even before William the Conqueror put on the crown at Winchester.[143] That the Bourbons never properly set the stage for a *French* revolution is evident both from 1793 counter-revolution in the Vendée and from the Republican reaction to it.[144] It was not enough for the Republicans to simply defeat the royalist forces there; the *Comité de salut public* had to destroy the region altogether (which they did with startling efficiency). The point is that in very important ways, France as the site of the event of the French Revolution emerged coevally with the event itself. And thus, the location of an event and the site of an event remain open to one another, just as the site of an event remains open to the event itself.

The openness of the site to location seems to be what Benedict Anderson has in mind with his contention that the French Revolution became a template for nationalist revolutions thenceforth. Like Badiou, Anderson sees a universalist quality about the French Revolution that cannot be reduced to the revolution's philosophical priming alone. Anderson, whose *gesamt* thesis is that the modern nation-state was made imaginable by the rise of vernacular print capitalism, attributes the universality of the French Revolution to the fact that, unlike major ideological uprisings of the past, this one occurred in print just as much as it did on the streets of Paris: "Like a vast shapeless rock worn to a rounded boulder by countless drops of water, the experience was shaped by millions of printed words into a 'concept' on the printed page, and, in due course, into a model."[145] The site of the event was a pure mediation, which lifted it out of its location and its historical moment. A further argument vis-à-vis Badiou could be made that the fact of the revolution's mediation in print was the supernumerary of the multiple elements of the revolution (something that was novel about the event), but whose novelty could only be named retroactively. Whether it was the event of an interpretive intervention into the event of the Revolution or a model indurated by the printer's press, both Badiou and Anderson seem to believe that the French Revolution became a sort of autochthonous abstraction, something totally outside the concrete instances of revolution, but to which the revolutions in France, as well as in Russia and elsewhere, referred.

Perhaps print mediation is what made the French Revolution durable enough to become a model for revolution in general; however, that is not the same as saying that print mediation made the Revolution universal, and it doesn't account for the actual modeling of the Revolution. I would argue—and I'm far from original in doing so—that both the universality of the Revolution as well as its modeling happened outside of France. Both the modeling and universalizing began instead in Saint-Domingue (Haiti). Without the Haitian Revolution, which led to the second independent republic in the Americas, the French Revolution might have been a slightly more radical species of the English Revolution, and subsequent revolutions of national liberation in the 19th century would have been perhaps less radical versions of the American Revolution.

For all the exclusionary products of modern nationalism (with which we continue to grapple), it is still clear that modern nationalism was the first ideology of the universal since the advent of Christianity, Islam, and at certain points, Buddhism. We can put ideologies of the universal into the following framework:

1. Christianity and Islam are *particular universalisms*. That is to say that although they wish to remake the world in their images, the world outside of Christendom or Dar el-Islam still serves a useful purpose, since proselytism is fully integrated into their identities and practices. A world without non-Christians or non-Muslims still needs particular institutional or textual authority in order to keep evil or heresy at bay, since the complete conversion of humanity does not abolish original sin or the Devil.

2. Communism (particularly with the addition of dialectical materialism) is an example of a *universal universalism*, in that a world without non-communists does not need a particular authority to prevent backslide. The authority of the state, which ensures its survival against non-communist systems, falls away like a spent booster rocket. Just as it seems like an impossibility for developed capitalist societies to return to feudalism or for

viviparous mammals to become monotremes, once communism is universal, it does not revert to its antecessor.

3. Modern nationalism is a *universal particularism*. The difference between nationalism and other ideologies of the universal, as Anderson makes clear, is that "The most messianic nationalists do not dream of a day when all members of the human race will join their nation…"[146] What nationalists do profess to believe is that every particular people should be sovereign. (Problems of course arise when there are Germans living in Czechoslovakia, Serbs in Bosnia, or Russians in Ukraine…and this is to say nothing about the contradictions of colonialism.) The particularism of nationalism, it goes without saying, did not need to be invented in Modernity, since sovereignty was already a well-developed concept. What did need to be invented in secular terms was the universality of particular nationalist sovereignty, or the idea that all of humanity is entitled to civic identity. Credit for this invention in practice is given to the French Revolution.

The traditional narrative of the Haitian Revolution, fashioned after the Carlylean Great Man thesis, focused on Toussaint L'Ouverture. L'Ouverture was styled as a sort of black Washington or Napoleon who seized his historical moment, which was presented to him in the wake of the instability caused by the revolution in France. The great Trinidadian Marxist historian C.L.R. James almost singularly overturned that narrative with his 1938 classic, *The Black Jacobins*. In it, James argued that the revolution in Saint-Domingue was in fact a key element of the French Revolution itself, and the expulsion of Napoleon's troops in 1804 meant that neither the Thermidorian Reaction nor 18 Brumaire were the beginning of the end of the Revolution. James saw the slave revolt in Saint-Domingue (which began before 1791) as an integral part of a dialectic that allowed the revolutionaries in France to identify the spirit of their own cause. Indeed, Robespierre himself articulated what was new and universal about the Revolution by acknowledging slavery as its chief contradiction.[147] Had the Constituent Assembly acted on Robespierre's 7 April, 1791 address (or perhaps had Robespierre suspected for a second that they would act), it would have been in the running for the most Hegelian moment in history. As it was, slavery wasn't abolished until 1794, by which time the white planters had made alliances with the British, and the Jacobin governor, Sonthonax, had already taken it upon himself to abolish slavery in Saint-Domingue. What we see between the years of 1791 and 1794 is not a spontaneous invention and subsequent spread of nationalist universal particularism from the site *France*, but the emergence of a modern nationalism by way of analogy, between France and Saint-Domingue, and between revolution and revolt.

The social structure of Saint-Domingue at 1789 was both as rigid as Apartheid South Africa and as labyrinthine as post-Civil War Lebanon. The hierarchy was very much after the Spanish colonial style. At the top was the equivalent of the Spanish *peninsular*, the European-born administrator.[148] Below that were two classes of creole: *grands blancs* (the while planters) and *petits blancs* (white overseers and laborers).[149] Below that were the *gens de couleur*[150] or free people of mixed race. Though, mind you, the economic power of the *gens de couleur* often rivaled, and sometimes exceeded, that of many *grands blancs*, let alone *petits blancs*. The French had a spectacularly elaborate flow chart for the classification of *gens de couleur*, based on precisely 128 shades.[151] If you do the math, that works out to a record of seven generations. There were separate names for you based on just about any amount of black or white contribution to your lineage, from your parents to your 5x great-grandparents. At the bottom, of course, were black slaves, but there were also the *maroons*, or slaves who had escaped inland, many of whom mixed in with the remnants of the native Taíno people. Take all of those strata and multiply them by the three provinces (North, West, and South), each of which had their own interests and power structures, and you might just be close to grasping the socio-political architecture of Saint-Domingue in 1789.

When revolution broke out in France, it might have found its echo in Saint-Domingue as a 1:1 correspondence with a little nuance. The *grands blancs* resented the French-born administrators for the same reasons the planters and merchants in the North American Colonies 13 resented the British. The British Mercantile System and the French *Exclusive* were essentially the same: trade monopolies and heavy duties imposed on products that were not manufactured or refined in the metropolis nation.[152] The *petits blancs*, on the other hand, saw what was happening in France as an opportunity to both usurp the *grand blancs* and dispossess the wealthy *gens de couleur*, all the while maintaining slavery. Presumably, once the *petits blancs* had done all of this, they would press for their autonomy from the French, just as the *grands blancs* were hoping to do. All of this is to say that if the whites in Saint-Domingue had acted as localized elements of the given domain French Revolution, the result would have been remarkably unnovel. It would have been a creole revolution on the order of the creole revolution that took place a little earlier in the thirteen colonies. Where would that have left the universalist legacy of the French Revolution? Again, probably as something like a crisis of monarchy, like that of the English Revolution. Modern nationalism's universal particularlism probably would not have been invented at that moment.

Nationalist revolutions might have continued to confine themselves to questions of civil rights rather than of human rights.[153] But when, in 1848, the spirit of the French Revolution made its way across Europe, the rights of workers, those of slaves, and the meaning made of the French Revolution were bound together. One of the first things the transitional government did after the collapse of the Louis Philippe monarchy, and just before the conservative backlash, was to re-abolish slavery in the colonies, calling it "a flagrant violation of the republican dogma..."[154, 155] And amongst the post-1848 demands for universal (male) suffrage[156] by young nationalists across Europe was the Wallachian nationalist push to end the 500 year enslavement of the Roma. The struggle for the rights of workers that also defined 1848 would have to be taken up in an internationalist discourse (a universal universalist movement), but the universal particularism of modern nationalism was moving from the margins of revolt to a political terrain, on top of which new conservativisms, liberalisms, and progressivisms would stand to face each other.

If there was an interpretive intervention that identified the French Revolution as a new thing, belonging neither to the domain *crisis of monarchy* (as in the English Revolution) nor to the domain *creole revolution*, it came not out of the universal inclusion of all the actors and events on the site France (which would include the colonies). The identification of the novel revolution happened because the revolution presented itself as a broken object to the people of Saint-Domingue. The French Revolution presented itself as having the quality of universal inclusion, and it functioned for those who would have assumed that they were already included in that inclusion as free French citizens, but it didn't function for black slaves. What the slaves saw was that they were separate from this revolution-thing. There were, of course, plenty of attempts in France by the *Société des amis des Noirs* and the Jacobins to include the slaves, but instead of waiting for inclusion, the insurgent slaves made an analogy between themselves and the insurgents in France, between the French Revolution and the slave revolt. The Haitian Revolution was neither a part of the French Revolution nor was it an inevitable result of the French Revolution.

Regardless of how *grands blancs*, *petits blancs*, or *gens de couleur* ended up interpreting their parts in what was happening in France, the Haitian Revolution began as a kind of slave revolt whose identity existed before 1789. The rebellion of the 1750s, led by François Mackandal was of particular importance.[157] Both Mackandal and Boukman (the initial leader of the 1791 insurgency) were *maroons* and charismatics whose authority came from divine revelation rather than national sovereignty. The revolt that L'Ouverture found in 1791 was, therefore, not just an assemblage of rebellious slaves in search of an identity, but an enduring thing of its own. L'Ouverture took the rhetoric of republican nationalism and analogized it to the revolt, and he did this while both speaking of the events in Saint-Domingue as a separate revolution[158] and not actually declaring independence from France. Just as Morton argues that ears hear *as* ears and digital recorders record *as* digital recorders, the Haitian Revolution was affected by the French Revolution *as* the Haitian Revolution. In making an analogy to the French Revolution, L'Ouverture and others recognized a disanalogy, an asymmetry between the qualities of the French Revolution and those of their own revolution, which was the problem of race. Out of the recognition of this asymmetry came a new universal—that national sovereignty begins from the entire (again, male) populace, regardless of race. And it was in the National Convention's 1794 abolition of slavery that the vanguard of the French Revolution both saw itself as a broken thing[159] and named its own universality. As Danton declared:

Representatives of the French people, until now our decrees of liberty have been selfish, and only for ourselves. But today, we proclaim it to the universe, and generations to come will glory in this decree; we are proclaiming universal liberty.[160]

Here, Danton is by no means creating the French Revolution's universalist legacy, but rather making the French Revolution's transformational encounter with the revolt in Saint-Domingue present, by arguing for the endurance of that encounter. If the Haitian Revolution was affected by the French Revolution *as* the Haitian Revolution, the reverse is also true—the French Revolution was affected by the revolt in Saint-Domingue *as* the French Revolution.

Naming, Presence, and the Epideictic

Modern nationalism is an ideology, and despite Destutt de Tracy's intentions in coining the term, an ideology is not a science. The non-scientific nature of nationalism is most apparent in the formal declarations of national principles from which constitutions are derived. Such declarations are deeply rhetorical and affective documents. The elements of a declaration cannot serve as logical domains for the elements of a constitution. Constitutions are interpretations of declarations, just as specific applications of law are interpretations of a constitution. The metaphors of declarational rhetoric, such as "life," "liberty," "fraternity," etc., would lose their universalistic power if they were deployed without an affective spirit. If "liberty," for instance, hung from discernible predicates, then its application would be a matter for technocrats and not for the political body in whose name the "liberty" was proposed in the first place (which is to say nothing about who is and who is not recognized as being part of that political body, or about who may and may not speak for that body).

Latour makes a similar argument about the difference between religion and science. He claims that the conflict between religion and science is based upon a sham-modern conflation of their respective functions. The idea that both religion and science exist to discover the truth of what is far away is, according to Latour, a "category mistake."[161] He argues instead that "Neither religion nor science is much interested in the visible," but "it is science that grasps the far and distant; as to religion, it does not even try to *grasp* anything."[162] That is to say science takes its tools out into the invisible world (not just into the tiny spaces of atoms and bacteria but into unimaginably large temporal places of universe formation and biological evolution) and it transforms that world into something visible. Religion, on the other hand, makes meaning out of how the present itself is transformed by what has become present (e.g. presence in Christian *Communion* or in Hindu *Darśana*).

Latour calls both religion and science "regimes of invisibility,"[163] but we may also extend Latour's distinction to a regime of visibility, like art. The art object, Heidegger contends, presents its world to us. We may bring a wealth of education, opinions, moods and tastes to our experiencing of the art object, but ultimately, we cannot *go out to* the object and render all that is invisible in it visible without losing touch with the object itself. In other words, if you analyze an art object like Van Gough's *A Pair of Boots* into domains such as chemical composition, artist biography, historical moment, etc., you might create some important knowledge. But no synthesis of that knowledge, no matter how exhaustive, can serve as the predicate for the art object; the synthesis would instead be a predicate for the discourse about the object. As an art object, *A Pair of Boots* is predicated by the world the painting itself brought with it.

When we make arguments about a work of art by analyzing it into its domains (be they geometrical, chemical, historical, or otherwise), we are employing *forensic* rhetoric. The forensic is the rhetorical mode that concerns the past, and it is the mode of all synthetic discourse. We have already identified the thing as a thing, and then as a thing of significance. Now we are trying to decide how the thing came to be, just as the forensic investigator tries to decide whether a death *was* a murder or an accident, whether the fatal wound *was* inflicted with a kitchen knife or a hunting knife, whether the killer *was* left- or right-handed, tall or short, and so on. All of it brings the death past the death itself and into known domains, such as categories of cause, weapons, and handedness. But the experience of encountering the art object, of identifying the thing as a thing of significance happens in the present, even as it pulls the future in with it. The encounter with the art object is not unlike that of the person who discovers the killed body in the first place. Folded into the recognition that she has encountered a killed body are both the immediate understanding that in the future she will have divided her life into the moment before and the moment after she came upon the killed body as well as the crushing sense of abjection[164] and moral failure she'll get when she catches herself not being taken over by what should be a normal emotional response, but instead asking herself how a typical person would react to the event. The nightmares she'll have in the following weeks, months, and years will repeatedly draw that moment of horror and abjection into the present, such that there will be little distinction between the present moment of the encounter and the present moment of the nightmare, and such that the encounter will be a terrifyingly non-local, temporally phased, self-similar object.

The moment of abjection in the art encounter no doubt pales in comparison to that of the killed body encounter, but it is that kind of moment that the work of criticism tries to draw forth and recreate, just as the nightmare draws forth the moment of encountering the killed body. Indeed, this is the difference between a mature work of criticism and a student report on a piece of art, the latter consisting primarily of analysis. The rhetorical mode for art criticism is the same mode employed for an Easter Sunday homily: the *epideictic*, the rhetoric of the present. The critic draws forth the moment of the art encounter by asking questions that double as affirmations of the value of art in general (e.g. "How does this installation transform our sense of space?"), just as the priest on Easter Sunday draws forth the moment of the Resurrection by asking questions that affirm Christian values (e.g. "How *is* our sense of hope transformed *now* that Christ *is* risen?").

What's true about critical and Easter homiletic rhetoric is also true of nationalist declarational rhetoric. The American Declaration of Independence is a good example of the epideictic mode, for although it spends a good amount of time arguing forensically that the king has in fact been an unscrupulous tyrant and an ass, it begins with the affirmation of values and proceeds to an argument about who the Americans are now that they have recognized their values in the face of such tyranny. This recognition of transformation is even more striking in Dessalines's 1804 *Haitian Declaration of Independence*. The first half of the document refers only to "our island," describing the cruelty of the French and the sacrifices of the

"Native citizens" of "this island."[165] Shortly after declaring of the French that "they have conquered but are no longer free," and concluding with the cry, "Anathema to the French name! Eternal hatred of France!" Dessalines performs a thaumaturgical naming of the nation: "Natives of Haiti!"[166] In both the American and the Haitian declarations of independence, it is clear that the authors are not making any arguments about what the nation is in essence (that's for the constitutions); they are drawing forth the moment in which the citizens identify the being of the nation and are transformed by it.

The epideictic rhetoric of criticism, Easter homilies, and national declarations does not create or identify its object. And although it's impossible to deny that something like a national declaration makes an intervention that affects the way citizens interact with the nation, intervention is not its primary objective. The primary objective of epideictic rhetoric is to argue for the endurance of a thing. Indeed, the textbook example of epideictic rhetoric is the eulogy. And what is a eulogy if not an assembling of memories of and praises for the deceased designed to persuade the bereaved that their friend, leader, or loved one leaves a legacy that continues to affect and transform in and beyond the present moment? Implicit is the notion that the deceased's legacy, as an enduring thing, will affect the community of the bereaved in *similar* ways, both from bereaved to bereaved and from moment to moment. In persuading the audience that the deceased's legacy is an enduring thing, the eulogist is representing the thing as symmetrical to itself and capable of affecting others in other moments, even as those others in other moments encounter the thing asymmetrically.[167] Thus, ontologically speaking, epideictic rhetoric is truer to the object than forensic rhetoric is.

What I'm trying to argue is that if you want to trace the identification of a new object of discourse, such as the French Revolution's universalist legacy, and therefore to understand how new such objects are identified prior to the analysis of their qualities into domains, artifacts of epideictic rhetoric are far better places to start than those of forensic rhetoric. Epideictic rhetoric is faithful to the encounter with that new object, which, being prior to the analysis of the object, is an affective encounter. Indeed, in the broadest sense of the term, the encounter is an *aesthetic* one. Furthermore, although Badiou's *interpretive intervention* is an incredibly useful concept, it must be said that the aesthetic encounter with the new object comes prior to the interpretive intervention. The identification of an object of significance comes with the aesthetic encounter, whereas the *decision* on its significance comes with something like the interpretive intervention (which Badiou characterizes as a decision). Thus, we must make a distinction between identification and decision. In the identification of an object, the one who identifies the object does so *as* an object, not as a knowing subject who encounters a pure concept and its endless string of known domains. The decision on the object's (or, *pace* Badiou, the *event's*) significance is volitional, and is therefore something someone does as a subject. And, of course, Badiou's argument is that the subject of an event emerges with such a decision, but it is not my intention to discuss the existence or necessity of the subject at this junction. The point here is that the identification of objects occurs between *objects*, and not between *subject* and object.

But we began our discussion of nomination and Badiouan sets by asking how new, non-traditional objects such as global warming can be identified without first being analyzed into objects from known processes. What about those objects which not only have not been identified as objects but which also possess qualities for which we have no concepts? Surely, we're dealing in a "regime of invisibility" with this question. But the kind of "grasping" for what is "out there" that Latour says is the work of science is not so different from the grasping that a constitution does at a declaration. Before any analytical work can be done, scientists must be persuaded that an enduring object has been identified.

Again, we can look to the artifacts of scientific discourse to see how this argument works. The research paper is the easiest place to start. Unlike the desultory screed you are enduring presently, scientific research papers have a pretty regular structure, consisting of an introduction, a methodology, a results and discussion section, and a conclusion. The introduction is rhetorically forensic, as it consists of locating the problem inside of previous research. And so is the results and discussion section, since it analyzes the research into known domains of knowledge. The conclusion is at least somewhat deliberative in that the authors typically propose specific kinds of research on the problem for the future. The methodology section, on the other hand, is epideictic. But it is so in a strange way, a way that sets it apart from all other kinds of epideictic rhetoric. The methodology section brings the observations or experiments to the present by describing the materials, the sites, and the techniques involved in the research. But instead of persuading the audience that the object of research is an enduring thing that repeats itself self-similarly, the rhetorical goal of the methodology section is to persuade readers that the observation or experiment can be repeated in a self-same way.

We have Robert Boyle to thank for the peculiar sort of epideictic rhetoric found in methodology sections. Boyle was one of those early modern scientists whose successes were due, in part, to the metaphysical and theological axes they were grinding. Boyle, like Newton, was a corpuscularianist. Against the Aristotelian hylomorphic currents in scholastic philosophy, modern corpuscularianists like Boyle argued that motion should replace form as the metaphysical primitive that pairs with matter.[168] In the "*modern* Aristotelian"[169] pairing of form and matter, the form of an object determines its potential for movement. For Boyle, the form/matter pairing would have involved a God whose creation was not immediate to himself, since, even if God created forms, it would be the forms that were immediately responsible for movement. If on the other hand God created the regular laws of motion by which material elements interact with each other, then all material forms could be reducible to that single, simple act of creation. (You can be forgiven at this point for sensing the Watchmaker God lurking just around the corner.) As a good Protestant with at least one foot dipped in Calvinism, the motion/matter pairing had an added bonus for Boyle:

> But to come now to the *Corpuscular* philosophy, men do so easily understand one another's meaning, when they talk of *local motion, rest, bigness, shape, order, situation* and *contexture* of material substances, and these principles do afford such clear accounts of those things that are rightly deduced from them only, [...] though perhaps the effect be so admirable as would make it pass for that of hidden form or occult quality.[170]

As with the Protestant imperative to experience the Word of God without an interpreting intermediary, the idea is that knowledge of the physical world should be clear and accessible to everyone. Indeed, in his own prose Boyle practiced what he preached, writing in simple English and consequently becoming a model for popular science writing. But it wasn't just that Boyle's corpuscular metaphysics laid the groundwork for a simple understanding of the physical world; the point was also that the simplicity of the metaphysics would be mirrored by a simple epistemology for his chemistry in which the basic conceptual building blocks ("local motion," "rest," "bigness," etc.) would be understood in the *same* way by everyone. What Boyle is doing is laying the foundations for a scientific community that comes together in the common *presence* of these concepts. It is not surprising, then, that Boyle was instrumental in the founding of the Royal Society.[171]

The Protestant imperative for accessibility and simple sameness extended further to Boyle's methodology. His emphasis on the repeatability of experiments served him philosophically and rhetorically. First of all, Boyle was fighting a metaphysical battle on a physical front. The key element in this front was his work on vacuums. The existence of vacuums was a crucial part of the corpusculianist argument because, if they existed, they would show that there could be a break in the material plenum,[172] which runs contrary to Aristotelian metaphysics. Although Boyle never claimed that he could create a perfect vacuum (in the metaphysical sense),[173] his experiments with vacuums demonstrated that there were differences between space inside and outside of a vacuum (e.g. sound does not travel and fire does not burn). Since the evidence for this argument couldn't travel by the normal vehicles of logical or mathematical proofs, the only way to make the argument mobile was to describe in painstaking detail the materials and techniques used in the experiments so that they could be repeated exactly as they were in other times and other places.

If experimental knowledge and the demonstrative knowledge of proofs were such different epistemic animals, they would have to travel by very different rhetorical vessels. Boyle would, therefore, ground his rhetoric of experimental knowledge in self-sameness. Just as he praised the basic concepts of corpuscularian philosophy for their simplicity and consistency, Boyle was quick to point out the opacity and inconsistency of the concepts used in scholastic argumentation, vowing that his work would be free of such incongruities:

> And it made me the more unwilling to stuff these papers with any needless School controversies, because I found upon perusal of several scholastic writers [...] that they do not always mean the same things by the same terms, but some employ them in one sense, others in another, and sometimes the same writers use them in very differing senses [...][174]

This lack of sameness in scholastic argument was not only a source of frustration for naïve, ordinary readers (amongst whom Boyle, perhaps a little disingenuously, counted himself), but it also rendered much of the knowledge generated in those "school controversies" superfluous. But the most significant way in which he wanted to distance the rhetoric of experimental knowledge from scholastic argumentation was in the matter of epistemic authority:

> And indeed there are many opinions and arguments of good repute in the Schools, which do so entirely rely upon the authority of Aristotle or some of his more celebrated followers, that, when that authority is not acknowledged, to fall upon a solemn confutation of what has been so precariously advanced were not only unnecessary, but indiscreet [...][175]

At this point in early Modernity, it was far from obvious that the mere ethos of a celebrated scholar might be less reliable than experimental evidence. Boyle answered the question of epistemic authority in two ways: modernistic pluralism and the multiplication of witnesses. Firstly, the reliance upon scholarly authority reeked more than a little of papistry. He pointed out that Scholastic arguments were often so tangled up with theological teachings and controversies within the Catholic Church as to become indistinguishable from them. But rather than launch into any theological arguments against Catholic dogma (and thereby getting tangled up in the controversies himself), the clever Robert Boyle took a noticeably modern, pluralistic (indeed, even a universal particularist) position, arguing that because many of the scholastic stances that are rooted in Catholic dogma are opposed by the perfectly legitimate "divines of other churches," the arguments themselves "would not be proper to be solemnly taken notice of by [Boyle]—whose business…is to discourse of natural things as a naturalist, without invading the province of divines by intermeddling with supernatural mysteries..."[176] As Boyle would have it, all churches had a right to the interpretation of their own mysteries. As a naturalist, his work wouldn't get bogged down in theological or political squabbles. Boyle managed to use the weight of scholarly authority against itself. It was a brilliant bit of rhetorical aikido.

But experimental knowledge still needed to appeal to authority of some sort, particularly if it was going to be argued by non-schoolmen or by people who weren't sons of the Earl of Cork. Recall Boyle's half-joking concern that the concepts of corpuscularian philosophy are so powerful in their clarity and universality that they might be mistaken for occultic tools. We tend to associate the occult with all sorts of fun stuff like magic and ghosts, but Boyle was concerned about occultism in the most quotidian sense of the term; it was the "covered up" part of *occult* that he sought to distance from experimental knowledge. Experimental knowledge in the 17th century still had more than a whiff of alchemy about it. And indeed, Boyle, like Newton, maintained a great interest in the transmutation of metals. Alchemy was unseemly and even dangerous not because of its non-Christian origins but because…what if it worked? At this time in Western Europe, mercantilism was at its zenith, and wealth was still confined to the amount of precious metals a nation could accumulate and keep. If a successful formula for transmuting base metals into gold and silver were disseminated, the game would be up for a young empire on the rise like England.[177] Punishments for those who falsely claimed to make transmutation work were severe, and so—understandably—alchemists were quite a druidic bunch. Knowledge was closely guarded and experiments were done in private. And as Shapin and Schaffer argue, the first way in which experimental science was to distinguish itself from alchemy was in the nature of the space in which experimental science was practiced, noting that "The terms 'laboratory' and 'elaboratory'…were very new in seventeenth century England."[178] The laboratory, according to Shapin and Schaffer, "was contrasted to the alchemist's closet precisely in that the former was said to be a public and the latter a private space."[179] Not only was experimental science to be on the up-and-up as regards its benefits to society, but rhetorical authority would come from the multiplicity of witnesses to the experiment.[180] The more witnesses to the experiment there were, the more reliable the knowledge would be, and so the more valid the whole enterprise would be. By detailing his experiments in such a way that they could be repeated as the same experiments elsewhere, Boyle was multiplying his witnesses to such an extent that the ethos of any one witness would be of little import to the epistemic value of the work. But of course, few experimentalists had the massive resources that Boyle had in order to replicate his experiments, and anyway, he was writing to a larger reading public (however limited it was) that would have had neither the interest nor the wherewithal to replicate them. Thus, the extensive detailing of methods and materials worked as a functional, if sleight-of-hand, performance of the experiments themselves, creating what Shapin and Schaffer call "virtual witnessing."[181] The experiment, then, emerges in discourse as a being in self-same repetition.

This completes the circle for Boyle. Again, there is a remarkable consistency that strings through his ontology, epistemology, and rhetoric, which modern science has inherited: the universe is populated by material elements that interact with each other according to the forces that, depending upon scale, are the same; the foundational concepts of this reality are the same; and the epistemic products of the practical deployment of those foundational concepts are made present to others by self-same repetition.

But there are a couple of limitations to this remarkable sameness. The first limitation is one that anybody who has thumbed through an interdisciplinary science journal over the past few years will recognize immediately. The problem, which has been exacerbated by the rising costs of science and the publish-or-perish imperative, is that experiments are not being replicated enough to check for intentionally or unintentionally erroneous data. This could not have come at a worse time for experimental science, particularly as the Right has managed so effectively to foment public distrust in the enterprise in recent years. What starts off as a public relations problem becomes a funding problem, which becomes an existential threat to anything but corporate science. There's a sense in which the epideictic rhetoric of the methods and materials section of the research paper is, at times, too persuasive for its own good. Because doing experiments and observations is so expensive, and because the pre-tenured workhorses of science are so pressured to publish new research, and because—let's face it—science-for-profit has little vested interest in safeguarding mechanisms like replication or peer review, the "witnessing" is becoming more "virtual" than ever. If the replication of experiments by others in other moments is not being conducted, or more importantly if it is *assumed* that it is not being conducted, then experimental science may be making a slow retreat back into the alchemist's closet, which will continue to leave it vulnerable to politicization.

The second limitation to sameness is in the growing importance of the science of complex systems, which, as I will argue, obliges us to reintroduce self-similar forms as metaphysical primitives along with self-same motion and matter. Key to research on complex systems is the development of stochastic models. In stochastic or dynamic modeling, the experiment itself is virtual, is capable of dragging its own presence to others in other moments. (Granted, input data need to be gathered from observations and experiments, the reliability of which will have to be determined by the old means of sameness.) For instance, if you want to build a predictive model for how a shipping lane will affect a grey whale population, you could input data about the average yearly birthrate of grey whales at a particular location, information about the population and hunting behavior of local killer whales, variations in ocean temperature, the probability that a ship will be in a certain location at a certain time, and so on. Each of these data will become actors with their own possibilities for movement at a given moment. In turn, the moments themselves are regular units of time that simulate instants or spreads of non-simulated time. The same simulation with the same probabilities can be repeated thousands of times in order to obtain a single probability of an event like a ship hitting a whale. In reporting on and interpreting the results of such a model, the usual norms of the methods and materials section apply. The model is still a fabricated thing and is therefore vulnerable to all sorts of bugs and errors like any experimental apparatus. But since the models are already replications of themselves to themselves, the question becomes not how to replicate the same thing for other witnesses, but how to replicate the model *differently*. It is not so much the elimination of error that the replication of a stochastic model is after, but the production of chaos. Stochastic models are replicas of complex systems, but they are not mere representations of complex systems. They share with complex systems the element of instability. So, any new element introduced into the model or system, no matter how small, has the potential to effect radical change.

I rather doubt the concepts of chaos and complex systems need explaining to anyone minimally familiar with the 1993 blockbuster, *Jurassic Park*.[182] Okay, the film was a bit on the nose. More than a bit, really. On the one hand, it's a good old fashioned *Frankenstein* story, replete with all of our modern Promethean anxieties. But on the other hand, it's not as much a cautionary tale about modern science going too far as it is a warning that we can no longer do the science that we are now capable of doing (e.g. bioengineering) in the same way that we had been doing modern science. It's the idea that no science can now be practiced or spoken of without acknowledging the transformational presence of complex systems.

In the story, Jurassic Park's creator, Hammond, is a contemporary alchemist who got his start engineering sleight-of-hand flea circuses. In secret, Hammond marshals the forces of the nascent science of bioengineering to transmute the genetic information of bullfrogs into dinosaur life. The DNA strand still had something of a Philosopher's Stone aura in the early nineties—and indeed, the key to creating the dinosaurs was locked inside of rare, fossilized amber stones, which contained mosquitoes, which contained dinosaur blood. The story's other heroes are two modern scientists: Grant, a paleontologist, and the paleobotanist Sattler. There is also a chaostician, Malcolm (played by the show-stealing Jeff Goldblum), who has the sleek and confident look of a time traveler from the not-so-distant future. The story begins as a revenge of the alchemist, whose work threatens to put the modern scientists out of business. But it quickly becomes clear, as Malcolm guessed from the start, that Hammond has created something that belongs neither to the alchemist's closet nor to the experimentalist's laboratory, but to the probability space of a complex system.

As the group sets off on its package tour of the park, we see them through one of three screens in the park's technology center. On the other two screens are a 3-D simulation of the tour and a model of an incoming weather system. As we see the simulation of the tour and the weather simulation side-by-side, we're of course meant to understand that the chaos of the real weather system is going to be folded into the events of the real tour, but it does so in an indirect, complex way. If there's a human villain in the piece, it's the petulant IT man, Nedrie, who plants a bug in the park's security system in order to give him enough time to reach a departing boat and hand over the dinosaur DNA he has stolen. In the bad weather, Nedrie gets lost in the park and ends up paying for his sins at the teeth of a truly righteous little toxic black goop-spitting dinosaur. Because Nedrie doesn't get back to debug the security system, the dinosaurs get free run of the park. Nedrie, therefore, is not so much of an antagonist as he is another agent of chaos, folded into other agents, such as the weather and the DNA of spontaneously sex-changing bullfrogs used to clone the otherwise all female dinosaurs. As Jeff Goldblum's Malcolm so memorably notes, "Life, uh, finds a way."

The last shot of the film has the survivors flying away from the island in a helicopter, with Grant looking out the window at a halcyon scene of pelicans gliding along the sea breeze. (In his work as a paleontologist, Grant had advanced the notion that birds evolved from dinosaurs.) Again, a bit on the nose, but lovely nonetheless. The easy takeaway from the story is that life cannot be manipulated and controlled like other objects we manufacture, that there is something about life that is irreducibly different from the molecules of which a living organism is composed. But what the film's final shot itself speaks of is the irreducibility of forms. Dinosaurs don't belong in our time not because they were wiped out millions of years ago, but because they currently do exist in another form (birds), that, unlike the park's dinosaurs, exist in some sort of balance and proportion with other current life forms. You can make new dinosaur organisms by combining fossilized DNA fragments with the genes of extant bullfrogs, and you can mechanically pepper in modifications for breeding and nutrition, but the *form* that is assembled from all of those materials is going to have its own potential for movement—limited, it seems, only by the profitability of the *Jurassic Park* movie franchise.

Complex systems and epistemic opacity

Complex systems tend to be scary things. They are associated with chaos, which is demonic. They are traffic systems, terrorist organizations, hurricanes, algal blooms, flu epidemics…and rampaging dinosaurs! Also, being 'complex,' they are epistemically "opaque."[183] It is on the epistemic opacity of complex systems—the irreducibility of a system to its parts—that philosophers and polemicists tend to be fixated. It's a cathexis point for various moral and political desires. A form without an agent directing it into being seems more natural and right than nature itself. For a New Atheist like Richard Dawkins, the idea of simple replications leading to complex forms makes reality more magical[184] than magic (or miracle) itself. For Mark C. Taylor,[185] the way global information capitalism seemingly emerges out of local selections of information from noise shows that it is a more durable and creative system than all other economic modes. And on the other end of the political spectrum, Michael Hardt and Antonio Negri[186] have synthesized Italian Autonomism and Deleuzean metaphysics to theorize emergent and creative political movements that escape the confines of sovereign representation by virtue of their epistemic opacity. For these and likeminded thinkers, the kind of opacity that opens up possibilities for the new is thought of in terms of domains and domain blurring. In particular, it is the blurring of the local and the global that holds the most fascination. The most emblematic image of the chaotic mechanics of a complex system is that of the butterfly flapping its wings in such and such a place causing a tornado in such and such a place. But the important epistemic difference between the study of chaos and that of complex systems is found in the emphasis in the latter on global-local feedback. It is not so much that a little mutation or innovation can cause a big species or system change, but that the local actor and the global phenomenon can transform each other. For instance, using a particular kind of social medium for political organization between local actors can lead to a new, larger movement, but in effecting this larger movement, the local actors have also changed the way in which the social medium is used, which, in turn, governs the way the local actors use it thenceforth. What is left unknowable or undecidable is whether the agency for movement resides in the global or the local domain. For Hardt and Negri, this blurring of agency signals the attenuation of national sovereignty, in which the top-down domains of local and global had been well defined. Here, the (local) national subject took the (global) nation as its predicate, with the political universe of modernity being a parallel repetition of the subject-nation domainal structure (again, universal particularism). But it seems to me that what collapses or gets blurred in complex systems is not just the local-global binary, but the whole notion that the domain is our one and only epistemic engine. What emerges out of the collapse or blurring of the global-local domain structure is new forms, be they political, technological, ecological, etc. The forms that emerge in complex systems cannot be reduced to any self-same interactions between elements of that system, and they furthermore carry with them their own potential for movement. We should, therefore, conclude that forms are indeed primary, and that they deserve to be reinstated alongside force and matter as metaphysical primitives.

In his philosophical writings, Werner Heisenberg argues that the history of modern science can be traced by way of the replacement of ontological terms, just as I have been arguing for in this book. Specifically, he asserts that modern science had taken the form-matter pair and turned it into the motion-matter pair, which then became the force-matter pair. Heisenberg goes on to argue that in the 20th century, the boundaries between force and matter were blurred, "since every field of force contains energy and in so far constitutes matter."[187] What we are once again left with, Heisenberg says, is *form* and matter: "The infinite variety and mutability of the forms of matter must be the immediate object of the investigation…"[188] In complex systems in particular, form and matter are relative to one another. Consider a bridge that an ant colony makes of itself in order to cross between two logs. The matter of this system is no more fundamental than the ants themselves,[189] and the form of the system is, of course, the bridge. From which of these does the potential for movement come? Clearly, the individual ants are interacting, and at the level of any two individuals, they are entering into a materially asymmetrical interaction (each ant is clutching the posterior of the other), while a state of similarity emerges between their formal interactions. It is this asymmetrical interaction into which their forms (individual ants being forms of ant-objects) enter that creates a new state of matter, which exists between the ants. The two ants have, therefore, become new matter for a form. These two clutched up ants are then linked up to other clutched up ants, at which point, the form of the bridge is acting upon itself. The bridge is acting self-similarly, since it is repeating the asymmetrical interactions between its matter-ants. If the matter-ants were interacting self-samely, then the identity of the bridge would be self-same; but then again, if the ants were interacting self-samely, there would be no form for the bridge, since all there would be is a bunch of pairs of ants clutching each other's posteriors, and therefore the ants themselves would not be matter at all. Thus, it is the self-similar form that repeats itself. The form is what endures. After all, the individual matter-ants may go on to clutch the bums of other matter-ants, but the bridge will continue to endure. The enduring, self-similar form is then also the agent of movement, since it alone is capable of interacting with other forms in an asymmetrical way in order to become matter for another form (think of two ant bridges linking up).

Finally, the form of the ant bridge is held together by the withdrawn Real Object of the bridge. Using Harman's terminology, I would call the form of the bridge which other objects encounter the Sensual Object.[190] We can also put the ant matter into Harman's scheme as the Real Qualities of the bridge. The bridge is really made up of ants, so in synthetic thinking, you could establish a predicative relationship between the bridge and the ants: this bridge is ants. But when form and matter are relative, the relationship is qualitative. As in: this is an anty bridge. If what had been the thing's predicate in synthetic thinking is actually the thing's Real Qualities, then, once again, we can say that the thing has shared in its own predication.

If the complex system that is the ant bridge is an object, how do we identify it? The ant bridge is a complex system, but with our normal means of perception, it's relatively easy to identify it as an object as compared to other non-traditional objects like global warming. As we're walking through the woods, we encounter an elongated, bristling thing between two logs. The elongation and bristling are Sensual Qualities. On closer inspection, we find that the elongation and bristling are really ants jostling around. Thus, we have noticed an object. We have encountered its SQs, and we have reasoned that the RQs (ants) are behind the SQs. We have done all of this without identifying either the Sensual Object (the form of the bridge) or the existence of the RO of the form.

But I've glossed over something. Didn't we notice an object? And if we did, would that not be either the SO or the RO? And if it's not the SO, then wouldn't it have to be the RO? What I'm going to argue is that what we have noticed was not the RO, but it wasn't the entirety of the SO *for* us either. I argue that what we have noticed as an object is actually just a sensual quality, one that is available to us when we encounter an object like an ant bridge, but one that is not available to us when we encounter non-traditional objects like global warming.

First of all, the "object" we noticed cannot be the RO. For one, the RO is withdrawn, and so we can never capture the whole of it with our senses. Furthermore, as Harman makes clear, Real Qualities "can only be the target of intellectual and never sensuous intuition."[191] This must go for the RO as well. It is never something we can *notice* as itself. But the "object" we noticed may not be all that the SO is for us. At least for humans and some other animals, mere "objects" are noticeable without being identified by either form or number. This is called *subitizing*. It has to do with counting crows, which we shall henceforth distinguish from the maudlin alt-rock band of the 1990s. There have long been stories of crows being able to count small quantities of things; however, as Hurford notes, what crows and other animals with similar abilities are actually doing is subitizing.[192] Subitization is the immediate awareness of a necessarily limited amount of discrete things in a given scene. Human ability to subitize is usually tested by flashing a number of dots on a screen, and then having the viewer recount how many dots there were as quickly as possible. When I tried it for myself, I was 100% accurate at up to four dots, but in the two scenes that flashed five dots, I guessed "six" each time.[193] According to Hurford, I did no better than a dog can do; however, I can take comfort in the fact that most humans can't subitize more than four things anyway.[194] Although subitizing tests ask participants to ascribe a number to the things they see, subitizing is distinct from counting because counting is an analytical practice that works in relation to a cultural system.[195] Numbers themselves play no role in the everyday practice of subitizing, except when testing subjects are asked to enumerate what they saw. But what is even more interesting about subitizing, as Lana Trick finds, is that spatial and sensible qualities do not play the same role in subitizing as they do in counting. Counting, on the other hand, does rely more on sequences that involve spatial and/or featural selection:

> [P]articipants select one group [of items] to individuate, then the next, until every group has been enumerated. When items are homogeneous, the basis for selection is necessarily spatial: A person might choose to start with groups on the left and work right, the groups on the top and work down, and so on. However, when items are heterogeneous, and heterogeneous in such a way that early vision could use heterogeneity to define different groups (as in grouping by similarity), an individual might form a strategy of selecting items by feature. For example, a person might select the red items first, then blue.[196]

Possibly because counting relies on the selection of sequence, moment-to-moment featural changes in items slowed down counting speed, but had no effect on subitizing speed.[197] On the other hand, "people do not seem to use the fast and accurate subitizing process to enumerate three concentric rectangles" (which is in the subitizing range), as the relative speed for three concentric rectangles is about the same as that for five to seven rectangles, which is in the counting range.[198] I would argue that this is because a selection of sequence strategy must be adopted (in-outwards or out-inwards) before the rectangles can be registered as discrete things. This makes sense given Dehaene and Cohen's research on simultagnosic[199] patients who were largely unable to count more than three items, while subitizing excellently for one to three items.[200] They found that the problem in counting stemmed from "a general deficit of serial visual exploration due to an inability to use spatial tags to refer to object locations."[201] In other words, without a spatial index, the test subjects could not be sure if what they were counting had already been counted. Thus, a spatial index would have to be constructed in the case of the concentric rectangles, which, on the surface, occupy the same space. Enumerating the rectangles would, therefore, call upon the counting mechanism rather than the subitizing mechanism.

It is worth noting that there is still some controversy among psychologists as to whether or not subitizing is actually a separate mechanism from counting. But if it is indeed as Trick says, "more than mere superstition,"[202] then it must be acknowledged that we can apprehend things without reference to sequence, space, size, color, texture, etc. And if what is noticed is not counted, then it is not an RQ.[203] And if it is not an identified form that we've noticed, then it is not *necessarily* the entirety of the SO that we have identified. Unqualified extension, it turns out, is simply another SQ, just like the shimmering blue of a lake with the sun overhead.

The temptation in identifying non-traditional objects like Morton's *hyperobjects* is to say that since they do not appear in the form of traditional objects, we have to speculate via the intellect on their forms, to induce the form of such an object from what is known of its RQs. The temptation, in other words, is to say that we analyze such objects from a known aggregate of processes. But again, just because we cannot notice the form of an object like global warming right in front of us as we would notice a shoe, that does not mean that the form of such an object is not available to us by sensuous intuition. As I have argued, even when we notice something like a shoe in front of us, we are not identifying its form but merely encountering one of its SQs.

One the other hand, at least for humans, identifying the form of an object (or the SO) is not always entirely a matter of sensuous intuition because we ascribe a name to the form too. The sensuous encounter with the SO and the naming of the form intermingle with each other to the point of indistinction within the space of an analogy. Thus, in the case of the ant bridge, it is quite impossible to separate the moment when the form of the object struck us as a bridge from the moment when we signified it as a kind of bridge. Before we identified by analogy the form of the bridge, we had to know that the object's RQs (the ants) were different from the RQs of a more familiar wooden bridge (an act of intellectual speculation), but the encounter between the SQs of the object and the SQs of the wooden bridge, out of which this analogy emerged, was a sensuous encounter. Thus, the SO does indeed emerge in an aesthetic moment. Naming the object as an ant bridge is an acknowledgement that there is an RO there, which is an act of the intellect; but that does not mean that when we get to the level of language, we are suddenly outside the realm of the aesthetic. We are of course used to the idea of poetic metaphors as aesthetic things, but as I shall later argue, even grammar emerges from aesthetic, analogical encounters. Where analogy is concerned, language itself fragments into SQs. Linguistic constructions can be the SQs of an object just like accidental perceptions of spatial extension, color, texture, smell, etc. can be. And since the apprehension of a particular SO does not require every kind of SQ,[204] we can identity new objects with any number of those SQs. And some kinds of SQs of some of those objects will not be available to us at all.

The SO of an object such as a complex system, whose unqualified spatial extension (that which is subitized) is unavailable to our immediate sensuous experience of it, might nonetheless be identified through analogy. In fact, analogy seems to be the most important means of identifying non-traditional objects without the unqualified spatial extension SQ. The growing importance of complex systems as objects of scientific knowledge throws us back, in a sense, to pre-modern Europe, when the cosmos was understood as an infinite series of similar forms. Benedict Anderson summarizes the pre-modern state of political, spiritual, and epistemic authority beautifully in terms of the difference between vernacular and Latin:

> The astonishing power of the papacy in its noonday is only comprehensible in terms of a trans-European Latin-writing clerisy, *and* a conception of the world, shared by virtually everyone, that the bilingual intelligentsia, by mediating between vernacular and Latin, mediated between earth and heaven. (The awesomeness of excommunication reflects this cosmology.)[205]

Latin was a *lingua franca*, a common and epistemically productive language for the intelligentsia, and would remain so long enough to be the medium for Newton's scientific revolution, but as a liturgical language it was also epistemically *protective*, just as a language like Kallawaya[206] both protects the knowledge of the shaman and the potency of that knowledge. As a liturgical language, Latin was a guarantor of a cosmology in which signs could make real interventions into the spiritual and physical world, and thus existed on the same ontological plane as the spiritual and physical. Signs could initiate the turning of bread into flesh, and they could also sever the soul from its creator. In this world, as Foucault[207] says, "it was resemblance that organized the play of symbols, made possible knowledge of things visible and invisible, and controlled the art of representing them. The universe was folded in upon itself..."[208] It was a world of self-predicating objects. Foucault gives the example—which might be my all-time favorite similitude—from Crollius of the imminently useful analogy between walnuts and brains:

> [W]hat cures 'wounds of the pericranium' is the thick green rind covering the bones—the shell—of the fruit; but internal head ailments may be prevented by the use of the nut itself 'which is exactly like the brain in appearance.[209]

Here, the walnut is not predicated of anything external to it. It is not predicated of its species or the self-same matter of its chemical make-up. As an object, it is predicated of its own form (its SO); but of course, it could have a form that was not predicated of itself as an object (its RO). Thus, it would be a mistake to say that, in this cosmology, the walnut is a type of brain or that the substance of the walnut is brain or the other way around. Here, God creates forms and things as they are. If there is a predicative jump for these things, it is to the *act* of God, but even that, as we shall explore in the next chapter, worked analogically. Besides the *act* of God, the walnut and brain did not share a substance, and they did not share a form. What they had were similar forms, though again, I would argue that the similarity was an emergent state of affairs.

Even if we wouldn't prescribe a walnut concoction for meningitis, it is hard to deny the simple aesthetic relationship between the walnut and the brain. They strike us as having similar forms because their SQs strike us as being similar. Remember that SQs are accidental, so there is no guarantee that, for instance, a worm would encounter similar SQs on either the walnut or the brain. The similar SQs of the walnut and brain, then, are a part of another SO entirely: the SO of the analogy-object. Because of its similar qualities, the SO of the analogy is self-similar enough to endure and to be speculated upon. Once we have apprehended the SO of the analogy by aesthetic intuition, we can begin to speculate intellectually on the RQs of the analogy. (These are linguistic signs, just as ants are the RQs of the ant bridge.) We can ask what sorts of categories of things the analogy's SQs suggest. Presumably, we would come up with the category *folds*, which is common to our descriptive metaphors for both the brain and the walnut. We could then go on to speculate upon the function of folds in either or both the brain and the walnut.

In the pre-modern world of similitude, the RQs of the analogy were the *act* of God, which like God could be felt and speculated upon—though never known in essence—but which nevertheless was revealed by God so that we could build knowledge out of the infinity of forms in His creation. Again, Foucault:

> [E]ach resemblance [...] has value only from the accumulation of all others, and the whole world must be explored if even the slightest of analogies is to be justified and finally take on the appearance of certainty [...] The only possible form of link between the elements of this knowledge is addition.[210]

This is actually not unlike what complexity scientists are doing. It is never enough, it seems, to create basic, self-same laws of complexity and then deduce the material world from the forces that derive from those laws. Knowledge of complex systems sustains and justifies itself on the constant accumulation of complex systems. Take, for example, the comparative metabolic systems of warm-blooded animals. Metabolism in warm-blooded animals is a self-similar system whose scale can be at least approximately analyzed onto a double logarithmic plot.[211] Beginning from the knowledge that small animals have higher metabolic rates than large animals, it was originally thought that metabolism would work in proportion to body mass. But that turned out to be way too high for larger animals. However, it did turn out that metabolic rates scaled at roughly three-fourths the difference in body masses.[212] This is an impressive finding in and of itself, but in order for it to mean anything as a complex system, it had to find an analogy elsewhere. Working in collaboration at the Santa Fe Institute, an ecologist, a biologist, and a theoretical physicist (respectively, James Brown, Brian Enquist, and Geoffrey West) analogized the metabolic system to the circulatory system, and found that the number of capillaries in animals scaled in a similar way to their metabolic rates.[213] But even this linkage must be added to something else in order to justify the knowledge that the analogy produced. The more seemingly far-flung the analogy, the more universal the knowledge. West, therefore, analogized the energy consumption of cities to the metabolic rates of animals, finding that cities at the larger end of the scale are more energy efficient than those at the smaller end, which is similar to the scaled efficiency of animals.[214] West's findings, if accurate, obviously have enormous practical applications for urban geography and city planning. But the point is that before this object could be available for speculation and analysis, the metabolic city—a nontraditional object by any reckoning—had to be identified as an SO, and that was done by analogy. Indeed Melanie Mitchell, one of the leading voices in complexity theory, argues that there will probably never be any "general principles" by which all complex systems are deduced and understood. She says instead that complexity scientists should be looking for "common principles" of complex systems.[215] What this means is that all complex systems will not have the same qualities, sensual or real, and therefore no set of qualities can be used to identify all complex systems. Synthetic thinking cannot lead us to the identification of objects that are unknown to us. And so, if analogy is the epistemic engine by which we will identify new objects, then we have to understand analogical thinking as a truly distinct process from synthetic thinking.

Chapter 3
Similarity and Reality

Reckless Etymologies

Philosophers and polemicists use etymologies for a couple of different rhetorical purposes. The first, more poetical purpose is to free a word from the semantic chains it has accreted in its lifetime of translation and usage, perhaps to reintroduce some ambiguity or nuance into the word's hardened familiarity. It might be pointed out, for instance, that *cosmos* shares the same root with *cosmetic* in order to reintroduce an aesthetic element into our understanding of the universe. The other purpose of etymology in argument is the sometimes naïve, sometimes cynical, and occasionally genuinely enlightening normative function. It's the argument that the way a word has been translated and used has been corrupted from the original, and that inasmuch as it has been corrupted, our thoughts too have rotted. One might point to Heidegger's calquing his way from 'truth' to ἀλήθεια [*alethia*] to *Unverborgenheit*. Or perhaps as a way of criticizing the ethos of individualistic, personal fitness in Western yoga practices, one might point out, snarkily, that *yoga* and the English *yoke* share the same Indo-European root, which means "union."[216]

It takes a lot to make the etymology of *analogy* truly interesting and worthwhile. There is a fair amount of overreach involved, almost to the point of being irresponsible. So here goes. The original Greek ἀναλογία [*analogia*] is so much less than it is, and a simple translation is going to be far more fruitful than any analysis of the word could be. Nevertheless, ἀναλογία is made up of a root, a prepositional prefix, and a suffix indicating an abstract noun. If we break it apart accordingly, it means "upon logic" or "by logic," or perhaps even "apart from logic." An adventurous etymological analysis might put ἀναλογία side-by-side with ἀνάλυσις [*analysis*], which means "up-loosening" or "unfastening" or "breaking up." If the prepositional prefix ἀνα- [*ana-*] is common to both analysis and analogy, and the ἀνα- in analysis connotes something like "toward" loosening, then the ἀνα- in analogy might mean something like "toward" ratio or "toward" logic. But what seems to be the case is that by the time ἀναλογία made its way to Aristotle, analogy was going *away from* logic rather than towards it.

Clearly, the prefix ἀνα-was highly productive in the number of ways it could affix itself to a root. But of course, the root λόγος [*logos*] carries more philosophical baggage than perhaps any word in the Indo-European lexicon. Λόγος comes out of λέγειν [*legein*], which superficially connotes speech, but also "gathering" or "arranging." Heidegger elaborates even further: "Λέγειν means 'to glean' [...], that is, to harvest, to gather, to add one to the other, to include and connect with one another."[217] This sense of bringing together certainly connects *analogy* to its early usage in mathematics, but Heidegger is keen to stress that the work λόγος does of expressing relationships is not posterior to its association with speech: "Asking how λόγος also came to have the meaning of 'relation' is therefore backwards; the order of things is quite the reverse."[218] The sense of relation and bringing together is fortuitous for the larger argument in this book because it means that the terms *analogy* and *analysis* do not just sound (conveniently) like opposites, but that at root they *are* opposites of a sort.

Analogy enters the written record as a mathematical term. For Euclid, it was a term of proportion and proportionality.[219] Plato seems to have been the first philosopher to employ the term outside of mathematics, though he does so as a conscious abstraction from its mathematical meaning.[220] Analogy was both calqued into the Latin as *proportio* and translated as *ratio*. The original Grecian *analogia* continued to be used in Classical Latin as a term of rhetorical grammar. Julius Caesar, in fact, composed a treatise on grammar entitled *De Analogia*, which was addressed to the great authority on the subject, Cicero. But as a philosophical term, the Grecian *analogia* had been largely washed out of usage by the time Vulgar Latin became the literary engine of western Christendom. Analogy appears in Romans xii, 6 in the Greek New Testament thusly:

> Ἔχοντες δὲ χαρίσματα κατὰ τὴν χάριν τὴν δοθεῖσαν ἡμῖν διάφορα, εἴτεπροφητείαν κατὰ τὴν ἀναλογίαν τῆς πίστεως.[221]

The passage makes its way into the Vulgate as:

> Habentes autem donationes secundum gratiam quae data est nobis differentes sive prophetiam secundum *rationem* fidei.[222]

And here's your King James:

> Having then gifts differing according to the grace that is given to us, whether prophesy, let us prophesy according to the *proportion* of faith.[223]

The idea is that each of us has received certain gifts by grace—including prophecy—but that the use of those gifts should not exceed faith in the God who has given us the gifts. We seem to be dealing with comparative quantities, but it's a comparison of two different kinds of quantities: use and faith. The Vulgate's translation of ἀναλογίαν into *rationem* certainly places emphasis on quantity; however, in his *Greek-English Lexicon of the New Testament*, Grimm suggests that ἀναλογία in this passage could be translated as "conformable."[224] Translating it this way would imply more of an aesthetic relationship between the different kinds, use and faith. Which actually rings truer to the spirit of Paul's admonition: the use of your gifts should resemble the form of your faith. Thus, in this instance, *analogy* would mean a coming together or a mutually affective contact of forms, which puts us closer in range with what Heidegger argued for in the root of the root of *analogy*. Clearly, this more subtle meaning of the term is lost when ἀναλογία is washed out in the Latin.

Probably the only reason 'analogy' remains in common usage today as itself rather than as some variant of *proportio* or *ratio* is because medieval theologians—most notably, the Thomists—found it a useful concept for understanding our own understanding of God and our participation in God's being. They might easily have used the Latin translation, but because Aristotle was the singular source of their understanding of the concept, the original Greek was preferred and preserved. For these scholars, analogy was more than just a term that Aristotle employed occasionally; Aristotle became the effective author of the term. Contemporary Anglophone literary theorists are obliged to use *jouissance* rather than *enjoyment* when employing the relevant psychoanalytical concept, because it can only be understood properly in the context of Lacan's system and his cultural milieu. Likewise, the reason we use "analogy" instead of some variant of *proportio* or *ratio* is because, for medieval scholars, the concept could only be understood properly in the context of Aristotle's system.

Thank goodness Thomas Aquinas, Cardinal Cajetan and others were such eccentric readers of Aristotle, or else we would have to look to another term entirely in order to have anything interesting to say about the thing we call analogy. Aristotle tends to hammer other philosophers for their use of analogical or paradigmatic arguments, but that doesn't stop him from employing plenty of what we would call analogical arguments himself, particularly in his tracts on the natural world. The closest we get to an understanding of analogy as such is probably in Book Delta of *The Metaphysics*, when Aristotle is defining sameness, difference, and likeness. Here, analogy falls into his understanding of difference:

> "Different" is applied (1) to those things which though other are that same in some respect, only not in number but either in species or in genus or by analogy; (2) to those whose genus is other, and to contraries, and to all things that have their otherness in their essence.[225]

Likeness, where we might expect to find analogy, covers things

> which have the same attributes in every respect, and those which have more attributes the same than different, and those whose quality is one; and that which shares with another thing the greater number or the more important of the attributes.[226]

Likeness, then, deals with attributes or qualities. That leaves analogy in the realm of functional similarity. So strictly speaking, things that have similar qualities, such as the brain and the walnut, would not bear an analogical relationship to one another, unless we could, through reason, show that the undulating shapes that characterize the brain and the walnut have a similar function. Aristotle gives us more clarity in his *Parts of Animals* when he discusses the differences between types of birds and between birds and fish. He brings up the possibility that if feathers are for birds what scales are for fish, then birds and fish might be part of the same, higher group. But this couldn't be, says Aristotle. Things that belong together in a genus are those things with like attributes that differ only "by excess" of those attributes.[227] So, even if two kinds of birds have different feather lengths, the different birds are alike in that they share the essential attribute of feathers. Furthermore, there is no common attribute shared by both feathers and scales, as far as Aristotle is concerned. All they have in common is what they are *for* their respective animals.

But this leaves open a giant question, one that would only become significant when analogy enters into Christian theological discourse: is analogy proper to both epistemology and ontology, or just to epistemology? As a purely epistemological thing, we could say that the feathers of birds and the scales of fish function for their respective animals *for* our inquiry into the parts of animals. Is it merely the case that because we know feathers serve a particular function for birds that we should treat scales as things which also serve a particular function, even if the function of scales has nothing to do with what feathers are for? Or does the analogy point to some sort of self-same function of functions? Aristotle even speaks of clear physiological correspondences as being "common by analogy," pointing out that "some animals have a lung," and "others have no lung but something else to correspond instead of it."[228] Here, it seems to be the case that if we find an animal without lungs, we should go looking for an organ that serves the same *function*, which would mean that the function is a cause of the organ:

> Just as the saw is there for the sake of sawing and not sawing for the sake of the saw [...] so in some way the body exists for the sake of the soul, and parts of the body for the sake of those functions to which they are naturally adapted.[229]

So, with regards to feathers and scales, analogy serves to stimulate inquiry (i.e. If feathers do x, then scales might do x, y, or z.). But as we have seen, analogy can also make specific things intelligible (e.g. lungs and lung correspondences). Aristotle is working without the benefit of evolutionary theory, but the metaphysical problem remains: is there a separate being of the lung function of which lungs and gills are both properties? Or are lungs and gills ostensive definitions of the lung function? Here, we wade into issues of reference and meaning, priority and posteriority, and univocity and equivocity, all of which were at the heart of medieval theological discourse on analogy.

At this point, the question of what it means to be healthy (or what *healthy* can be) takes center stage. It begins at the beginning of Book Gamma of *The Metaphysics*, as Aristotle is attempting to describe what a science of being as being would do. All that follows comes out of the following ambiguity:

> Everything which is health is related to health, one thing in the sense that it preserves health, another in the sense that it produces it, another in the sense that it is a symptom of health, another because it is capable of it.[230]

This little teaser came to be known as the "*pros hen*"[231] ambiguity.

The question that the Thomists grappled with (and with which Thomist scholars still grapple) was whether Aristotle is talking here about analogy or equivocation, or, as the earlier Boethius had it, analogy as a *kind* of equivocation. What was clear was that Aristotle was getting at different ways of talking about being and what the proper subject of being was. To restate it more concretely, medicine can produce health; and urine can be a sign of health; and a diet can preserve health, but only the animal is the proper subject of health. All of these things can be said to be healthy, but, once again, only the animal is the proper subject of health. Likewise, for Aristotle, only a substance can be the proper subject of being. Qualities as beings, such as the *healthy* of healthy urine are secondarily being—the *healthy* is attributed to the urine, which is merely an indication of the health of the animal. Thus, all of those other healthies reference one *healthy*, which is the healthy of the animal who alone is capable of actualizing health, rather than simply causing it or indicating it. We can say that all of the other healthies reference the healthy of the animal, without which none of the other healthies would have meaning. And we can also say that the healthy of the creature is prior to the other healthies.

For Aristotle, the *pros hen* ambiguity was simply an illustrative example meant to set up his real analysis of being as being. And for moderns, all of this talk about health and piss might seem like a bit of anachronistic silliness—or, to give it a little more credit, a trivial semantic game. But for the theologians, it was deadly serious.

Thomas the Realist

The *pros hen* ambiguity first of all indicates that being is not univocal. To say that the animal is the proper subject of health does not mean that the healthy urine simply belongs to the greater being of the healthy animal. The obvious place to go to next is to say that *health* is here a term of equivocity—that is to say that when we talk about the healthy urine and the healthy subject as the same thing, we are simply in error because they are two totally different kinds of healthy with causes and effects that have nothing to do with one another. Again, Botheius saw the *pros hen* as a particular kind of equivocity, but Aquinas did something radical by arguing that analogical terms neither point to some underlying univocity nor are they just another species of equivocity. Analogy, for St. Thomas, is a third mode on equal footing with both univocity and equivocity. It is, we might say, an *included* middle.

Univocal terms, Thomas says, can be exemplified by "when *animal* is predicated of a man and a donkey."[232] Both, in other words, are animal. When *dog* is attributed to both animal and a star, we're dealing with an equivocal term.[233] A healthy body, a healthy drink, and healthy urine are, on the other hand, analogical because the healthy objects "though diverse by meaning and definition, bear on some one common meaning."[234] Which is to say that the intelligibility of *health* as such is dependent upon all of those terms bumping into one another. The difference between univocal terms and analogical terms is obvious—a symptom of health is not the same as something that causes health. But the difference between equivocal terms and analogical terms is much subtler. Clearly, the term for dog the animal preexisted the term for dog the star. And thinking about dog the star in no way contributes to the meaning of dog the animal. However, the same cannot be said for healthy the animal and healthy the urine. Although healthy the animal may have preexisted and been attributed to healthy the urine, the attribution of health to the urine made *health* intelligible in an entirely new way.

The majority opinion in modern Thomist studies holds that Thomas limited his analogical mode to attribution and proportion. The argument is that analogies of attribution contribute to our very imperfect understanding of God, and that analogy as such belongs only to the human linguistic realm. This too is the way Kant understood the intelligibility of God.[235] For instance, the diverse ways in which we experience goodness can contribute to our conception of God's goodness, although our concept of goodness has nothing really to do with the goodness that is proper to God. Thus, analogy once again becomes another shade of equivocity.

But it seems to me that if St. Thomas had meant for analogy to apply only to names and proportions, he might have said something to that effect. But he doesn't seem to have done so. In fact, as Steven Long[236] points out, Aquinas does have something to say about the analogy of being as being. But because Aquinas discusses the analogy of being as being in his early writings (*De veritate*), modern Thomist scholars tend to take the absence of that ontological discussion in his mature work (e.g. *Summa theologica*) as a sign that St. Thomas dropped this line of thinking altogether. As for the meager presence of the discussion in the *Summa*, Long answers, "Indeed, one might think, Thomas already explicitly answered it in *De veritate* and so had no reason to raise it again, especially since there is no contradiction between the two treatments."[237]

Certainly, there is no reason to think that the problem Aquinas was addressing with his ontological notion of analogy of proper proportionality had gone away by the time he was older. In fact, it's still very much a problem with philosophers and theologians to this day, though perhaps with different stakes and implications. It's very much the same univocal-equivocal question that Deleuze and Badiou debated so intensely toward the end of Deleuze's days.[238] What was at stake in the Deleuze-Badiou debate was the emergence of the new. In Badiou's equivocity, new modes of being are reliant upon the persistence of a totally non-self-same *Void*, whereas newness in Deleuze's univocity consists of purely different iterations of the same. What was at stake in Thomas's time was the very nature of God. The cultural hybridity of early Christianity brought it into contact with the existing debate in Greek thinking, which went back to Parmenides, and even further, to Thales. But by the time St. Thomas picked up the debate from Averroes,[239] it had been distilled through a robust Islamic notion of the transcendent. Obviously, univocity would be out of the question. Had God's will not been separate from his creation, the creation would have emerged coevally with God. But equivocity too presented a couple of serious problems for a transcendent God. For one, equivocity might imply an interdependence between the being of God and the beings of creatures.

Secondly, as Aquinas asks, if the distance between God's being and the beings of creatures is greater than the distance between the beings of creatures and non-being, then how could we know anything about God or conform to God's goodness?[240] This is once again like the question of how dog the star can contribute to the meaning of dog the animal in any analytical sense. Medieval theologians were prepared to take on mountains of intellectual labor in order to avoid these pitfalls of equivocity. Duns Scotus, for instance, came up with a perfectly reasonable solution to the problem by attributing concepts such as *goodness* to univocity, so that particular differences could be deferred to haecceity.[241] Indeed, we can trace the intellectual lineage of Deleuze's ontology of difference and Hardt and Negri's political concept of the *multitude* right back to Scotus's solution to the equivocity problem. Aquinas, on the other hand, turned not just to analogy of nominal attribution but to analogy of ontological similarity.

Again, Aquinas argues that non-being is closer to the beings of creatures than the finite beings of creatures are to God's infinite being. We're of course sweeping infinitesimals under the rug,[242] but you can see how there could be no discernable ratio between a finite and an infinite as there can be between two finites. So, analogy of proportion is out of the question when it comes to the relationship between God's being and the beings of creatures. And analogy of attribution deals only with the ordering of terms, so that's out too.

To be clear, Thomas's ontological notion of analogy begins with the similarity between God's knowledge and our knowledge. But for Thomas, the act of knowing is not cordoned off from being. Knowing is subject to the same Aristotelian division of act and potential that sculpting, cooking, or building are. Knowing, like sculpting, is the act of the substance that is knowing or sculpting. That substance is also limited by its potential in what it can know or sculpt. There is a gap of non-being between the act of knowing and potentially knowing, and that's why we finite creatures, with all of our limits, are closer to non-being than we are to the limitless being of God. So we find ourselves back at the second danger of equivocation: if God's knowledge is pure act and our knowledge is an act-potential dialectic, then how would we know anything about God at all? In this case, it would make just as much sense to be an agnostic as it would to be a believer. Clearly the *Doctor Angelicus* could not be happy with that. The solution to the problem is to argue that the being of creatures is analogy all the way down. So, knowing, sculpting, and cooking are obviously not the same thing, but they are also not predicated of being as such, because the being of created substances is divided into act and potential. Thus, knowing, cooking, and sculpting are not only not the same as each other, but they are not the same as themselves either because the division between act and potential is sutured by non-being. We can therefore say that they are all *like* each other in the same way that they are *like* themselves. God, Thomas argues, is uniquely self-same in this respect because "just as His essence is the same as His act of being, so is His knowledge the same as His act of being a knower."[243] Nevertheless, just as there can be an analogical similarity between being and non-being, there can also be an analogy between God's being and the beings of creatures. Whereas the relationship between created being and non-being can at least be understood logically as a 1-0 binary (though even that is an analogical understanding), the relationship between God and created beings can only be grasped aesthetically, "as when sight is predicated of bodily sight and of the intellect because understanding is in the mind as sight is in the eye."[244]

Clearly, the above analogy can be understood as an analogy of proper proportionality rather than an analogy of proportion, and it can be notated as such:

Body : Mind :: Sight : Intellect

What this analogy of proportionality lacks is the coefficient that is prior to all four terms that one would see in an analogy of proportion. And yet, I also don't think that Thomas is simply setting out to achieve equivalence by other means. In his conception of analogies of proportionality, Thomas is not holding out for an as-yet-named term that predicates the two relations. He is calling attention to the fact that no such name exists now nor will ever exist. Thomas's ontological notion of analogy is not an equivocation deferred; it is radical similarity. What Thomas is arguing for in regards to knowing (and therefore to being) is quite similar to the case I referred to in the previous chapter of the existential copula in the Arabana language. One doesn't say "There *is* object *x*" and "There *is* object *y*." Rather, one says something closer to "There *sits* object *x*" and "There *stands* object *y*." The syntax of the two statements suggests some similarity between the two objects; yet, there is no sense in which object *x* and object *y* share in the same being. There is no "is" between them, but that doesn't mean that there cannot emerge a relationship between them.

St. Thomas authored a well-known prayer for students in which the supplicant petitions God, "Grant me the talent of being exact in my explanations and the ability to express myself with thoroughness and charm." I pray that the reader will forgive the following summary of Aquinas's solution, for it is thoroughly without charm: God has knowledge and the creature has knowledge; the creature has knowledge of God, but the nature of that knowledge is only an impression of God's knowledge. The two knowledges share no more nature than a haystack does with a Monet painting (actually, less so). And yet, impressive paintings of haystacks exist. To be sure, the relation between thing and image is, for Thomas, an asymmetrical one, in that the impression of the thing does not affect the thing in the way the thing affects the impression. I have neither the space nor the expertise to go into the subtleties of Thomas's take on *imageo dei* except to say that although the thing (God) has no definite relation to the image (the creature), the relation between the two is nonetheless real as are both the thing and the image in and of themselves. All that is to say that although Thomas Aquinas is often erroneously called a rationalist, he is firmly in the realist camp and similarity is a central part of his realism.

So how did similarity and reality get to be so opposed to one another in modern philosophical thought? That's the question I'll be taking up in the next chapter. My argument there is that under the great influence of empiricism, similarity was not merely dismissed in considerations of reality, but that the rejection of similarity was indeed central to the formulation of reality in modern philosophical thought.

Chapter 4
Empiricism and the Problem of Similarity

The title of this very book is *The Being of Analogy*, and it is of course a riff on *analogia entis* [the analogy of being], which has been attributed to Aquinas.[245] As I have pointed out, analogy and its relation or non-relation to being is still taken seriously by Thomist scholars to this day, though it is a debate largely confined to theological studies. Linguists and cognitive scientists too maintain an interest in the topic of analogy, and I'll discuss that conversation in depth later on in the book. But for the last major consideration of being and analogy in philosophy, one has to go as far back as Vico's arguments on historical movement (though Vico seems to be enjoying a bit of a renaissance in recent years). For the most part, Vichian historiography survives only inasmuch as it was appropriated by Hegel and reformulated as a dialectical synthesis, where it was then distilled into structuralist anthropology. So while analogy and similarity were not altogether rejected in Continental philosophy, they were effectively forgotten. This is not true, however, for empiricism and its twentieth century scions, which include philosophies as diverse as neonominalism and Deleuzianism. For those thinkers, the entire edifice of their reality stood on the exclusion of similarity. For the neonominalists (as was the case for Kant), the only way to speak properly about an objective reality was to confine aesthetic phenomena, such as similarity, to the active subject. As for Deleuze, he did away with the primacy of the active subject altogether. And while he was at it, he relegated similarity to representation, both of which would be enervated with the now defrocked subject. All of this is to say that if we really want to rediscover the relationships between being, knowing, and aesthetics, we need to look at how exactly similarity became such as sticking point for the empiricists.

At least up until Deleuze, modern empiricists ejected similarity by wedging a *frame of reference* between being and knowing. There would have been no room in Aquinas's ontology for something like a *frame of reference* to say anything useful about being or knowing, since knowing is itself a way of being and because there is no univocal or equivocal predication of being. Even *time*, which is the ultimate frame of reference, cannot be predicative of being for Aquinas. And indeed the idea that we do not share the same created time with that of God is one of the things that made Thomas unpopular with the millennially minded church authorities of his time.

David Hume could not say much about the metaphysics of time, but the experience of time was sufficient to create a frame of reference that would eject similarity from reality. Hume acknowledged that time as such was infinitely divisible[246] and that the mind was limited in its capacity to grasp such an infinity. The *experience* of time, however, could be analyzable as discrete idea-units. What is common to the real infinite divisibility of time and the experienced divisibility of time is succession:

> 'Tis a property inseparable from time, and which in a manner constitutes its essence, that each of its parts succeeds another, and that none of them, however contiguous, can ever be coexistent.[247]

There is an asymmetry between ideas of time and time itself, which is characterized by duration or speed, but this does not contradict the basic principle of succession. The sense of duration of an object, however, can bypass our understanding of successive parts and can therefore override our experience of time.[248] In such cases, Hume might say that the idea of the object produced is a low-fidelity recording of the sense impressions of that object.

As a matter of fact, the language of digital recording is a good way of talking about Hume's notion of similarity or *resemblance*. Hume's primary division of the human mind is between impressions and ideas.[249] Both impressions and ideas are further divided into the categories of "simple" and "complex."[250] Hume's system begins from the "general proposition" that "our simple ideas in their first appearance are deriv'd from simple impressions, which are correspondent to them, and which they exactly represent."[251] Thus the simple idea is a recording of the simple impression in perfect fidelity: "all perceptions of the mind are double, and appear both as ideas and impressions."[252] But fidelity begins to suffer in memory. What I'm referring to as "fidelity," Hume casts in intensive terms, such as "force" and "vivacity." And it's easy to see here how Deleuze found in Hume a forerunner to his own philosophy. Yet, what exactly Hume meant by "force" and "vivacity" is unclear. Perhaps because he was describing an aesthetic experience, those terms were meant to be left evocative and unanalyzed.

What is more certain is that a high degree of self-sameness of the perception (impression + idea) is necessary to produce the experience of force and vivacity. Ordinarily, when we think of a memory losing the vividness of the initial impression, we think of *loss* and *fading*, as if the impression is actually losing material, like an old man shedding hair and bone density. But Hume's thinking on this process is strikingly more sophisticated, prescient even. First of all, because impressions are always prior to ideas, an idea of an impression (a memory) coming back around to form another impression cannot be the same as an impression recording itself as an idea, and so the self-sameness of the perception is compromised. Second—and here's where Hume seems to anticipate information theory—the idea in the memory does not lose its vivacity because it is shedding intellectual energy or mass; rather, the information in the idea becomes distorted by the *addition* of noise. That is to say, the idea is placed into proximity with other ideas that begin to resemble it. The more the idea begins to resemble other ideas in circulation, the more diffuse the information of the idea becomes. Memory, therefore, has an entropic quality about it. But because this loss of fidelity in memory is not a net loss of stuff *per se*, the loss of fidelity can lead to the production of new ideas:

> When a quality becomes very general, and is common to a great many individuals, it leads not the mind directly to any one of them; but by presenting at once too great a choice, does thereby prevent the imagination from fixing on any single object.[253]

So, what is lost in the vivacity of a rerecorded impression is gained in a new abstract idea, which looks very much like a negentropic[254] process. Remarkable!

Given his understanding of how new, abstract ideas are formed, David Hume should be celebrated as one of analogy's great philosophical champions. But on the other hand, it seems that Hume is only thinking in terms of serial similarity or analogy of proportion. The resemblance Hume is thinking about is "resembling perceptions in the chain of thought."[255] That is to say that diverse ideas may share the exact same quality, and on the basis of the repetition of that self-same quality, a new, abstract idea is formed. Hume's *resemblance* is a multiple iteration of the Same within its frame of reference, which consists of ideas as discrete units.

The Neonomalism of Quine and Goodman

The quantizing of impressions and ideas is exactly what W.V.O. Quine and his fellow neo-nominalist Nelson Goodman had in mind when they sought to banish similarity from philosophy once and for all. As Quine argues, "it is a mark of maturity of a branch of science that the notion of similarity or kind finally dissolves…"[256] Goodman was less delicate: "If statements of similarity, like counterfactual conditionals and four letter words, cannot be trusted in the philosopher's study, they are still serviceable on the streets."[257] Sticks and stones, Nelson.

Quine maintains that empiricism is still the proper practical foundation of science and that empirical science is still based in sensory evidence and that "all inculcation of meanings of words must rest ultimately on sensory evidence"[258] as well. The ideal move, then, would have been to create a grammar of sensory experience that could then be transmuted into sentence and set logic, just as Carnap had attempted to do. Sense impressions could be differentiated as distinct semantic units, just as ideas could be unitized for Hume. No doubt, as Quine recognized, this would put the "epistemological burden to psychology."[259] The weakness of such a program is obvious. Since psychology too is a science supported by sensory evidence, it would also have to begin from the very grammar of sense units that it was responsible for naming. So, the hot potato gets passed back into the philosopher's tender hands. Quine's solution is to wedge in a frame of reference. This time, the frame of reference could not itself reference any of the transcendent notions of space or time with which Kant had tried to sew up Hume's system. The grammar had to be immanent in the sense impressions themselves rather than what sense impressions reference in reality.

What Quine comes up with is *ontological relativity*. So, the problem with going out and looking for a frame of reference for sensory experience is that you very quickly run into infinite regress. The experience of the color red can reference a certain range of the wavelength of light (620-750 nm), which can further reference electromagnetism, which can reference the electroweak force, etc. But, says Quine, the infinite regress of reference does not negate the meaning that is produced at each stage of reference, or that which emerges from the relationship of any subject to its predicate. So, in saying that the impression of red is the detection of light within a given wavelength range, you are not getting at the ontological foundation of that impression. And while you are not making a really real statement, you are making a really meaningful statement. And if you impose a frame of reference onto a set of statements about sensory experience (e.g. color is made up of varying wavelengths of light), then you are both making a meaningful statement and also referencing the limits of meaning.

The infinite regress of reference is on one side of the problem, but on the other side is the seemingly infinite divergence of sensory experience itself. The only way to make sensory experience epistemically productive, Quine argues, is to collapse it into self-same units, thus binding meaning to an ontological frame of reference at one end and a psycholinguistic frame at the other. And Quine sees the enormous analytical potential that supposedly came with the advent of the alphabet as evidence for the viability of such a program:

> Consider, to begin with, the linguistic phenomenon of phonemes. We form the habit in hearing the myriad variations of spoken sounds, of treating each as an approximation to one or another of a limited number of norms—around thirty altogether—constituting so to speak a spoken alphabet. All speech in our language can be treated in practice as sequences of just those thirty elements, thus rectifying small deviations.

> Now outside the realm of language there is probably only a rather limited alphabet of perceptual norms altogether, toward which we tend unconsciously to rectify all perceptions. These, if experimentally identified, could be taken as epistemological building blocks, the working elements of experience.[260]

It seems like a seriously quixotic project, but Quine was writing amidst a renaissance in the anthropology of analytical thought. One of Quine's great philosophical nemeses, Noam Chomsky, was reversing longstanding behaviorist theories of language and thought with his nativist approach to grammar in which human language could be reduced to a limited hierarchy of self-same structures, the result of a single mutation event in relatively recent human evolutionary history. Quine, meanwhile, enthusiastically deferred to the then nascent field of *evolutionary epistemology*, which was championed by behaviorists and philosophers of science, such as Karl Popper. In historical support of the evolutionary epistemology program was the work of the classicist, Eric Havelock, who proposed that the great divide in human thinking between oral and literate societies came not necessarily with the advent of writing *per se*, but with the Greek formulation of the alphabet. It is this thought-technology that Quine is referencing in his vision of a system of "epistemological building blocks."

For Havelock, the invention of the alphabet was the great aperture through which analytical thinking and the prospect of universal literacy flowed. Havelock pointed out, for instance, that because the alphabet is both limited and arbitrary—that is, no single grapheme represents a semantic or syntactic unit—alphabetical writing could be learned early on and without specialization. Havelock went on to explain the revolution in Greek philosophy—the development of a voice for *being* as such—in somewhat ontogenic terms. Just as with Jacques Derrida's *grammatological* approach to the speech-writing divide, Havelock argued that Greek discourse about speech was presupposed by a discourse of writing, the kind of which was shaped by the alphabetical system. He pointed out, for instance, that *grammata* and *syllabai* were both Greek terms of writing,[261] and that indeed even as Aristotle used *gramma* for "sound unit" in general, it first denoted "letter."[262] Likewise, Havelock argued that the Greeks' most deeply analytical ontology, atomism, was voiced in the discourse of the alphabet:

The Greeks themselves perceived that the twenty-three or so signs of their own invention now furnished a table of elements of linguistic sounds, and accordingly when their philosophers later came to propose an atomic theory of matter, thus explaining the variety of physical phenomena as the result of a combination of a finite number of primary elements, they saw the analogy with what the alphabet had done to language and likened their atoms to letters.[263]

This is precisely the kind of revolution in thinking that Quine has in mind with his project to determine the "epistemological building blocks" of sense. Just as any alphabet only approximates the individual phonemes in a given language, despite phonological variation amongst actual speakers, Quine's system is content with real variations in sensory experience, as long as ambiguity and similarity are cast out at the epistemological stratum.

If sensory impressions are at all like alphabetizable phonemes, then the atomistic model of sensory experience is immediately in trouble. It is commonly assumed that when the Greeks constructed their alphabet from the Canaanite-Phoenician alphabet (descended from Semitic syllabaries), their big innovation was to add vowels, which meant that when a reader encountered a consonant cluster, she would not have to infer the vocalic particulars of the word from context or memory. But actually, as Havelock pointed out, what the alphabet really introduced was the idea of the consonant.[264] This seems strange because Semitic alphabets were little but consonants. But in the syllabary, the consonant (or what we now call the consonant) was a consonant plus a vocalization, or a syllable. Our *names* for consonants are still vocalized, whether we call a /z/ a "zee," a "zed," or a "zeta," but the phoneme to which they refer is a non-sound, a stop brought on by varying degrees of friction. It was the recognition and representation of these negative spaces of vocalization that allowed for vowels to become positive entities in the alphabet. Now of course, no working orthography captures perfectly the phonological variations present within a language or between speakers—and Quine recognized this—but the bigger problem with taking the atomization of phonemes as a model for the atomization of sense impressions is not just that letters are approximations of really distinct sounds, but that the things to which letters refer might not be really distinct in the first place. Since at least the 1950s, linguists have debated as to whether or not phonological segmentation is a real psychological phenomenon, and if what we think of as the phoneme is really the "the smallest possible quantum of language."[265] Therefore, it cannot really be said for certain that the invention of the alphabet was the discovery that there were real atomizable differences between consonants and between consonants and vowels. Consider a glide consonant, such as /w/, which produces only as much friction as the vowel /o/, and whose status as a voiced or voiceless phoneme is uncertain. There are also liquid consonants, such as /l/ and the rhotic /r/. In both consonants, there is no tap, stop or fricative to firmly obstruct airflow, although airflow is compressed around or above the tongue. The reason why adult Japanese English language learners famously have a hard time producing distinct /l/ and rhotic /r/ sounds is because Japanese does not contain liquid consonants and so adult speakers sometimes process them as one phoneme. Then to what exactly do we pin the reality of liquid consonants? Their status as consonants in the way most other consonants are consonants is uncertain. If what distinguishes them from other consonants is that they compress air rather than stop or restrict air, then we might say that the /l/ and the rhotic /r/ are two species in the same genus, which is different from either the genus vowels or the genus consonants. What divides the two as separate species in the genus may not be a preexisting psychological processor but multiple, similar experiences of using each phoneme.

This line of thought is labored, tortured even. I know. But the point is that if phonemes are a kind of sensory impression or enough like sensory impressions that a grammar of sensory impressions can be modeled on an atomistic orthography (like an alphabet), then similarity cannot be excluded from the reality which that model is referencing. Atomizing reality for the purposes of creating a productive analytical discourse of experience or whatever else is fine, but in doing so, you cannot put your science or its metaphysical foundation in the realist camp.

Untangling Similarity and Class

We've seen at least one case in which the exclusion of similarity does not bring an epistemological program any closer to a realist metaphysics. But if we dig deeper into the neonominalist program, we find that similarity is only a secondary target for exclusion. What neonominalists really abhor is classes, or the idea that categories name entities that exist in reality.[266] And indeed it seems to me that the assumption that similarity is inextricably bound to class or kind has gone largely unchallenged in Western philosophy regardless of how much reality a particular school apportions to classes. I will argue that in an object-oriented ontology, class and similarity need not be bound in such a way.

When Quine and Goodman opened their joint manifesto for a new nominalism with the exordium, "We do not believe in abstract entities,"[267] there was much dropping of monocle and wringing of hand. Both Quine and Goodman expressed some regret for saying this and much more regret for leading with it.[268] After all, an entity like a goblin might be considered an abstract entity, and Quine and Goodman's program certainly would not exclude entities like goblins, provided they exist in relation to an appropriate frame of reference. Indeed, if Quine had reason to suspect that a phoneme did not reference any individualized thing but rather a distribution of similar things, he would have argued—with a perfectly straight face—that a goblin is more real than a phoneme. Again, what the nominalist's realism truly abhors is classes.

The abhorrence of abstract entities such as classes was, for instance, the basis for Goodman's disagreement with his famous former student, Noam Chomsky. For many socio- and cognitive linguists, Chomsky's problem is that his program is too rigidly analytical. It's quite rare to hear charges that Universal Grammar is not analytical enough; yet, that was precisely Goodman and Quine's problem with it. Goodman once composed a dialogue between the characters Anticus and Jason (lately, of *Argonaut* fame) in which Jason had recently returned from an encounter with a strange group of nomads from "Outer Cantabridgia" who claimed to have discovered secret commonalities between all languages.[269] Anticus (Goodman) suspects that what Jason (Chomsky) has brought back is "more fleece than golden."[270] Along with their secret to languages in general, the nomads have constructed a new language, "Grubleen," which "no human being could acquire…as an initial language."[271] The existence of Grubleen was supposed to show that those languages which were initially acquired contained elements that were reflective of structures innate to all human minds, and thus that there existed a firm distinction between natural and artificial languages. But since, as Jason admitted, there could be no experiment in which a child would be isolated and forced to learn only Grubleen, the nomads' hypothesis was impossible to prove or disprove. Furthermore, Anticus pointed out that children learn a system of symbols before they ever acquire their initial language. And since children learn that system of symbols just as naturally as they do their initial language, Anticus wondered, what is so especially natural about the initial language?

Besides the lack of falsifiable claims, Goodman had two problems with Chomsky's nativist argument. The first was that under Universal Grammar, all distinctive elements of each human language can be reduced to a limited number of syntactic classes which exist prior to the individual elements of a language. So, for instance, all recursive utterances would be effects of an upward merging operation in the human language faculty. Once again, classes: bad. The other problem Goodman had was that one symbolic system could be more natural and, therefore, more real than another. Goodman claimed that his primary ontological pledge was to individuals (which either excluded or subsumed classes). But actually, the ontological pledge was to systems, since systems were what were predicated of qualities, which, in turn, were predicative of individuals. Reality, for Goodman, consists of the relationship between individuals and their system. (The legacy of this type of program in contemporary structural realism is obvious.)

Goodman contrasts his notion of realism to photographic realism.[272] Here, Goodman is drawing upon his first life as an art dealer and critic. So, the simplistic measure of realism in visual art is how close, say, a painting approximates photographic reality. But of course, photographs themselves are not perfect representations of reality, since photographs are only representations of a given reality (e.g. a picture taken from a particular place and angle). This is to say that naturalism is a poor substitute for realism. Which is an admirable position as far as I'm concerned. The world, says Goodman, is "many ways,"[273] so the best a realism can hope for is a frame of reference that eliminates as many unnecessary abstractions and unobservable concretes as possible. For Goodman, as for Quine, this is the system-individual structure.

Goodman is very clear on how individuals are to be characterized: "to treat entities as individuals for a system is to take them as values of the variables of lowest type in the system."[274] Here's an illustration. Let's say we have in a system three apples. One apple is 2 parts red and 1 part green. The second apple is 1 part red, 1 part green and 1 part yellow. The third apple is 2 parts red and 1 part yellow. The system references only the colors of the apples and not the apples themselves. So in this system, there are three distinct color combinations, and so there are three individual entities. There is a possibility of having 3!(3 − 1)! or 12 entities in the system, but the system would not admit additional entities, such as *all mostly red apples*, since *all mostly red apples* would be a class and not an individual. And here we see how similarity is anathema to neonominalist philosophy. The apple that is 2 parts red and 1 part yellow has nothing to do with apple that is 2 parts red and 1 part green because the apples are themselves mere collections of qualities and not entities over and above their qualities. In the fourth of his "Seven Strictures on Similarity," Goodman writes dismissively that "Anything is in some way like everything else…"[275] Thus, if we took similarity to be real, nothing would be definable as an individual and so nothing definite could be said about the world. But this is only true if qualities were the only entities, in which case similarity would be nothing more than a repetition of the same. Again, the repetition of the same quality seems to be what Hume had in mind with his metonymical notion of *resemblance*. If two ideas shared an exact same quality, then a third, abstract idea might emerge.

And yet, there are no grounds on which to assume that similarity should be reduced to such arithmetical terms. Nor is there any justification to assume that similarity belongs only to classes and not to individuals. Both assumptions presuppose that objects are collections of either atomic material or parsable qualities. And it is true that if objects were simply collections of these things, then similarity would be a matter of simple proportion. So, the two apples that were ⅔ red would be proportionately similar to an orange that was ⅔ orange and ⅓ yellow, or perhaps even to an orange that was ¾ orange and ¼ yellow (in that it is > ½ a single color).

Thus, if we do suppose that objects are mere collections, then Goodman is quite right to claim that everything is ultimately similar to everything else in such a way that similarity becomes a useless concept. But if objects are real unto themselves, then similarity cannot be discounted on those grounds.

The other glaring problem here—the problem that Cajetan took great pains to redress—is that when we talk about similarity (or analogy) as such, we're attributing the name to several different things that, when put alongside one another, look, well, like apples and oranges. So, similarities of proportion and similarities of proportionality not only denote different phenomena; they belong to entirely different philosophical categories. Proportion can never be anything but epistemological, whereas proportionality can refer to relations of being. When we refer to the proportional similarity between the two apples that are ⅔ red, we're only describing a particular state of affairs. And indeed, this kind of description can lead to perfectly useful scientific questions, such as "Why are most of the apples I observe mostly red?" In other words, similarities of proportion are good tools for helping us think about correlation. And, of course, static models are difficult to build without similarities of proportion (static models themselves having more descriptive than predictive power). Similarities of proportionality, on the other hand, are relevant to ontological questions, such as those of causality. For example, observing that two out of my three apples are mostly red says nothing about the real relationships between the apples. However, if I dropped one of my apples on the cement floor, I could say that the potential of the apple to be dented becomes similar to the floor's act of being hard and flat. Indeed, once the apple collides with the floor, it may even take on a flat dent on its side, an impression similar to the floor's flatness. We cannot say that the floor was totally responsible for the apple's dent (nor was it all gravity's fault), since the apple had the potential to be affected by the floor as an apple.

But of course, none of that makes any sense unless you understand objects as being with their qualities instead of being *from* their qualities. The assumption that similarity deals only in classes or kinds and not in individuals also presupposes that objects are mere collections of individual entities, which are more real than objects, but which are somehow not themselves objects. It is true, as Hume thought, that thinking of similarities (or *resemblances*) effects abstract ideas or generalizations. But of course, any sort of induction projects itself onto classes in one way or another. Even if you are making a prediction about the behavior of a single object, you are still at the very least classifying time (e.g. $Past_{1, 2, 3...}$ and $Future_{1, 2, 3...}$). Analogies of proportion and analogies of proportionality project themselves onto either classes of qualities or classes of objects. So, if I come across a rock with relatively flat perpendicular surfaces, I may think to myself that the rock has chair-like qualities, and I may perhaps use the rock as a chair-like object. Analogies of proportionality may project themselves onto both classes of qualities and classes of objects, as in Yukawa's analogy of the photon and the π-meson. But whatever analogies project themselves onto, they always begin with objects. The analogue-objects may be abstract objects or they may be parts of a larger collection, such as Aristotle's feathers and scales, but they are objects with qualities. They are objects that have been up to something. Even when qualities alone are entered into analogies, either they are never unaccompanied by their objects or else they enter into the analogy as abstract objects themselves. For example, I can say that the grey of this building is like the grey of the clouds overhead. But both greys are chaperoned. Or I can say that blue is to purple as yellow is to green, but I cannot do so without assuming that each of those colors is an object and that it has been up to something with its own qualities. Thus, similarity begins with the ontological position that mid-level objects are just as real as atomic material or collections of individuals and that their being does not come from their qualities.

The Neonominalism of Sellars

Quine's proposal for an orthography of sense presupposes that sense experiences are discrete enough to be structurally isomorphic to occlusions and vocalizations which themselves are supposed to be discrete enough for symbolic representation. What Quine seems to be trying to reconcile here is a commitment to the senses as the foundation of knowledge with a concession that propositionality is the mode of existence for knowledge, all while keeping at least one toe dipped in realism. Sense experiences must be real and some sort of representable category of sense must be *real enough*, since propositional knowledge is projected onto categories. The hope is that sense experiences are both discrete and universal enough to be real categories—discreteness and universality being the ingredients of a category. The challenge is to turn private knowledge founded on private sense experiences into the building blocks of public scientific knowledge. The alphabet is such a tempting model for this project because it has proven itself a productive medium capable of operating across the discrete/universal—private/public matrix. Again, my problem with this is that there is no reason to assume that phonemes and sense experiences are self-same, discrete, and totally accessible to our knowledge.

A far subtler and more persuasive approach to the problem of realism and categories comes from Wilfred Sellars, who like Quine and Goodman identified with nominalism, but whose thinking was also tinged with Thomism. Sellars's approach was in fact to move categories away from sense experiences. This is far more consistent with an ontology which holds that real things in the world are non-propositional in nature. Since sense experiences are real, Sellars thought, they are not of categories and they do not know themselves. Thus, "The vocabulary of sense does not include abstract singular terms (formal universal)."[276] Instead, "The intellect somehow forms these words from their predicative counterparts."[277] The existence of categories, for Sellars, is tied to intellectual reflexivity, which thus excludes the realm of sense from the realm of knowing. As such, "sense is a cognitive faculty only in the sense that it makes knowledge possible and is an essential element in knowledge, and that of itself, it knows nothing."[278] Knowing as-such precedes knowing-that in Sellars's program, and knowing as-such exists in the realm of the *meta*, specifically of the metalinguistic. The trick is how we get from the linguistic to the metalinguistic. For Sellars, as we'll see, metalinguistic knowing as-such proceeds from a linguistic knowing-how, but first we have to deal with the problem of knowing as-such.

As is common in mid-twentieth century philosophical thought experiments, Sellars imagines the cognitive limitations of a sophisticated robot. The robot travels around its environment, records events in their locations and times, and even makes inferences based upon observed patterns. The repetition of a certain spatiotemporal event, such as a flash of lightning, gets recorded onto the robot's tape. Here, Sellars argues that the robot has a picture of lightning without actually knowing lightning as-such by virtue of the fact that there is a material correspondence between the lightning and the record of the lightning:

> Thus the robot would contain a picture of the occurrence of a particular flash of lightning *not* by virtue of the absolute nature of lightning existing immaterially in the robot's electronic system, but by virtue of the correspondence of the 'place' of a certain pattern on the tape in the system of patterns on the tape to the 'place' of the flash of lightning in the robot's spatiotemporal environment.[279]

It is hard not to think here that the robot has some representational knowledge of *lightning*, since there is a pattern on the tape, which should constitute a signifier (Sellars provides us with signifier '::'). Yet, Sellars insists that without an immaterial concept of *lightning* as having an absolute nature, the signifier '::' is merely a material correspondence to the material sensation of lightning. The concept belongs to an entirely different order of discourse, that of the formal universal, or the category, which itself is not part of material reality. Reason, for Sellars, is thus predicated on the division of objects and concepts.

It's relevant that Sellars uses the irrational robot as an illustration because it shows us that at least when he is talking about materiality, he is thinking of substance, and not about something that could be reduced to something more fundamental, such as mathematical structure. Otherwise, the digital computer would have the possibility of being admitted into the realm of rational beings. Here, we can think about a simple kind of Turing machine, one that, as usual, works through individual cells either unmarked (*blank*) or marked with the symbols '1' or '0'. Using just a few simple rules, the machine could, for instance, calculate whether there were an even or an odd number of cells marked with a given symbol, such as '1'. Mitchell provides us with just such a set of rules:

1. If you are in the *start* state and read a 0, then change to the *even* state, replace the 0 with a *blank* (i.e., erase the 0), and move one cell to the right.

2. If you are in the *even* state and read a 1, change to the *odd* state, replace the 1 with a *blank*, and move one cell to the right.

3. If you are in the *odd* state and read a 1, change to an *even* state, replace the 1 with a *blank*, and move one cell to the right.

4. If you are in the *odd* state and read a 0, replace that 0 with a 1 and change to the *halt* state.

5. If you are in the *even* state and read a 0, replace that 0 with a 0 (i.e., don't change it) and change to the *halt* state.[280]

Let's say the machine's head is in the *odd* state when it reads the 0, so it erases the 0, writes a 1, and goes into its *halt* state. This simple Turing machine, which is far less impressive in its capabilities than Sellars's robot is, has nonetheless created a bit of propositional knowledge. Its output symbol "1" has said something about the number of 1s in the machine's input. If we just consider the "1" at output as standing in for the 1s at input, then all we have here is a signification in the same spatiotemporal frame, just as the sensation of lightning merely gets recorded as an "::" on the tape of Sellars's robot. But the "1" at output in the Turing machine also signifies a category to which the 1s at input belong, the category of the set of odd numbers, which *in itself* possesses distinctive properties in relation to, for instance, the set of all natural numbers. The trick here is that you must accept that a) mathematical structure is more fundamental than material substance and that b) mathematical categories are both real and exist outside of linguistic mediation. The obvious objection would be that the proposition, "1s (input) are odd (output)" is not a proposition for the machine itself, but rather for the one observing the machine. Of course, the output of this machine, and even the rules of the machine themselves, could be coded as the input for another machine, which itself may or may not have the same rules as the first machine. Which also means that the procedural rules that got us from a given number of cells marked 1, 0, and unmarked to the proposition "The 1s are odd" could have been coded into a machine operating on our Turing machine. The procedures behind our procedures behind our proposition could, in theory, regress infinitely, leaving us to wonder about the exterior origins of the procedural rules.

If we think of the human mind as a propositional knowledge-making machine, then at least the Chomskyan UG program has an answer to the problem of the infinite regress of rules. There is an outside to the rules, which is the modular language organ(s), which itself has some material exteriority whose form emerged in evolutionary movement (even if the nature of that form remains unclear). But Sellars finds his way back to the material by a different route. Sellars puts the monumental burden on himself of explaining knowledge on two sides of an equation: 1) the relationship between knowledge and materiality, and 2) the relationship between knowledge and procedure. The fact that Sellars is able both to set up this problem and offer a pretty consistent solution certainly puts him in the running for one of the most important and underappreciated philosophers of the 20th century. As to the procedural side of the equation, Sellars adopts a behaviorist solution to the problem of infinite regress, which itself is at least consistent with the material side of the equation, but I'm going to work may way back from the procedural to the material.

One of the most important things to keep in mind about Sellars's epistemology is that knowledge is a normative enterprise, and it is normative precisely because it is projected onto the immaterial. This is a crucial sticking point with regards to the contemporary debate about Harmanian, Latourian, and Deleuzean metaphysics because it is where the most notable Speculative Realism expat, Ray Brassier, makes his stand against all three brands of metaphysics. The argument is that for knowledge (and here we're talking specifically about scientific knowledge) to move closer to the way things really are, it must be corrigible (opening up a space for this corrigibility being the job of philosophy). This requires that *knowing*, although of reality and about reality, cannot itself be *part* of reality. One of the things this project further requires is that knowledge and information be completely separate entities.[281] Collapsing one into another, according to Brassier, leads to a cynical, postmodern reduction of knowledge (and, ultimately, of truth) to power, as he has accused Latour of doing.[282] Such a collapse leaves philosophy, as traditionally understood, out in the cold. The way of keeping the two separate is to keep information at the level of the senses (the order of the real) just as Sellars does,[283] such that it can be constituted as matter, objects, actants, or whatever else you want. So again, sense-information is the real (matter, object, etc.) foundation of knowing, but knowing leaves that realm, passing "from looks and glimpses to referential verdicts."[284] Contrary to traditional empiricism, then, sensations do not "terminate as mental objects."[285]

The argument that sensations do not terminate as mental objects is part of Sellars's overall attack on the so-called "Myth of the Given" in traditional empiricism.[286] The idea behind the myth is that secondary properties coming off of an object get reassembled as a mental object with no more mediation than that of the senses by which they were perceived. As we've seen with Hume, the repetition of resemblant properties, either by direct perception or by the negentropic process of the memory, coalesce as abstract mental objects, allowing for a proposition, such as "Xs are Y" to be made. But Sellars argues that although this might explain the predicative relationship between Xs and Y, it does nothing to explain predicative relationships as such. There is not an easy continuum between sensing X, thinking *there is an X*, and proposing *Xs are Y*. It is not the repetition of the same process. Sellars believes instead that the distributive operation *means* says something interesting about the nature of linguistic predication. *Means*, here, is distributed across five operations:

a) Meaning as translation

b) Meaning as sense

c) Meaning as naming

d) Meaning as connotation

e) Meaning as denotation[287]

Roughly speaking, a) is meaning from word to word; b) is the expression of a concept (word *as* concept); c) is a concept that provides meaning to another concept; d) is the name of a concept that refers to its properties, and e) refers to things of a certain property, though it in itself does not name a class of things. What I believe is important here is the fact that all of these operations are interrelated—perhaps analogically extended—but that one cannot be subsumed under another. Particularly crucial is that the semantic operation of *means* not be subsumed under *denotation* alone, and that denotation not be an immediate relation between a class and a thing. Thus, there cannot be a direct line between operations *d* and *a*. Let's take one of Sellars's most well-known examples of operation *a*, translation: "*Rot* means 'red'".[288] Here, *Rot* is not the German equivalent of something denoting an abstract entity, *red*. When we give the *means* operation "*Rot* means 'red'," even if we might be picturing a red thing as we're saying it, we are of course only dealing at the level of tokens, like Gertrude Stein's rose. This is pretty uncontroversial. However, Sellars goes on to argue that in this instance *Rot* itself does not denote an abstract entity, which we might think of as redness. It is instead a *distributive singular* term. Distributive singular terms, as William de Vries nicely characterizes them, "are grammatically singular but distribute their references across an entire class."[289] Before it is referred to as a class, *red* is a prototype that is distributed across observational statements of red things. The distribution itself does not refer to anything, let alone the class *red*. Once again, Sellars is internally consistent in a most ingenious way. Remember that for Sellars a sensation cannot itself be a given fact, since a sensation in and of itself does not refer to anything. Likewise, the distribution of a linguistic token cannot itself refer to anything like a class. So to say that something is green is not merely to relate a sensation (having been given in repetition) to a given name for that sensation: "An awareness of an item *as* green is a response to the item *as* green. But it isn't an *awareness* of it *as* green simply by virtue of being a response to it *as* green."[290] In order to know the thing as being green, there must be metalinguistic knowledge (knowing-how) of "green" which takes the shape of predication. Here's the takeaway. Language is not structured the way it is because thinking is structured predicatively. It is the other way around. Which is why Sellars thinks we mistakenly take the observable world as bearing some propositional structure. Thinking, Sellars argues, follows speaking, both logically and ontologically.

The objection on the grounds of a logical correspondence might be that we can think without using inner words or sentences. To this, Sellars answers that speech can be an act without being actualized:

> Just as to be flammable is not to contain a hidden flame, nor an electron's propensity to jump to another orbit, a concealed jumping, so propensity to verbalize is not an "inner" verbalizing. It may be accompanied by verbal imagery, but does not require it, and is certainly not identical with it.[291]

Therein too lies the ontological correspondence between speaking and thinking, and it could almost be straight out of Aquinas, except that for Sellars, acting (and thinking is acting) is the absolute negative of being. Thinking is always removed but projected towards something that is being. As was made clear before, a sensation is not knowing, but a response to a sensation too is not knowing, since real awareness and response are very different things:

> An iron filing can be said to respond to a green magnet *as* a magnet. It doesn't respond to the magnet *as* green, and, indeed it would respond in the same way if the magnet were of any other color.[292]

He goes on:
> But though the filing responds to the magnet *as* magnet, we don't say, except in a metaphorical way, that the filing is *aware* of the magnet *as* magnet.[293]

Such awareness must be removed once more from both the sensation and the response to it. Thus, a statement like "This is green" is to "express observational knowledge," but it too is not knowing "as-such." Rather, it is a "*symptom*" of a *sign*" of the presence of a green object.[294] But, adds Sellars, "the perceiver must know that tokens of 'This is green' are symptoms of the presence of green objects in conditions which are standard for visual perception."[295] Knowing is knowing '*that* this is green.' What seems to be going on is a modeling from an atomic picture of a green thing to a fact "*that* this is green." In other words, knowing is knowing facts, and facts are not given to the senses, so a fact is a meta-picture.

I'll return to the relationship between knowing and "going meta," but Sellars must also explain *how* observational knowledge is expressed. Knowing *that* this is a green object "presupposes that one knows of the form *X is a reliable symptom of Y.*"[296] The "*that* this is green" is already embedded in a ruled system of language. The first thing to know about Sellars's notion of language is that rules in language emerge from patterns. Rules are meta-patterns. Here, Sellars is a behaviorist all the way through. Somehow, we go from the normal to the normative, the normative itself being a precondition for public knowledge. So how do we get there? Remember that Sellars's robot can make inferences based upon patterns, but does so only because certain rules were programmed into the robot from the outside. It's a sort of Chomskyan robot. But in Sellars's view of language acquisition, since there is no set of rules that might constitute an *a priori* metalanguage (which Sellars takes to be a contradiction), the learner "conforms" to rules rather than *obeying* them.[297] By *conforming*, I take Sellars to mean distributed imitation (which I would assert is *translation*), which, of course, would obviate any prior metalanguage. As a behaviorist, Sellars argues that conforming to rules is governed by selective rewarding for appropriate rule following.[298] There is thus, as de Vries points out, a further distinction between "*ought-to-do*" and "*ought-to-be*,"[299] the former belonging to the realm of rule-conforming. In and of themselves, these *ought-to-dos* would remain as simple imperatives, no different in kind from those which any communicating organism can express. But as it is, they pertain specifically to language, which provides the opportunity for metalanguage. There seems to be a feedback loop between language patterns and pattern-conforming behavior, out of which explicit rules emerge, which in turn produces an awareness of how linguistic utterances ought to be rather than an imperative for what a speaker ought to do. There is an *expectation* that an explicit *out-to-be* will result in a speaker doing what they ought, and thus an awareness of what effects language can have in the world (and, therefore, an understanding of language as being different from the world). The real distinction between an imperative and an *ought* concerning language itself presupposes the existence of deontic modalities in language (e.g. the subjunctive), which in turn gives us the potential for theoretical language. We can go from the idea that something in particular should or might be the case to positing that an entire framework of that particular should or might exist. And it is precisely this kind of theoretical perspectivalism that science is most actively engaged in.

Once again, thinking is both normative and outside of being for Sellars. Once a rule-conforming individual enters the metalinguistic realm of rule awareness, a rational agent emerges. The rational agent is a critical user of language because of the normative tools she has at hand. But there are a couple of major problems stemming from Sellars's (albeit nuanced) reliance on behaviorism. For one, it does very little to explain the evolutionary emergence of human grammar as such—and this is what I'll be addressing in the next chapter. Second, it seems to me that the *habit* of conforming to rules simply replaces innate grammar (or UG) as an exteriority for language. Habit, if you will, becomes the linguistic version of the unmoved mover. Thus, when the learner is conforming to patterns of rules, she is engaged in an activity of distributive imitation, but habit somehow obviates that activity, and then the learner is in the metalinguistic realm of the rational. In other words, the end of distributed imitation marks the beginning of rational thinking. There are a couple of reasons why this shouldn't be the case. For one, while I do not subscribe to Chomsky's single mutation event version of grammaticality (something I believe can be explained in terms of neural entrainment, episodic memory, and grammaticalization itself), the behaviorist would still have to address Chomsky's original objection regarding the so-called *poverty of the stimulus*. It goes like this. Children receive positive stimuli in the form of sentences spoken by adults that would be deemed appropriate or correct, but they do not receive much in the way of negative stimuli from which to judge and generalize correctness. An analogy to negative stimuli would be when a child hears adults use curse words and then repeats them. The child's parents might then say, "You shouldn't be saying 'fuck,' Noah." The child then has a set of parameters for socially appropriate language. Under the poverty of the stimulus argument in UG, children are given no such parameters for grammar, which would mean such parameters are innate.

Take a look at this example of a supposedly innate *subjacency constraint*. Notice that the formation of a WH-question[300] does not always entail moving the argument of an embedded clause (in this case, 'Sam') to the front and replacing it with the WH-:[301]

1. a) Bob believes that Jill married Sam.
   b) Who does Bob believe that Jill married__?
2. a) Bob believes the rumor that Jill married Sam.
   b) *Who does Bob believe the rumor that Jill married__?[302]

Children do not infer 2b from 1b, nor do adult speakers ever utter 2b in order to tell children not to say it (with the exception, perhaps, of linguist parents). The avoidance of such utterances in adult and child speech is explained either by the presence of an innate logical constraint or by a pragmatic consideration of what information such a question would be eliciting. As Michael Tomasello points out, "Sam" would be the potential focus of 1b, whereas "Bob" would have to be the potential focus of 2b, but since Bob (and his believing) is already information given in the question, the question itself makes no sense.[303] *Focus*, by the way, is a pragmatic rather than a formal linguistic phenomenon. If even child speakers are sensitive to such pragmatic considerations, an innate formal constraint, such as the subjacency constraint, is not needed. As per the Sellarsian program, a decision about relationships, such as topic and focus, can only occur at the rational, metalinguistic level. But how do we enter that realm without either innate formal constraints, adequate stimuli, or a prelinguistic capacity to grasp such relationships? I would argue that we do have the capacity to analogize pragmatic linguistic relationships from prelinguistic relationships. This includes distinctions between episodes in time (even without a concept of *time* as such), deictic relationships, as well as object-based analogical relationships. And the theoretical capacity to grasp such relationships amongst prelinguistic humans (apes can certainly grasp them) points to a linguistic structure in which the topic-focus relationship is more primary than the subject-predicate structure. Meaning that the way from prelinguistic communication to human language is less steep than either the generative grammarian or the verbal behaviorist would suggest.

There is also the problem in the Sellarsian program of normativity and modality. For Sellars, the acquisition of deontic modality is evidence of a fundamental transformation from the *ought-to-do* imperative to an *ought-to-be* awareness of language as-such. They are evidence of a distinction between a real order and an intentional order. Again, for Sellars, to say "This is green" is, on the one hand, a material performance sanctioned by the *ought-to-dos* of linguistic training, its phonological and syntactical rightness having been selectively reinforced into habit. However, it is also an *ought-to-be*, a token of the metalinguistic "*that* this is green," which the speaker put into a relationship with a symptom of the presence of a green object. Expressing the token "This is green," in other words, presupposes the deontic modal "should," as in "This is green" *should* be a symptom "of the presence of green objects in conditions which are standard for visual perception."[304] In other words, "Knowledge of any particular fact, e.g. that this is green, presupposes that one knows general facts of the form *X is a reliable symptom of Y*."³⁰⁵ Putting the general fact in a necessary relationship with the particular observation constitutes the knowing of a particular fact, which is an act in the order of intention (as opposed to the order of the real). Inferential acts in the order of intention are normative, so they "never become *obeyings* of *ought-to-do* rules."³⁰⁶ In other words, such acts are totally distinct from the mere conforming to linguistic rules, conforming being in the order of the real. To conform to linguistic *ought-to-do* rules is to imitate linguistic patterns, and so to infer is never to imitate patterns, even as the form of the inference statement itself conforms to such patterns. What this means is that the inference (and the reasons potentially given for the inference) can be called into question, even while the form of the statement is correct. This distinction between the normality of form and the normativity of content opens up a space for reason and corrigibility in the Sellarsian program. Thus, pursuing rational discourse, the kind with which science is ideally engaged, involves making the normative content of a statement explicit, which itself involves a normative decision on the language one is using. But I think such a distinction between the normal and the normative comes out of a mistaken universalization of modality in Western European languages, such as English. While deontic and epistemic modalities may be related by analogical extension, they do not belong to the realm of the normative in the same sense. English speakers, for instance, are not obliged to use epistemic modality when formulating a proposition. They may either say "I saw that the rabbit chewed up the carpet" or simply "The rabbit chewed up the carpet." Using epistemic modality would seem to be an act of volition, which would put it in the realm of the normative. But of course in other languages, epistemic modality such as that in the inferential mood (e.g. Turkish) and in evidentials (e.g. Eastern Pomo) are obligatory. Thus, the line between conforming to rules (imitating/translating patterns) and making decisions with the awareness of rules as-such (the normative) is considerably more blurry. But we need not go to languages with the inferential mood or evidentials in order to see the normality of epistemic modality. It is also built into various genres through which English speakers communicate in different contexts. Conforming to the rules of many academic writing genres, for instance, involves various forms of hedging, such as "It seems to me," "I would argue that," etc. Such utterances, of course, indicate a reflexive awareness of the rules of the genre as-such, which for Sellars would demonstrate that they are being deployed from the metalanguage (or meta-genre), but that kind of meta-level awareness is not simply achieved once habit turns conforming to rules into obeying rules as-such. Meta-level awareness is achieved over and over again by the imitation/translation of patterns. Thus, there is no reason to make a fundamental distinction between the real-normal and the epistemic-normative. Nonetheless, I hold with Sellars that cognition does not begin from a prelinguistic access to categories that correlate to reality as it is. Rather, categories emerge out of analogical relationships between objects perceived (be they visual, auditory, metaphorical, etc.), which are themselves aesthetic phenomena.

It goes back to Sellars's theory of distributive singulars, which is brilliant and absolutely correct. Let's return to "*Rot* means red'", but this time let's switch from German to a language with a different mode of nominalization, like Kalderash Romani: *Lolo* (in K) means "red" (in E). When I say "*lolo*" in Kalderash, I am already using a particular (thematic) instantiation of *red*, that of the masculine adjective form. The masculine, as is so often the case, is taken as the universal unmarked form, and a Kalderash speaker would not use the root *lol-* in a sentence. There is either the unmarked *lolo* (to talk about its function in translation), the marked masculine *lolo* (as in *o lolo shon*: the red moon), the marked feminine (as in *i loli phabai*: the red apple), or the plural (as in *e lole phabaya*: the red apples). But the nominalized *red* must be constructed analytically: *lolimos* (*lol-* + *-imos*: abstract nominalizer), which is *also* the equivalent of the concept *redness*. This more clearly demonstrates Sellars's argument that the distributive singular precedes the name of the formal universal (nominalization and/or name of the concept), since here the formal universal is either hidden grammatically (*lol-*) or it is constructed analytically (*lolimos*). Before the category *red* exists, there are distributed singular instances of red things. There is a slide of red things before *red* can come around and describe those things and before *red* can describe itself. This is true, but I think it's a bad example. If we're not careful, we might be assuming that all of the resemblant red things are resemblant because they share one self-same quality (red) which exists independently of the objects themselves and to which we have immediate sensual access. As such, we would find ourselves back at the dreaded myth of the given. Circumventing the myth of the given, we can say that the self-same category or domain *red* was analyzed from what we found similar about red things, not from a self-same quality that we encountered with each and every object. The similarity we found in the qualities of those objects was ineffable and aesthetical before it was effable and analyzable, and so we needed no language to characterize the particular relationship of similarity (to say what that relationship of similarity was predicated upon) in order to grasp relationship. Relationships of similarity do not need to be predicated of a given category before they form the basis of a new category.

Again, *red* is a difficult example because we have a hard time distinguishing between the distributive singular and the formal universal when the latter is already in regular usage. So let's think about ineffable things, like faces. Say someone asks you the peculiar question, "What is my face?" You'd probably have a difficult time giving a satisfactory answer. You could talk about shape, function, and material, but those somehow wouldn't get at it. The ineffability of the face is precisely why coming across different people with a similar type of face can be such a weird and uncanny experience. Occasionally there are given predicates for classifying facial types, such as ethnic stereotypes or comparisons to one familiar face. But that involves analysis form one or more categories which we have taken to be self-same and given (e.g. the epicanthic folds or the freckles of an Irish face). But then there are those faces that you recognize to be of a certain type before you can ever analyze them as being Chris O'Dowd-faces or Irish faces or whatever. It is at this time, before you subject the relationship of similarity you've grasped to an existing self-same category, that the opportunity for the poiesis of a new category emerges. It is this sort of aesthetic experience which I would assert is the beginning of knowledge. The emergence of an idea of a new category begins to look like the emergence of any other new object. Naming the category would then involve a distributive imitation or translation of another name such that, for instance, "Chris O'Dowd" becomes "*a* Chis O'Dowd." The name of the new category is an imitation, a translation, and, above all, a *distortion* of the existing name.

Familiarity, Fame, and Going Meta

Timothy Morton describes the birth of a new object as *anamorphosis* or distortion.[307] The objects in contact become distorted and the new object takes on the distorted form. When multiple idea-objects possessing similar qualities come into contact, they create a distortion, an object with a form similar to the contacted objects, but one that finds itself looking out into a new and asymmetrical context in relation to the objects around it. I'm describing the metaphysics of such an event, but it can also be described in psychological terms as what Hofstadter and Sander call "conceptual slippage."[308] Hofstadter and Sander use the abstraction "shadow" as an example of this process.[309] The most basic kind of shadow we're likely to think about is a light shadow cast by our own bodies. But we may also observe the phenomenon of rain falling on the land on one side of a mountain and not on the other side. The impression of this phenomenon has a similar form to the impression of the first shadow, but their contexts, the material with which we perceive these different shadows interacting, are asymmetrical to one another. These two ideas of *shadow* in contact may create a third, distorted image of what *shadow* is and the contexts with which it can interact. The third shadow may interact with other impressions, such as an x-ray image of a shadow in a lung. Or, the other shadow metaphors may face each other as metaphors, which may produce a distortion of those metaphors. The third metaphor that arises as a distortion might be *shadow* as a class. Though again, what has emerged is a classy metaphor and not a class itself.

We can see a comparable process in the more clearly visible medium of internet memes and metamemes. For being relatively young, I'm pretty internet-old, a little slow to take notice of the latest trends and innovations. The first time I came across the phenomenon of memes was in 2010, when I was looking on YouTube for videos of Oasis concerts.[310] During my search, I came across the Hitler *Downfall* meme. The meme features a scene taken from the 2004 German film *Downfall*, about the final days of the Nazi regime. In that scene, Hitler is being told by his staff that the war is all but lost, to which Hitler reacts with a violent, almost childish outburst. The dialogue is in German and the meme's creators write in their own English subtitles that feature Hitler blowing up about a variety of pop culture events.

In the one I stumbled upon, Hitler was losing it over Oasis's key members, the brothers Gallagher, finally calling it quits. Others around that time included Hitler cracking up over Alaska Governor Sarah Palin's resignation and Hitler reacting to Kanye West crashing Taylor Swift's acceptance speech at the 2009 MTV Video Music Awards (in which Adolf Hitler calls Kanye West a "douchebag"). The meme was already a couple of years old by the time I discovered it, and it had long since gone *meta*, with memes such as Hitler finding out that he's become a meme and Hitler being told that Constantin Films was asking YouTube to remove the Hitler memes. The memes themselves are repetitions of the similar which are projected into asymmetrical contexts (e.g. Oasis Hitler vs. Sarah Palin Hitler). And so, as a *hyperobject*, the Hitler meme is self-similar in nature. But what is the relationship of the meme to its metameme?

In Postmodernity, going *meta* has become a substitute for wisdom. Or rather it has become the go-to means of performing wisdom against the homogeneity of mass culture. Timothy Morton describes this ethos best with his phrase: "Anything you can do I can do *meta*."[311] It's an ethos born of a near universal insecurity that there is nothing new under the sun. Television writers and advertisers are so good at what they do, so quick to pick up on a new idiom and spill its cultural capital all over the place that by the time you integrate it into your own lexicon, your grandmother's best friend Ruth has already used it in two Facebook posts, one about immigrants bringing the Ebola virus across the border and the other describing the lunch buffet on her latest Caribbean cruise. (They're out of crab legs by 11:15!)[312] So elusive is novelty that when we encounter the new, we feel as though we are being taken in, so much so that it becomes something to be defended against. We go meta to discover the name of the demon who is deceiving us before exorcising it. Indeed, the point of naming a demon in an exorcism is to identify it as a separate entity from the body it is possessing. The naming is not a means of gaining control over the demon (there's no hope of that); it's merely a way to drive a wedge between possessor and possessed. This is what we do when we go meta. We're powerless to either make or recognize anything new, so we simply extricate ourselves from (what we see as) the illusion altogether.

The logic is that the meta-thing is equivocal to the thing. It is knowledge of its object of knowledge. At this point, the whole thing begins to look like a dialectic. And yet, at least in the case of the Hitler meme, is would seem like the form and material of the metameme are hardly different from those of the meme. They are both clips from a particular scene in *Downfall*. They both contain English subtitles that diverge from the film's original German dialogue. And they are both produced in the medium of YouTube. But perhaps the distinction is phenomenological. The Hitler memes look to the Oasis breakup, the Kanye West incident, etc., whereas the Hitler metameme looks to the Hitler meme itself. But here again, the relationship between the Hitler meme and the Hitler metameme is one of similarity. In order to be a meme that could be deployed in different contexts—as in the Oasis breakup and the Kanye West incident—the Hitler meme needed to be self-similar. Which is to say that its constituent memes needed to be famous for another in order to be in similar ways and project themselves onto asymmetrical contexts. The Hitler metameme made itself similar to the famous Hitler memes, and because the Hitler memes were famous, they could also serve as a context, just like Oasis and Kanye West. Thus, the Hitler metameme is neither the same as nor different from the Hitler meme but analogous to it.

We should talk about fame. What I hoped to have shown in the discussion of the Hitler meme and its metameme is that the move from thing to meta-thing does not begin from an equivocal ontology, and therefore that the meta-thing has not emerged from a dialectical recognition. But also, unlike in the case of Humean abstraction, the relationship between the thing and the meta-thing does not begin as metonymy either. Relationships of *meta* begin with fame. And we can think of fame in two ways. First, we can think of it in terms of familiarity (though, etymologically, *fame* and *familiarity* are unrelated). Familiarity can be thought of as multiple things sharing one or more qualities. So, in a familial relationship of familiarity, you will share one or two of the same parents. Or, you might be familiar to a coworker because you share the same office building. Maybe one particular coworker is more familiar to you because the two of you share the same manager and you've worked together on some of the same projects. We can analyze familiarity in terms of the number and frequency of shared individual qualities. The more the same qualities repeat between things, the more familiarity is amplified.

Fame, as you might expect, is quite a different thing from familiarity. David Bowie and I don't share very much, but he is famous to me. In fact, if I somehow got to know Bowie, and he became more familiar to me, he'd probably be a little less famous to me. Also, if I did meet David Bowie, and I acted as if we were familiar, he'd probably be a little turned off. As it is I would most likely just stand frozen, brandishing a pallid grin, trying desperately to keep my knees from buckling. So, he'd still just be famous to me.

In her poem "Famous," Naomi Shihab Nye calls attention to the subtle differences between fame and familiarity by identifying relationships of fame that we might otherwise think of as being familiar:

The river is famous to the fish.

The loud voice is famous to the silence,
which knew it would inherit the earth
before anybody said so.

The cat sleeping on the fence is famous to the birds
watching him from the birdhouse.

The tear is famous, briefly to the cheek.

The idea you carry close to your bosom
is famous to your bosom.
[...][313]

These are all relationships of proximity, which makes characterizing them as "famous" instead of 'familiar' seem wonderfully strange. Also, none of these things is a person, which turns the familiar concept of fame into something altogether uncanny.

And of course the overlapping in mass culture of fame and familiarity is one of the most common tropes of postmodern art. Take, for instance, Andy Warhol's *Campbell's Soup Cans* or the most famous barn in America in Don DeLillo's *White Noise*.[314] In the novel, people come from all over the country in order to get their pictures taken in front of the barn. The barn is not famous because it is the site of some great or terrible event but because it is the most photographed barn in America. The barn, like a reality television star, is famous for being famous. And of course, the more people get their pictures taken in front of it, the more famous it grows. One of the things we're grappling with here is the question of authenticity. Warhol's soup cans seemingly come into existence as mechanical reproductions, representations without an original presentation. Warhol's representations are therefore just as much presentations as the represented cans are. Likewise, DeLillo's barn has lost its identity as a functional object and is now only identifiable as a pure repetition. But of course the anxiety about authenticity only comes about when it's assumed that there is an ontological gulf between representations and the things represented. If you begin with this equivocal scheme, and you find that the representation has somehow managed to traverse that ontological gulf, then you might find your reality in crisis. One response to that crisis, the Deleuzean response, is to assert a univocal ontology in which the original barn was never actually itself—it was differentiation all the way down—and representations of the barn are just repetitions of difference, ontologically indistinct from the internally differentiated barn.

The other response is to argue that the simulacrum or meta-barn is a separate object from the actual barn, an object that does not depend upon the existence of the actual barn in order to interact with other objects. But then the question arises of whether or not the being of the meta-barn is predicated upon pure repetition alone. If the meta-barn is just a pure repetition of an original, familiar image of the barn—if it is self-same—then what accounts for its unique interactions with others (e.g. tourists)? What accounts for its fame? Again, relations of familiarity involve the accretion and repetition of the same qualities between things. Relationships of fame, on the other hand, come from one thing imitating another. After all, I don't go karaoking with David Bowie; I karaoke Bowie. And when I do karaoke Bowie, I do it poorly and with much exaggeration. The goal is not to copy Bowie perfectly;[315] the goal is to imitate the Bowie beneath Bowie: the *sublime* Bowie. That's the famous Bowie. Any movement from thing to meta-thing, from idea of an individual to idea of a class, and from analogue to analogue involves an element of the sublime.

Here, Longinus is not only instructive but foundational. In his *On the Sublime*, Longinus draws a distinction between *grandeur* and *amplification* in works of oration and art. For effect, a speaker may "wheel up one impressive unit after another to give a series of increasing importance."[316] Such is amplification. Amplification, Longinus claims, deals in extension whereas grandeur—a necessary ingredient of the sublime—deals in elevation. In argument, amplification means to either repeat certain phrases or manners for effect or to elaborate on all of the details of a case so as to present a sense of totality. But sublimity, which is carried forth by grandeur, "exists often in a single thought."[317] We can say that amplification reiterates and grandeur reverberates. Thus, the end of amplification is familiarity—familiarity with the talking point that gets repeated in a news cycle, familiarity with a chain store layout, etc. The end of grandeur is fame. A thing of grandeur brings along with it a mood that sticks to us and causes fascination well after it has come into contact with us. We may repeat familiar talking points in an argument but, Longinus argues, we imitate the sublime and strive to similarly reproduce it in other contexts.[318] Fame is when we sense something imitable but ineffable (i.e. the sublime) beneath what is familiar. Thus, a thing of fame can never be represented, only imitated.

If there is something good about this age of reality television stardom, it is that it lays bare the unrepresentability of famous things. In the past, we might have gotten away with providing predicates for the fame of famous people: Why is Princess Dianna famous? She is beautiful and royal and glamorous. Why is Albert Einstein famous? He is the creator of relativity theory. But when we ask why such-and-such reality star is famous, we may either say that she is famous for being trashy or that she is famous for being famous. The first predicate gets us nowhere because *trashy* is a term of banality. And even when we add a superlative to *trashy*, the statement becomes so confounding that it can only be said in irony. Thus, the statement "She is famous for being the most trashy" is an ironical comment on fame rather than the famous reality star. The predicate, "is famous for being famous," gets us a little closer to representation, but it's almost beyond analysis. It would be like trying to make the proposition "All bachelors are bachelors" instead of the proposition "All bachelors are unmarried." We could do the Heideggerian thing and say that bachelors *bachelor* and the famous *fame*, but those aren't really representations either. The fame of the reality star is the imitation of the reality star. It's dressing up like the reality star for Halloween. It's using the reality star's catch phrase. It's an aspirant reality star aping the behavior of the famous reality star. The closest we ever come to a representation of fame is distributed imitation.

Metaphors and meta-things too are distributed imitations. When Michael Corleone says "You broke my heart, Fredo," or when Mickey Goldmill says "You're all heart, Rock," the metaphor *heart* represents nothing. It certainly does not represent the four-valved organ in the chest, but it also doesn't represent any of the other obvious candidates, such as the self or the soul or whatever. Had Mickey said instead, "You're all *soul*, Rock," we might have been led to believe that the *Rocky* franchise was about dancing. And it should be clear to anyone who's ever seen *Rocky III* that Rocky is an exceptionally poor dancer. The metaphor *heart* imitates all that cannot be represented about the idea of the soul. The idea of the soul is, therefore, famous to the metaphor *heart*. It is clear then that the metaphor *heart* leads a separate life from the idea *soul*. *Heart* is up to something on its own, but it is similar to the idea *soul*. And because it is up to something independently from the being of the idea *soul*, we cannot say that *heart* merely exists in reference to all that encompasses the idea of the soul.

What's true about metaphors and meta-things is true for other interobjective relationships. To borrow Shihab Nye's language for one of Harman's favorite images, the cotton ball is famous to the fire. The fire, as Harman says, burns the cotton ball, but it does not get at all that the cotton ball is. Instead, the fire is affected by the cotton ball *as* the fire. Indeed, as it's burning the cotton ball, the fire even takes on a shape similar to that of the cotton ball. The fire, in its way, is not representing the cotton ball but imitating it. Unless your ontology is strictly process-based, you will be obliged to accept that the fire has endured beyond its relation with the cotton ball. And having been in contact with the cotton ball, and having been affected by it, the fire has taken on properties similar to the form of the cotton ball. Here, as in the relationships of similarity between the metaphor *heart* and the idea *soul*, and between the Hitler meme and the Hitler metameme, we are nowhere dealing with frozen, representational abstractions. Each of those objects has the capacity to affect other objects *as* objects. So, with regards to the neonominalist argument, you cannot throw both abstractions and similarity out of your reality as part of a package deal.

The Deleuzean Rejection

The other major refutation of similarity in recent philosophical movements comes from Deleuzeanism. Deleuze's problem with similarity is not unlike that of neonominalists. The problem, once again, is that similarity supposedly creates abstract identities that exist outside of and prior to the emergence of the thing:

> Analogy is the essence of judgment, but the analogy within judgment is the analogy of the identity of concepts. That is why we cannot expect that generic or categorical difference, any more than specific difference, will deliver us a proper concept of difference.[319]

The main distinction between the neonominalists' objection and that of Deleuze is that for the latter there is no individual thing for an abstract identity to pre-empt in the first place. My own contention is that identity is real but that it does not exist prior to the object. Nevertheless, if an object is complete for another object, then it does indeed have something like an identity. In which case, identity is an aesthetical phenomenon rather than an analytical one. As for identities that exist outside of and prior to the things they identify, such as classes, I agree that there is no such thing except for the *classy* ideas themselves, which are also objects.

The subtlety of Deleuze and Guattari's critique of similarity and analogy is commendable. They acknowledge the classical distinction between analogies of proportion and analogies of proportionality, whereas someone like Goodman appears only to equate similarity with analogy of proportion. Deleuze and Guattari point out that both kinds of similarity helped to structure a cosmology that moved through mimesis,

> either in the form of a chain of beings perpetually imitating one another, progressively and regressively, and tending toward the divine higher term they all imitate by graduated resemblance, or as the model for and principle behind the series; or in the form of a mirror Imitation with nothing left to

imitate because it itself is the model everything else imitates, this time ordered by difference.³²⁰

In both of the instances Deleuze and Guattari describe, the ordering term or difference prohibits the production of the new. They argue that the first kind of mimesis—the ordering of relations by a divine term, such as God or Man—has melted away from science. So in the social sciences, there is no longer an effort to trace symbolic archetypes or totems to a single analogy between, for instance, man and animal. Instead (and Deleuze and Guattari are clearly referring to structuralism), "the identification terms" gets replaced with "an equality of relations."³²¹ In other words, analogies of proportion are no longer as epistemically productive as analogies of proportionality:

> If we note, for example, that the warrior has a certain astonishing relation to the young woman, we refrain from establishing an imaginary series tying the two together; instead, we look for a term effecting equivalence of relations [...] The result is a homology between the virgin who refuses marriage and the warrior who disguises himself as a woman.³²²

This example, which Deleuze and Guattari pulled from Jean-Pierre Vernant's history of war in Ancient Greece, seems far removed from any ordering principles in modern science, and certainly the thrust of their attack is directed towards the stucturalist understanding of social evolution in which greater complexity descends from simple relations. But this is also an attack on the modeling model of science, which includes generative linguistics, whose "object is an unconscious that is itself representative, crystallized into codified complexes laid out along a genetic axis and distributed within syntagmatic structure."³²³ The argument, in other words, is that generative linguistics is a reproduction of the Cartesian theatre in which whole linguistic utterances are projected upon an existing stage in the mind, complete with blocking instructions. Language—and by extension knowledge—becomes an acting out of reality, rather than a production of reality. And thus knowledge always has to work its way backwards to reality, backwards to the individual linguistic utterance, backwards to the actual object of scientific inquiry.

The idea then is that similarity is always a backwards looking enterprise. It is the idea that relationships of similarity are constituted by a prior relationship of representation. Similarity, for Deleuze and Guattari, preserves an equivocal ontology. And yet we have already seen how Thomas Aquinas envisioned an ontology of similarity as a way of circumventing the problems posed by equivocity, even if it was a rearguard action against the specter of univocity (which Duns Scotus and then Deleuze would come to embrace). But what Aquinas suggests is that relationships of similarity need not be reduced to a structure of mutual dependence between a term and its mode of representation. Relationships of similarity, as Deleuze and Guattari point out, do employ mimesis as a vehicle of movement, but there are different ways of looking at mimesis. In the Platonic mode of mimesis—the mode to which Deleuze and Guattari are no doubt referring—the many are an imitation of the One, and the creative imitation of an object is at least twice removed from the One. Thus, the artist is further away from the truth than the philosopher is. The fact that what the philosopher produces is a closer imitation of the truth shows that all production of the new can be traced back to a limited number of originary forms. But there was also a competing mode of imitation that predated and, in a few instances, surpassed Plato: the sophistic mode.

The sophistic mode of imitation was not a reproduction of, for instance, original principles in persuasive speech. Sophistic teachers of rhetoric had students memorize the teachers' own compositions, great poetical works, as well as famous speeches, such as Pericles's funeral oration (probably penned by his sophist lover, Aspasia).[324] The idea was that first of all, the student might select lines and images to use at the opportune moment in their own orations. We might say that what the students were doing was distributive copying. But the students were also to use existing works in a way we might think of as imitation rather than copying. That is to say that instead of producing what Quintilian would later refer to as "the shadow of substance"[325] (or counterfeits), students of the sophists would imitate the essence of other works as a way of producing new oration entirely. This is why the development of mnemonic tools was so important to the sophists. Memory was obviously a key technology in the performance of oration, but just as Giambattista Vico would point out a couple of millennia later, memory and imagination are inseparable,[326] and therefore so are mimesis and production. And while Plato famously defended memory against writing with one hand, he subverted memory as a mode of poetic production with the other.

The sophistic mode of mimesis was an object-to-object imitation, rather than an idea-to-object imitation (à la Plato). The notion of mimesis as idea-to-object imitation no doubt begins with Pythagoras, but also with Isocrates (a sort of self-loathing sophist), who begins to establish first principles of rhetorical practice. Though Isocrates continued to advocate for memorization and imitation, he did so as part of the distributive copying function. Dionysius of Halicarnassus would resurrect object-to-object imitation for literary composition in the first century BCE, and Longinus recovered the idea of imitating essence for rhetorical invention of the new in the second century A.D. While Longinus, with his notion of the sublime, may have been the only one of these thinkers with something metaphysical in mind, it is clear that the notion of mimesis to which Deleuze and Guattari are referring was relatively late on the scene, and that imitation and similarity have not always precluded difference and novelty.

Perhaps Deleuze would have looked a little more kindly on the sophistic mode of mimesis, but of course, similarity is fundamentally at odds with his univocalism. From this point of view, analogy "retains in the particular only that which conforms to the general (matter and form), and seeks the principle of individuation in this or that elements of the fully constituted individuals."[327] Again, when Deleuze speaks of the "general" with regards to matter and form, he is assuming that matter and form exist within pre-constituted limits, such as a most basic subatomic particle and the limits that particle can impose on forms, or perhaps a firm division between basic elements and forces and the limits such a division imposes upon form. However, as I argued with regards to the identities of objects in complex systems, matter and form are relative to the object of which they are a part. It is therefore the individual object that imposes limits upon matter and form, rather than the other way around.

Deleuze goes on to describe the most fundamental distinction between analogical being and univocal being:

> By contrast, when we say that univocal being is related immediately and essentially to individuating factors, we certainly do not mean by the latter individuals constituted in experience, but that which acts in them as a transcendental principle: as a plastic, anarchic and nomadic principle, contemporaneous with the process of individuation, no less capable of dissolving and destroying individuals than of constituting them temporarily; intrinsic modalities of being, passing from one 'individual' to another, circulating and communicating underneath matters and forms.[328]

It's early days for Deleuze, and he's not yet talking about desire as that which is "circulating and communicating underneath matters and forms," though he is referring to intensities which neither emanate from individuals nor are constituted within the experiences of individuals. It's clear that in order to avoid pre-constituted limits on being, the kind of which he associates with Platonism and *State* philosophy, he must sneak under matter and form rather than go above them, since above them he sees only the general and the same. And so he is incapable of seeing the creativity in object-to-object similarity.

The Wasp that Imitates the Orchid

The beauty of Deleuze's partnership with Felix Guattari, as many have pointed out over the years, is that the arrangements of their arguments so closely resemble the theses of their arguments. In *Thousand Plateaus* in particular, the reader finds something called an "Introduction." An introduction, as traditionally understood, is a scaled representative model of a book. And within the introduction, we expect to find a thesis, which is a scaled, representative model of the introduction. Yet when the reader looks at the "Introduction" to *Thousand Plateaus*, she is reminded of the opening lines to Coleridge's "Limbo."[329] It's not an intro; yet name it so. Instead of a book that can be referred back to its scaled representation (an introduction), and instead of an introduction that can be referred back to its scaled representation (a thesis), the book simply moves by heterogeneous images sliding past one another, leaving engraved plates rather than ordered *topoi* in

their wake. Arguing with it is a great exercise in polemical gymnastics. You
don't grapple with a thesis and try to undermine its support. You instead
find an image with enough intensity that it can be felt throughout the work.
Then you play with it.

The Wasp and the Orchid is one of those images. The lip of the orchid
flower on which its pollen is exposed is shaped like the thorax of a female
wasp. The male wasp grabs the orchid's labellum and attempts to fly away
with it so as to mate in flight. And in doing so, the wasp distributes the
pollen from false mate to false mate. For Deleuze and Guattari, this is
a powerful illustration of deterritorialization and reterritorialization, the
production of difference underpinning the production of life:

> The orchid deterritorializes by forming an image, a tracing
> of the wasp; but the wasp reterritorializes on that image. This
> wasp is nevertheless deterritorialized, becoming a piece in the
> orchid's reproductive apparatus. But it reterritorializes the
> orchid by transporting its pollen.[330]

They speak of images here, but caution that the orchid isn't really
"reproducing [the wasp's] image in a signifying fashion."[331] And this is
true enough. There is no sense in which the orchid is somehow creating an
exterior image of the wasp from some general blueprint of a wasp. Again,
the mimesis that Deleuze and Guattari are arguing against here is Platonic
mimesis, but while attempting to abrogate it they are also affirming it as
the true mode of mimesis. But I argue that what we normally think of
as mimicry or parody is really just context-free conformation, and if we
think about imitation as an object-to-object phenomenon, we see that the
orchid's labellum is similar to the female wasp's thorax not because the
orchid is projecting an image of the wasp's thorax but because the male
wasp is conforming itself to the orchid's labellum. The male wasp is being
affected by the orchid's labellum as the male wasp. It is the wasp imitating
the orchid, not the other way around. The first part of any imitation is when
an object encounters another object whose own form is asymmetrical to
the encountering object's form. The encountering object may then conform
its form to the other object's form as it intercourses with the object. This
happens whether the object is an orchid's labellum or an actual female wasp.

The orchid, in turn, has evolved to imitate the male wasp's imitation; it has been affected by contact with the wasp *as* the orchid. In practical terms, this means that the orchids whose labella were imitated by male wasps reproduced more successfully than the orchids whose labella were not imitated. As such there is no need for an exterior, signifying image of a wasp for the orchid to copy, and there is no need for a "becoming-wasp" or a "becoming-orchid."[332] And yet, the orchid's labellum and the wasp's thorax are similar.

Instead of imitation, Deleuze and Guttari argue that what is going on between the wasp and orchid is "a capture of code, surplus value of code, an increase in valence, a veritable becoming…"[333] As I argued in a previous chapter vis-à-vis Harman's position on object-to-object interaction, objects themselves possess greater valence than any number of their interactions. And so the wasp is able to be affected by the orchid, to the point of taking on a similar form, without fleeing from its own waspness. In the Platonic mode of mimesis, which Deleuze and Guattari affirm by abrogation, the surplus of being is in the signifying image of the wasp that the orchid is reproducing. For Deleuze and Guattari, the surplus is in the creative destruction of deterritorialization, the "surplus of code" that emerges in reterritorialization. As they explain later on, there is a literal surplus of information in the process of genetic coding, wherein "a single segment may be copied twice, the second copy free for variation."[334] They might be referring to replication slippage, which, if it results in nucleotide expansion, may have truly deleterious consequences for the organism (Huntington's disease in humans, to name one). Gene duplication is also a mechanism in speciation, although it might not be the most powerful mechanism. It is not as though Deleuze and Guattari got it wrong. They were scarily astute readers of scientific literature across the disciplines. The problem is that, at least in this case, they pledged their metaphysics to a science that was in its infancy when they were writing. Indeed, they relied most heavily on Francois Jacob's still wonderful book, *The Logic of Life*, which encapsulated Jacob's work from a time when the science was in its embryonic stage. Genetics is still no more than a toddler, but there are a couple of things learned from, for instance, the sequencing of the human genome at the turn of the millennium that pose problems for Deleuze and Guattari's reading of gene expression.

The important part of Deleuze and Guattari's reading of gene expression is the eclipse of matter and form as a primary ontological relationship. The supposed transcendence of form over matter gives way to the immanence of content and expression, which corresponds to the broader notions of deterritorialization and reterritorialization. When they speak of codes that move between organisms and viruses, between orchids and wasps, and between states and institutions, Deleuze and Guattari are preserving the reproductive power of codes while jettisoning the representational aspects of codes (again, in their unduly narrow conception of similarity, pure representation and similarity are bound up together). Gene expression seems like a great place to start because the nucleic sequence is both organizer and material, insofar as nucleotides form amino acids, which form proteins, which form enzymes, which in turn initiate biochemical reactions in cells, which direct the energy for reproduction. The nucleobases that constitute nucleotides are four in number: cytosine, guanine, thymine, and adenine. The different configurations of these nucleobases that manifest themselves as coded sequences of nucleotides are organized by simple affinities (one could read *desire*), namely those between cytosine and guanine and between thymine and adenine, which are obviously further coded by the electro-chemical affinities between constituent elements of those molecules. Code, therefore, is not equivocal representation, but univocal desire all the way down.

The difference, for Deleuze and Guattari, is not between stuff and pure information (or stated differently, ideas) but between content and expression, which are really two modes of the same stuff. The two modes, while flatly the same stuff, act on different strata, the multiplicity of strata replacing the dimensions of matter and form.[335] So in order for this model of multiple strata running through flat stuff to work, the stuff has to be "linear" and "unidimensional."[336] Thus, Deleuze and Guattari proclaim, "The essential thing is *the linearity of the nucleic sequence*."[337] The problem is that they conflate the linearity of the nucleic sequence with the linearity of protein production from genes (which again is understandable, given the state of the science):

The real distinction between content and expression, therefore, is not simply formal. It is strictly speaking real, and passes into the molecular, without regard to order of magnitude. It is between two classes of molecules, nucleic acids of expression and proteins of content, nucleic elements or nucleotides and protein elements or amino acids.[338]

So, triplets of amino acids (or codon units) combine as polypeptides that build proteins, the polypeptides folding in different ways to constitute the form of the protein.[339] This seems like a flat, regular, and linear path, except that it is now known that there are about four times as many types of proteins as there are genes (at least in the human body). It turns out that some genes code for multiple types of proteins and some genes don't code for any. Separate but related to this is the astounding lack of numerosity and diversity of genes in living organisms, despite the obvious morphological complexity and diversity. Given the asymmetries that exist between genes and proteins and between genetic diversity and morphological diversity, it becomes harder to posit something like gene duplication as the prime mechanism of speciation, or the "surplus value of code," as Deleuze and Guattari have it.[340] The large sequences of DNA that are not involved in the coding of proteins are surplus, but they are not superfluous. These DNA strings may become attached to certain proteins, which, in turn, inhibit or enable RNA molecules in binding to the DNA gene sequence further down the line, thereby either facilitating or preventing transcription and reproduction.[341] The morphology of a particular part of a body is thus largely determined not by the presence or absence of a particular functional gene, but by the form of the expression of a functional gene, which is affected by the patterning of those non-coding regulatory genes. So morphology, or the diversity of forms, is an effect of a complex system of regulatory gene patterns, which itself is formally diverse.

To be sure, the science of evolutionary developmental biology, which is concerned with regulatory genes and morphology, is far from entering its own age of majority. And so by drawing upon it for a metaphysical argument, I am committing the same sin that Deleuze and Guattari committed. It can't be helped. Still, the point is that differences between content and expression do not simply exist between different strata of the same stuff. Diversity of forms matters on each stratum, whether it be at the level of nucleotides or at the level of proteins. Form and matter, as I contend, are relative to the object, so that different objects possess different matters and forms, and the relationship between matter and form does not disappear at sufficiently large or small scales. And while deterritorialization-reterritorialization is a truly excellent way of conceiving of novelty, I would argue that deterritorialization happens at the level of form and matter, in which the form of one object may become the matter (or the real qualities) of another object that has form unto its own. Thus, a new object emerges out of the contact between wasp and orchid for which the forms of wasp and orchid are matter. The contact out of which the new object emerges is, in turn, initiated by the wasp imitating the form of the orchid's labellum (again, not the other way around), thereby making the form of the new object self-similar. In such instances, object-to-object similarity initiates novelty. As I will argue in the next chapter, object-to-object similarity initiates novelty in knowledge and language according to the same rules of object-oriented metaphysics.

Chapter 5
Grammar and Emergence

> What particular similarity does our metaphor affirm? More generally, what resemblance must the objects a term metaphorically applies to bear to the objects it literally applies to?
>
> I do not think we can answer this question much better than we can answer the question what resemblance the objects a term literally applies to must bear on each other. In both cases, a reversal in order of explanation might be appropriate: the fact that a term applies, literally or metaphorically, to certain objects may itself constitute rather than arise from a particular similarity among those objects. Metaphorical use may serve to explain the similarity better than—or at least as well as—the similarity explains the metaphor.[342]
>
> Nelson Goodman,
> "The Fourth Stricture on Similarity"

It seems to me that the question of whether similarities constitute metaphors or whether metaphors constitute similarities is a bankrupt one. Such a question takes for granted the notion that language is intrinsically referential, which it is not. The assumption is that a metaphor either references a real similarity between objects in the world or that a metaphor references another metaphor which references a unique object in the world, thus replacing similarity with supervenience. But language is grammatical, not referential. There can be no epistemically productive relationship between metaphors without syntax, which means that a relationship of reference is just the syntax you don't see. We're used to thinking of metaphors as being particular kinds of objects and grammars as being systems of rules which regulate the interactions of metaphors. As I will argue in this chapter, however, grammars are every bit as much objects as metaphors are and that they are both products and producers of analogy, just like metaphors.

Elsewhere, when Goodman talks about images and the things those images reference and represent, he talks about goblins. The idea is that we can say that such-and-such is similar to a goblin, or that we may even call someone or something a "goblin" based upon perceived similarities between the person/thing and a goblin. But since goblins don't really exist, all we have for comparison is a representation of a goblin. The argument is that the metaphor *goblin* comes before anything else that we might think of as being *like* a goblin. Again, what this suggests is that metaphors have emerged by means of reference alone. By this logic *goblin* might have emerged when someone pointed to a scary shadow or pointed out something that went bump in the night. Reference, therefore, would precede analogy in concept formation. And indeed, the dominant position in cognitive linguistics is that chains of increasingly abstract metaphors branch out from references to familiar items, such as body parts. To be sure, as Morris Swadesh pointed out in the 1950s, terms for body parts are among the most durable words as languages undergo change over generations. For instance, virtually none of the common English words for body parts used today come out of the post-Norman lexicon. And even in a much more historically textured language like Kalderash Romani, most terms for body parts are still Indic in origin. Nonetheless, reference does not a language make. Moving from reference to metaphor requires syntax. What is needed for metaphors is a context-free relationship between references, the kind that we see in human syntax. Without syntax, Mickey could have not come near telling Rocky that he was "all heart."

Pragmatic Relations and the Origins of Human Language

Reference and syntax have a tangled relationship in the pre-linguistic world. It's clear that non-human animals recognize classes of things, though they of course do not recognize class as such. Vervet monkeys, for instance, have distinct calls for leopards, eagles, and pythons, each of which elicits a distinct response: run up the tree for a leopard; dive under a bush for an eagle; watch the ground for a python.[343] As James Hurford argues, the existence of such classes, as opposed to the mere existence of a threat, could be indicative of proto-predication, which is to say that if a class of leopards exists, then there should also exist "leopardy-motion" and "leopardy-smell," though these predicates are not articulated in vervet communication.[344] If we take the reference-first approach, we would have to conclude that the leopard is already atomized into smell and motion before a whole leopard is conceived of. Put another way, the vervet monkey encounters the leopard as a bundle of qualities; it would be a Humean monkey.

But it might be otherwise. David Kimmerer has suggested that although an animal might first recognize something like the motion of another animal (a modality-specific feature), the encountered animal is experienced as a whole object, with different sensory modalities coming together in what Kemmer calls a Convergence Zone (CZ). Here he provides the example of a dog running across a field:

> [T]he following stages of processing can be distinguished: first, activation patterns across visual feature maps are detected by modality-specific CZs that store purely visual information about dogs; these modality-specific CZs then feed forward to a cross-modal CZ for the more general concept of a dog; next, the cross-modal CZ triggers the engagement of related modality-specific CZs in other knowledge domains; finally, the various modality-specific CZs may, depending on the task, generate explicit representations across the appropriate feature maps—e.g. auditory images of what dogs typically sound like, motor images of how one typically interacts with them (like reach out and petting them), somatosensory images of how their fur feels, and so on. The evocation, whether

conscious or unconscious, of some part of the large number of such neuronal patterns, over a brief lapse of time, constitutes activation of the conceptual knowledge pertaining to the category of entities at hand, namely dogs.[345]

Thus, whether your ontology begins with processes, events, or qualities, pre-linguistic predication—if Kemmerer is right—begins with objects, and the conceptual atomization of qualities probably does not begin until we get full language.

But what's more important is that syntax itself does not begin with atomization and analysis. The study of the relationship between human proto-language and full language is a highly speculative endeavor, but it begins with a basic division between the catastrophists and the gradualists. The most notable catastrophist, of course, is Chomsky. Chomsky really does not have much to say about *how* human language came about but rather *that* it was a single mutation event that occurred sometime around 50,000 years ago and that it survived as a selective advantage.[346] 50,000 years ago (the beginning of the Upper Paleolithic) is an attractive date because the archeological record sees a significant uptick in technology, culture, and population, beginning in southern Africa. But while the date is tempting, it does cut rather close to the settlement of Australia, which may have begun even before the Upper Paleolithic (the number of settlement waves being unclear as well). The gradualist school, on the other hand, takes a more explicitly Darwinian approach, most notably with Steven Pinker and Paul Bloom arguing that grammatical rules began accreting around 400,000 years ago, successively gaining selective advantage until a more or less modern grammar emerged in the Upper Paleolithic.[347] But once again, the gradualist approach does less to explain the *how* than it does to explain the *that*.

The gradualist approach makes more intuitive sense than the catastrophic approach if we consider language as a specific product of evolution; however, its primary weakness, as Derek Bickerton points out, is that syntax "does not consist of a simple aggregate of rules." Rather, it "consists of a small handful of principles which interact systematically with one another."[348] Thus, any mutation resulting in a new rule would also have to be a meta-mutation of the existing aggregate. Bickerton instead takes on an *exaptionalist* approach, in which language does not go directly from reference to grammar. In exaption, grammatical categories are derived from basic thematic relationships, such as that between agent, patient, action, and goal. The centrality of thematic relationships comes out of the idea of reciprocal altruism as a competing social technology to the alpha-hierarchy structure. In reciprocal altruism, members of a community may share food and favors (e.g. grooming) instead of acting within the trickle-down system of the alpha-hierarchy.[349] Keeping track of these favors, however, would require a different sort of memory than what is needed in an alpha-hierarchy. It's pretty clear at least that chimpanzees and gorillas, in addition to humans, possess what is called *episodic memory*.[350] Episodic memory consists of events inclusive of actors, actions, and relevant objects, though there is no need for an event to be remembered in reference to an associative or abstract timeline. Episodic memory, being context-free, is enough to account for who in the group shares food and favors and who doesn't, thus helping to build stronger or weaker relationships along those lines. So, instead of immediate relationships of Me and You, and Me and That, you have a way to think of Me and Her, and of Her and Her, and so forth. With the regular diversity of thematic roles comes a more defined structure of different kinds of predicates. And thus, as Bickerton states, "the existence of thematic roles and their obligatory nature potentially yields the basic building blocks of syntax: the phrase and the clause."[351] The "obligatory nature" of thematic roles to which Bickerton is referring has to do with how many *arguments*[352] a given verb takes. Here, Bickerton argues that the thematic roles become "Janus-faced," because they function syntactically but do so with respect to their semantic context.[353] Again, the number of arguments a predicate can take on depends upon the meaning of the predicate verb. So, for instance, as a verb *sleep* is intransitive, which means that as a predicate verb it takes only one argument:[354]

John(*a*1) sleeps(*p*).

*John(*a*1) sleeps(*p*) the bed(*a*2).

A verb like *give*, on the other hand, takes three arguments:

John(*a*1) gave(*p*) Mary(*a*3) the ball(*a*2).

*John(*a*1) gave(*p*) the ball(*a*2).

As Bickerton says, "there is no language in which the verb that means 'sleep' takes two obligatory arguments, the verb that means 'break' takes three, but the verb that means 'give' takes only one."[355]

Thus in order to convey information about the different combinations of agent, theme, and goal in multiple, specific events, there had to be in place a small set of combinatorial principles that delineated arguments from predicates, and then different classes of predicates and arguments. With these basic phrasal principles in place, phrases could then be combined into higher clauses using other kinds of delineative markers, such as prepositions. At this stage, the building of sentences from thematic relations and then from argument-predicate relations, and then from phrasal and clausal relations is beginning to look recursive or self-similar. And indeed, the mechanism to which the latest iteration of Chomsky's generative program (the Minimalist Program) is anchored to recursion. Recursion has been the focus of the most public spat linguistics has seen in quite a while, with Daniel Everett arguing that recursion cannot be the unifying mechanism for all human language since, at least in Pirahã (a language spoken in the Brazilian Amazon), as Everett claims, there is no recursive embedding of phrases.[356] If the recursive mechanism is the expression of a catastrophic mutation event, and if that event was the birth of full human language, then it would be difficult to imagine any particular language casting it aside, having once used it in the distant past. However, if the recursive embedding of phrases is not a requirement of language but a benefit of a growing working memory augmenting the existing capacity to parse and merge arguments and predicates and then phrases to other phrases, then higher level recursion, such as phrase embedding might be an optional grammatical technology. Indeed, in other areas of grammar, particular languages are unevenly complex, possessing greater or fewer elements of syntagmatic redundancy.[357] Furthermore, the expression of the basic grammatical division between agent and theme is not universally distributed across documented languages.

The characterization of thematic roles as facing both the syntactical and the semantic seems to me to be correct. Furthermore, there is evidence to indicate that the less syntactical and more pragmatic relationship between the topic of a sentence and its focus both precedes and gives rise to the relationships between noun and verb, and then to that between subject and predicate.[358] All documented languages mark the distinction between topic and focus, either by morphology or by position, whereas a few languages do not mark the subject-predicate distinction. To explain, most of the time in English the subject and the topic occupy the same position. Occasionally, however, pragmatic concerns override this convention. So, if I were to describe a non-specific event like a truck hitting a dog, I would say it just like that: "A truck hit a dog." Here, *truck* is both topic and subject, and *dog* is both focus and direct object. But if I were to report this thing happening to my dog, I'd be much more likely to say, "My dog got hit by a truck." Because who the hell cares about the truck? That was my dog![359] There is evidence, for instance, that children who are acquiring English internalize the topic position before they ever internalize the subject position in that they frequently prefer the oblique "me" over the strictly subjective "I" (e.g. "Me wanna go home.").[360] To be clear, topic-focus relationships are not the same as thematic relationships (the latter being concerned with the agent and patient of an action), but in both cases syntactical structure cannot so easily by extracted from pragmatic-semantic concerns.

Formulaic Sequences and Phonological Similarity

But whether the Janus-faced thematic roles get analyzed as a subject-predicate division, a noun-verb division, or a topic-focus division, the question remains as to how exactly the members of those classes of words acquired enough meaning to be categorized along syntactical lines. The answer, again, is that analytical categories have captured analogical relationships. Alison Wray offers, in my estimation, the most persuasive explanation as to how, in proto-language, these classes of words came about. Wray's program is called *formulaic language*, and it begins from the somewhat counter-intuitive position that words which were both semantically significant and syntactically functional came out of whole language chunks. Wray points out that human language is full of phrases that, on the surface, contain divisions between argument and predicate, as well as phrase-delineating markers such as prepositions. These chunks, however, are not analyzed grammatically, but instead are stored in the memory as whole lexical items.[361] The chunks, or "formulaic sequences,"[362] are idiomatic, although they should not be conflated with idiom, since some idioms are large enough to be produced by grammatical analysis. Formulaic sequences might be as small as a simple collocation. For instance, in American English, one rarely hears the adjective *merry* when it is not adjoined to *Christmas*. Other formulaic sequences appear to be more complex. I have used a couple in this chapter, such as "*X*s that go bump in the night" and "*X* a *Y* does not make." The syntactical and morphological structures of these sequences are necessarily rigid, and in order to alter them, the whole sequence needs to be analyzed. So, for instance, I can replace the *things* that go bump in the night with *X*s that go bump in the night without analyzing the sequence; however, if I replaced *X*s with something singular, I would need to analyze the sequence instead of spitting it out of my lexicon: "*A creature* that *goes* bump in the night."

There are a couple of reasons why formulaic sequences persist in language. For one, they are pretty economical:

> Formulaic sequences are rarely the *only* way of expressing a given idea, but they are undoubtedly very often the *preferred* or *normal* way. Although *Do not step on the lawn* and *Please perform an act of kindness for me* are comprehensible, we are much more likely to encounter *Keep off the grass* and *Would you do me a favor?*[363]

The immediate recognition of such simple, chunked directives will have a selective advantage over possible alternatives because, if they are heard as wholes, the recipient is less likely to mishear any one lexical component, which might otherwise render the entire utterance incomprehensible, thereby requiring that the sender repeat herself.

I would speculate even further that formulaic directives function as grammatical agents. Just as a corporate memo might read, "*It has been decided* that part-time employees will no longer receive health benefits," *Keep off the grass* defers the agency of the sender either to some amorphous body of authority or to the authority of custom. Likewise, some formulaic sequences perform wisdom without the need to engage directly with the details of a situation: *It's like making a silk purse out of a sow's ear.* The other reason Wray gives for the persistence of formulaic sequences is the performance of identity. Not only would the *sow's ear* sequence project conventional wisdom or common sense, but it might also serve the rhetorical purpose of ingratiating the speaker with her audience. Indeed, 2000 years ago, Cicero broke with rhetorical convention when he encouraged speakers not to engage in oratory hotdogging, but to lay on the rusticisms so that the audience might identify with the speaker instead of merely being impressed by the speaker. That tradition persists among politicians today, particularly in the United States, which identifies itself as a nation of yeoman farmers just as Rome did.

Both the economy and the identity functions explain the persistence of formulaic sequences, but not necessarily their function in protolanguage. Various chimpanzee cries are similar enough that they can be grouped into broad categories, such as directives, expressives, etc. Wray explains:

> Chimps use their noise/gesture system to effect changes in their world, maintain social structure and express the place of the individual within it. But they do not harness it as an entity in its own right, either as a means of accessing other information (e.g. mnemonics) or as a processing shortcut.[364]

Wray argues that although chimpanzees appear to express a state of affairs, such as "thirsty," this cannot be isolated from the manipulative subtext, "give me a drink."[365] This is important because instead of referencing a concept, a chimpanzee is expressing thematic relations with an unsegmented utterance.

But how might the thematic roles existing in episodic memory have been mapped onto a semantic memory that is able to express the segmentation of roles? Again, Bickerton's argument that the graduated increase of neural entrainment accounted for a progressively greater capacity for combining segments, but it doesn't explain segmentation itself. Wray invents a few holistic utterances that do not have a clear referential function but which would be used for interpersonal manipulation, similar to the chimpanzee utterance:

> *tebima*: give that to her
> *mupati*: give that to me
> *kumapi*: share this with her
> *pubatu*: help her

As she explains, "There is no part of *tebima* that means *give* or *to her*. Simply the whole thing means the whole thing."³⁶⁶ "But," Wray contends,

> if in two or more sequences there were chance matches between phonetic segments and aspects of meaning, then it would seem as if there was a constituent with that meaning. So if, besides *tebima* meaning *give that to her*, *kumapi* meant *share this with her*, then it might be concluded that *ma* had the meaning *female person + beneficiary*.³⁶⁷

Here, we would at least have part of the focus of a grammatical sentence. (Note that *female + beneficiary* is morpho-syntactic as well as semantic.) We would have a foothold on semantic memory. Described in metaphysical terms, we have the emergence of a new object that did not have to be washed through an analytical or atomic stratum in its emergence. The pressure for such chance segmentations probably would have come from the burden on the memory of an increasing load of such holistic utterances, perhaps as reciprocal altruism created a greater complexity of social roles, or perhaps as semantic memory capacities were unevenly distributed amongst individuals.

Bickerton's argument about thematic relations crossing from episodic into semantic memory is in basic agreement with Wray's scheme; however, he disagrees with the notion that holistic utterances would have emerged without a synthesization of predetermined references.³⁶⁸ The argument here is that either *ma* would have appeared in all situations in which a female beneficiary was involved—in which case, *ma* would have been synthesized already—or that *ma* would have occurred in a potentially innumerable set of situations, some of which involved a female beneficiary and some of which did not. Bickerton further argues that an unanalyzed protolanguage would not have a sophisticated phonology, so "how could speakers judge whether any pair of phonetic tokens represented 'the same' or 'different' syllables?"³⁶⁹ But we need not look for a self-same phonological match. As I pointed out in the last chapter, there are good reasons to suspect that phonemes themselves are distributed objects, so that even the most atomistic orthography could not capture the psychological reality of phonemes. Furthermore, the utterances *tebima* and *kumapi* need not have been self-same in their phonological structure. Even speakers within a single dialect may employ *accent suppression* differently for the same words or phrases.[370] One speaker might say *tebima* as a whole unit, perhaps stressing only the first syllable, whereas another might, without any consideration of meaning, say `tebi `ma. What's more, another individual may hear `tebi `ma and the front stress-only `kumapi in similar contexts and still make an analogy between the `ma in `tebi `ma and the ma in `kumapi. Indeed, *ma* could be made meaningful in an analogy between *kumapi* and *tebimuh* or *tebina*. Furthermore, formulaic sequences are commonly produced and heard in different ways. For instance, one person might say "Once *in* a while" and the other may hear "Once *and* a while" or "Nip it in the *bud*" and "Nip it in the *butt*." Each version of these sequences will function equally well until they are analyzed, usually by a gallant crusader for linguistic purity with whom it is always such a pleasure to be trapped on a long car ride. What is needed for analysis is not an exact match between the same set of phonemes in the same kind of situation, but only similar phonemes in similar situations. We need not exhaust ourselves looking for one and the same atom of sound or meaning that is repeated exactly in *ma* (Situation 1) and in *ma* (Situation 2). There is no reason to think that the 'match' between *ma*, `*ma*, *muh*, and *na* in situations 1, 2, 3, and 4 would not be a matter of aesthetics and analogy rather than an analytical determination. This level of analogy-making in pre-linguistic humans would probably not have been out of bounds, since baboons have been shown to recognize similarities between shapes[371] and chimpanzees can even recognize relations between relations (analogies of proper proportionality).[372]

There are a couple of conclusions that we might draw from all of this. One is to reaffirm the now rather orthodox generative notion that syntax and semantics are indeed not independent from one another. In other words, context-free reference does not come free of grammatical relations. On the other hand, grammars do not appear on the scene as abstract modules of rules—they are indebted to pragmatic relationships that emerged with a particular social technology (reciprocal altruism). Furthermore, the analytical structuring of a grammar out of thematic relations was indebt to the emergence of analogies that brought together several loosely related pragmatic situations and phonemic sets.

Embodied Metaphors and Disembodied Grammars

We are used to lumping together analogies with metaphors as if the development of a metaphor is part of the same process as the creation of an analogy. And indeed, we could think of a metaphor as an ossified analogy. It could also be argued that metaphors are sometimes over-ossified and lifeless. Recall George Orwell's complaint about the so-called "dead metaphor" *toe the line*.[373] Already in Orwell's time, it was being written as *tow the line* as often as it was being written as *toe the line*. Meaning, of course, that the imagery of feudal military service had been washed out completely. We need not go so far, as Orwell did, to say that *tow the line* represents the death of *toe the line*. As soon as *toe the line* became a metaphor, it was imitating previous iterations *as* a metaphor and not as the image of a feudal military practice, just as *tow the line* imitates *toe the line*. Reference to anything outside of language is not a necessary precondition for meaning. Shared intention, in which a speaker (or in this case, a writer) successfully guesses that a metaphor is not out of bounds in pursuit of a rhetorical goal, is enough for meaning. That said, I certainly take Orwell's point about being attentive to the poetics of one's own language.

To be sure, analogies drive metaphors and metaphors may even be, as Chaim Perelman and Lucie Olbrechts-Tyteca claim, "condensed analogies,"[374] the imitation of one idea by another being hidden to various degrees. And as I will argue, metaphors can be classified as being either opaque or transparent, and the more transparent a metaphor is, the less hidden its analogicity is. But what I want to argue at the moment is that the relationship of analogy to metaphor is not simply about the creation of labels for things. Analogies drive past labels and onto grammars. As we have seen, phonological analogies may have been a key factor in the morpho-syntactical parsing by which human grammar moved from protolanguage. But analogies also drive the creation of grammars of labels of things, and those grammars, as complex system objects, themselves become agents driving the creation of other analogies in a self-similar fashion.

One of the more prominent and enduring challenges to the generative grammar program has been what is sometimes called *generative semantics*, a linguistics based in cognitive psychology and neural science. George Lakoff is probably the most prominent figure in this field, and he is best known for some of the extraordinary and controversial claims he has made about conceptual framing and political orientation. This work has been vastly oversimplified into frozen dinner notions of "Republicans think in terms of *X* and Democrats think in terms of *Y*." But at the heart of it all is a commitment to the idea that cognition is deeply embodied. Naïve arguments about conceptual frames and politics are the public face of generative semantics, but it grows out of a critique of the scienticization of politics found in early works like Haig A. Bosmajian's 1974 *The Language of Oppression*, which traced the grammar of Nazi rhetoric back to metaphorical frames of health and the body.

Lakoff's own argument with the Chomksyan version of Universal Grammar is part of a larger critique of Western philosophy that extends from Plato to Descartes to Chomsky, in which the essential parts of humanness (namely language and thought) are located in structures divorced from sensorimotor experience. Complimentary to his cognitive linguistics program is Lakoff's philosophical program, which he calls *Experimental Realism*. Lakoff lays out the cornerstones of this position as:

a) a commitment to the existence of the real world

b) a recognition that reality places constraints on concepts

c) a conception of truth that goes beyond mere internal coherence

d) a commitment to the existence of stable knowledge of the world.[375]

There is something, if only in name, that would ring familiar to the philosophies of Speculative Realism. Certainly, principles *a* and *c* are in agreement with what is common in SR, and depending upon what is meant by "world" (Lakoff does not clarify), *d* might be as well. But it is the "recognition that reality places constraints on concepts" that, while fine on its own, introduces another version of Kantian correlationism when applied to generative semantics. While Lakoff dismisses the notion that our knowledge of the world is derived from a correlation between real structures and principles of an abstract language mechanism, he advances the notion that cognitive linguistic structures radiate outwards in an asymmetrical, one-way direction from sensorimotor experience. And while I agree that analogies from embodied experience are a key source of human metaphor-making (in addition to phonological analogies from pragmatic relations), I again argue that the grammars that emerge from these processes are objects on their own and that they need not be continuously replenished by human sensorimotor experience alone to affect human knowledge making.

What brings the linguistics of generative grammar in line with other sciences is its claim to predictability. In other words, if we can detect the presence of a certain structure, we can formulate a principle in which another structure will or will not be present. For instance, if it is observed that verbs are at the front of verb phrases, it is likely that complimentizers (such as *that* or *which*) will be at the front of compliment phrases and vice-versa.[376] This logic is most apparent in the Principles and Parameters program, in which a limited number of deep structures operate as binary switches. What this means for linguistic typology is that geographical location and historical filiation produce only superficial effects on linguistic diversity. The real instruments of linguistic diversity are supposed to be predictable from the binary system of switches. For instance, the distance between English and Spanish is measured not by tracing each language's roots back through the Indo-European tree, but by the distance of a few switches.

Here's a pretty common illustration of the phenomenon.[377] In English, you can express the following statement in a few different ways:

>John often kisses Mary.
>John kisses Mary often.
>Often, John kisses Mary.

The first two mean nearly the same thing, while the third, with *often* as its own clause, could mean something slightly different, as in John does kiss Mary often, though it might be slightly out of character for him to do so. What English lacks in grammatical forms and cases, such as the frequentive verb, it sometimes makes up for in word order. But the one way of saying this that would seem awkward or perhaps even nonsensical to an English speaker would be:

>*John kisses often Mary.

On the other hand, it's perfectly fine to say it that way in French or in Spanish:

> Jean embrace souvent Marie.
>
> Juan beso normalmente Maria.

In both French and Spanish, the *verb-attraction* parameter is switched on, meaning that the adverb *often* moves up the tree to attach itself under the verb. (In English, the verb-attraction parameter is switched off.) And if the verb-attraction parameter is switched on, a further switch is presented: the *pro-drop* (variously, *pronoun-drop* or *null subject*) parameter. Thus, in French, as in English, a verb must take a noun or a pronoun as its subject:

> It's raining.
>
> Il pleut.
>
> *Raining.
>
> *Pleut.

The equivalent Spanish sentence, on the other hand, is free to imply its grammatical subject:

> Plueve.

Predictability works pretty well in some cases, but if predictions are made from universal principles, the whole program is jeopardized when exceptions are found. This occurs, for instance, Everett's contention that Pirahã lacks both recursion and a counting system.

In his generative semantics, Lakoff replaces the notion of predictability with *motivation*. In this way, the science of linguistics is not located in a unified system of principles that makes structural output predictable, but in the physiological apparatuses that motivate linguistic structures. The difference is that although clear correlations can be established between the physiological and the linguistic, the specific ways in which the linguistic extends itself outwards from the physiological are not predictable. But, of course, what this means in reverse is that any linguistic element—say, a metaphor—theoretically can be traced back to a particular physiological motivation.

Lakoff claims that physiological motivation can account for many of the problems that have stumped generative grammarians in the past. For instance, why should existential *there*-constructions be so similar to deictic *there*-constructions if the two are derived from completely different syntactical principles? (Recall the difference between the object-dependent existential copula in Arabana and the English deictic construction from Chapter 2.) So, the following sentences can have two very different meanings, although on the surface, they only differ by the use of a proper noun:

> (Deictic) There's Harry on the porch.
> (Existential) There's a man on the porch.[378]

As Lakoff points out, the real difference between the two becomes apparent when you try to add elements like negability or reversal tags:[379]

> (Negability) There's not a man on the porch.
> (Reversal Tag) There's a man on the porch, isn't there?
> (Negability) *There's not Harry on the porch.
> (Reversal Tag) *There's Harry on the porch, isn't there?

What is obvious is that in the deictic, *there* is an adverb but in the existential, *there* becomes the subject. Thus, in order to negate *There's Harry on the porch*, you need to move *Harry* up to the front, in which case it becomes clearer that *Harry* is the subject and *there* is the adverb:

> Harry is not there on the porch.

Another notable distinction here is phonological. An English speaker is much more likely to stress the *there* in the deictic utterance than in the existential. In the deictic, we already know that Harry exists; the important thing is that he is *there* on the porch. In the existential, the existence of the man is the new information, and so while *there* is the subject, it is swallowed up by the topic.

These are just a few of the degrees of difference between the two *there*s. And yet the superficial similarity between the two *there*-constructions is undeniable. And one should not underestimate superficial similarities. They can bring about some truly profound effects. Lakoff and others argue—persuasively—that the deictic is more basic than the existential because the existential is always perceived to be located in some proximity to the speaker.[380] The existential *there* emerges from analogy to the more central concept of the deictic *there*. Once again, conceptual extensions radiate from a center of embodied experience.

The idea of central-radial categories threads its way through the logic of generative semantics. It largely comes out of Eleanor Rosch's work on prototypes in psychology. It's a pretty Aristotelian-sounding idea, in that general categories proceed from ideas of specific things. The difference, of course, is that in prototype theory, the specifics and generals are entirely psychological in nature. The other key difference in prototype theory is that membership in a general category is not determined by a set of common properties. Instead, one member exemplifies the category as a whole concept. So, instead of the general category *vehicle* being predicated by the combination of thing + transport + wheel, etc., it is simply predicated by *car*.[381] *Car*, in this case, is both a middle category and the basic category. It sits between larger categories, such as *vehicle* and small categories, such as *sports car*.[382] The category of *sportscar* is thus not predictable from *car*, but it is motivated by *car*.

We can also see the prototype effect in marked and unmarked categories. Actually, *unmarked* is marked in relation to *marked*, which is itself unmarked. Here's something a little less Lewis Carroll: In judgments of height, the basic ends of the spectrum are *tall* and *short*. However, only *tall* can stand in for height in general.[383] No one asks the question, "How short is she?" unless it's a response to something like "My sister is *so* short..." Questions of height are thus raised in specifically marked contexts. This phenomenon of markedness carries with it more pernicious consequences as well, as for instance in gendered or raced marking. *Actor* is unmarked with respect to *actress*, but since the days of air travel, *steward* has become marked with respect to *stewardess*; and since the honorific *master* has fallen into relative disuse, it is now marked in relation to *mistress*. Marked or unmarked, none of this works in women's favor. Also, if a white American has a bad experience in a restaurant or a movie theater, and the offending parties were also white, she is unlikely to complain about the annoying *white* guys there. But she is at least somewhat likely to identify them by race if the offending parties happened to be minorities, with that particular case sticking in the memory as it supports existing stereotypes. Once again, white is unmarked.

Our most basic verbs, nouns, and even prepositions are analogized from our most familiar sensuous experiences, which become prototypes for other metaphors. Those sensuous experiences are lived in three dimensions.

And just as Kant used this fact as a primitive for universal reason, Lakoff and Johnson see it as a launching point into more abstract concepts, such as quantity, time, and relations. They note the widespread conflation of increase in a quantity with upward direction ("Prices rose today"), the conflation of time with directional motion (forward for future and backward for past), and the conflation of similarity/difference with spatial proximity.[384] Morpho-syntactical systems too are motivated by familiarity and prototyping. Consider the particular class of irregular verbs in English that includes *run, sing, ring,* and *drink*. As Pinker observes, children will often overgeneralize the regular past tense rule and apply it to irregular verbs, creating words like *runned*.[385] But they are not likely to overgeneralize irregularity. For instance, there is an asymmetry in the tensed forms of the verbs listed above:

> sing/sang/sung
> ring/rang/rung
> drink/drank/drunk
> **rin*/ran/run

This would indicate either that irregular verb forms are each learned as exceptions to the regular rule or that there are other rules for irregulars, in which case there would only be a small group of exceptions, such as *run* to produce from memory alone.

Here, the generative grammarian faces a dilemma. The epistemological agenda of generative grammar is to push minimization as far as it can possibly go. The idea is to envision a system capable of producing the maximum amount of information from the smallest number of rules. The assumption is that memory and linguistic processing exist as separate mechanisms and that it takes a lot of work to go from one mechanism to another, just as it takes a lot of work to move information between processor and memory in a computer. So, in the case of irregular verbs, it becomes a question of where to minimize: the rules or the exceptions? Ultimately, generative grammar abhors exceptions, so they are what must be minimized at the cost of adding rules. Adding rules provides relief to the memory but that burden gets transferred onto the theoretician who must explain how the rules work together and what psychological or physiological bases there might be for such rules. The alternative to this epistemological agenda is to think of exceptions not as threats to an elegant, minimal structure but as extensions to a self-similar network. Let's consider some more irregular verbs in English, such as *spin, win, sling, string,* and *dig.*[386] Joan Bybee and Carol Lynn Moder find that a few of these verbs are stronger representatives of the category than others, namely those that:

a) begin with an *s*, followed by one or two consonants

b) those that end with an *–ng* (velar nasal)

c) those with a short *i* (lax high front vowel).[387]

These attrbutes do not constitute a rule because if they did, most words would be an exception in one way or another. Rather, each verb in the group is similar to another by at least one of the three attributes. Furthermore, this self-similar network has affected verbs that wouldn't otherwise share the *i-u* tensing pattern, such as the verb *bring*, whose past and past perfect tense commonly appears as *brung*.

Lakoff sees the prototype effect working in the irregular category that Bybee and Moder identified. Because *string, sling, swing,* and *sting* all share each of the three attributes of the group, they would be the prototypes from which all others in the category are shaped. But I see no reason why this should be the case, unless it can be shown that the supposed prototype members have been more familiar to speakers than the non-prototype members (if we are to follow the same logic of prototyping seen in metaphorical categories). As it is, there is evidence that irregular verbs used less frequently get regularized with the *-ed* morpheme at a much faster rate than more common irregulars.[388] Note that *swing* is sometimes tensed as *swinged*, but a less prototypical irregular like *win* is almost never tensed as *winned*.

While there is no denying that basic metaphors began with analogies from our embodied experience, I don't believe that corporeal familiarity remains at the center of a grammatical system. Grammars are more than expressions of abstract principles and they are also more than their relationships to an embodied mind. They are complex objects capable of affecting the economy, organization, and distribution of knowledge, and they cannot so easily be reduced to an identifiable set of conceptual relations.

Women, Fire, and Dangerous Things

The most enduring illustration of radial categories in generative semantics is based on Robert M.W. Dixon's famous 1972 study of Dyirbal (a northeast Australian language). It's where Lakoff gets the title of his 1987 book *Women, Fire, and Dangerous Things*. The title refers to Dyirbal's grammatical gender system. Unlike the masculine-feminine-neuter classification of nouns known in several European languages, Dyirbal has four genders which approximate to masculine (*bayi*), feminine (*balan*), edible plants (*balam*), and everything else (*bala*). Not only is this an interesting noun classification system in its own right, but the fact that Dyirbal has a gender system at all is pretty exceptional for languages in the Pama-Nyungan family, which might mean that it is relatively recent development, hence the attachment of some elements to existing oral tradition.[389]

In the masculine gender (*bayi*) are of course men, but there are also common animals like kangaroos as well as the moon. The feminine gender (*balan*), on the other hand, contains among other things, women, the sun, and fire.[390] It's easy enough to trace the motivation of some of these items to an embodied, conceptual center. The sun and the moon can certainly be seen as opposites, just as man and woman can. It doesn't take a great leap to get from sun to fire, just as it is easy to go from sun and fire to the hairy mary grub, "whose sting is said to feel like sunburn,"[391] and which is also classed as *balan*. Fire and the hairy mary grub are harmful things, and so it's not difficult to see how they might pull other harmful things into their grammatical orbit. Epistemically, this is pretty economical. Common names for things are not always reliable sources of information about the properties of a thing that would be most relevant for human contact. For every *poison ivy* in English, there are several *snow-of-the-mountain*s, snow-of-the-mountain being just as irritating to the skin as poison ivy, though perhaps a little prettier to look at. Navigating your way through plant life is much easier when all you must do is match the classed noun with the thing instead of matching the noun to the thing to its relevant properties. But on the other hand, a grammar like Diyrbal is profoundly uneconomical in its production, since it does not appear to begin with an ordered set of principles. This is true too for simpler grammatical genders like those found in European languages. There is no consistently principled reason why, for instance, *the mustache* should be *la mustache* (feminine) in French and *el bigote* (masculine) in Spanish (though, clearly the etymologies of the two words are quite different). Similarly, there is no principled reason why *water* in Dyirbal should be classed as *balan* alongside sun and fire, and why most birds too should be classed as *balan*, while hawks, which are considered harmful, should be classed as *bayi* alongside harmless animals.[392] Those classifications emerge out of a multiplicity of analogies, though we should not make the mistake in thinking that a class is the result of a series of analogies that is coherent and principally different from the series of analogies found in a neighboring class.

Lakoff grants that mythological models can themselves form domains of experience, though not as fundamental as those which emerge from embodied experiences,[393] such as that of danger. This explains why, for instance, crickets are classed as *balan*. There is a mythological connection between crickets and old women, which is perhaps less fundamental than the idea of birds as spirits of departed women. But presumably, in the logic of generative semantics, myths too can be traced back to particular kinds of embodied experience. Again, Lakoff is very careful not to grant any predictive powers to the prototype-radial categories program other than the claim that some categories are predictably more fundamental than others and that the system is a one-way, outward projection from those categories. The strongest claim, then, is that to be able to trace categories back through the chain of experience, "all we would need to know is which domains of experience are relevant for categorization and then we would need specific knowledge of the domains."[394]

But I'm not sure if any grammar could be that transparent, even if we had access to the information above. To be sure, consistently labeling domains of experience as they are connected directly to mammalian life in three dimensions does not present too many problems. There is still a lot to be learned about the physiology of consciousness, language, and socialization, but let's say we have a baseline. But if your scheme makes the distinction between what is more and what is less fundamental, then you have a giant gulf to cross between, on the one hand, those concepts that have been analogized from but are analyzable into a set of physiological constants, and on the other hand those concepts that must be analyzed to the analogies from the primary set of embodied experiences. Having constructed the second and third orbital ring in your radial model, you must continuously multiply your principles of fundamentality in order to preserve the orbital pull of your most basic domains of embodied experience. So, let's say there is a minimal number of categories analogized from embodied experience, which might include the categorical division between male and female. We'll put that number at x. Can we assume that each categorical division in the first orbit will correspond to a single categorical division in the second orbit? Because we're dealing with domains and not with pairs, we should assume not. So, if one of our categorical divisions in the first orbit is male/female, which gets analogized to the division moon/sun in the second orbit, evidence would have to be presented to show that there is no equally fundamental analogy to the <male : female :: moon : sun> analogy. This would seem to me a difficult task. But even if each categorical division in one orbit were analogized into just two divisions in the next, we would already have arrived at a number of $y = x^2$ for the set of divisions in that next orbit. Each member of set y in the subsequent orbit would have to be traced back to a division in set x of the previous orbit. This would grow cumbersome and increasingly speculative in very short order.

Of course, generative semantics does not claim that it works quite this way. At least in Dyirbal, there is evidence that new members of a class do not necessarily enter the class by similarity to members in the outer orbits of the class. For instance, pipes are classed as *balan* because they are concerned with fire, which is more fundamental than other members like the hairy mary grub. And presumably, the more central the member, the more analogies it will pull into the class directly, so the exponential model $y = x^2$ model may be overestimating the challenges to the program. Nevertheless, there is some unevenness in how some members enter into the domains of experience of other members. So, while pipes are classified with fire in *balan*, cigarettes are classed in *balam* with edible plants, perhaps because the whole smoking object is seen to be consumed, whereas only the tobacco is consumed in the pipe. Indeed, it is not terribly uncommon in language for the activity of smoking to be represented by the same (or a similar) verb as that for the act of drinking and/or eating.[395] But there are other examples in which the relationship between the member and its domain of experience is considerably murkier. It's common in many cultures for there to be an ontological division between fire and water. However, in Dyirbal water is classed in *balan* with fire. Lakoff argues that the category *water* belongs to the domain of experience of fire (and is therefore less fundamental than fire). This is because water extinguishes fire, according to Lakoff.[396] To be fair, Lakoff makes it clear that "these are speculations of an outside analyst,"[397] since neither Dixon nor the speakers Dixon worked with could offer a systematic explanation for the particulars of the grammar. Since there does not exist a cultural universal in which water belongs to a particular domain of experience, all that can be done is try to guess which relationship with another kind of object constitutes the most basic experience of a given kind of object, like water. Water, after all, could also have served as a prototype for dangerous things, followed by fire, and then by the sun, at which point the moon would have been classed as *bayi* with men. Certainly, the waters of northeastern Queensland hold more than their fair share of dangerous things.

The point is that it is difficult enough to identify the entire motivation for a single category, and so trying to analyze the chains of a system of analogies back to a single set of primitives is pretty impractical. Furthermore, there is no reason to suppose that all members of a class were pulled in by conceptual similarity alone. The possibility that some members were pulled in by phonological similarity cannot be ruled out. There are, in fact, several examples of phonologically similar nouns occupying the same class, such as:

> *garri*: sun
> *garri*: hairy mary grub
> *garram*: gar fish
> *yarra*: fishing line[398]

These apparent phonological similarities do not rule out the productiveness of conceptual similarity either, but they do suggest a grammar that behaves more like a complex system being driven by multiple actors in unpredictable ways. Barring the acceptance of either the strongest possible version of Universal Grammar or the most literal interpretation of the story of Babel, it must be conceded that grammars do not have a single point of origin to which the whole of their beings can be reduced. And human sensory experience, no matter how universal in its own right, cannot serve as this reduction point either. As an object, a grammar interacts with itself and with other objects. And like a city, a grammar is beyond its physical infrastructure and the interactions of the people within.

Alice Didn't Know Tuvan

There is a danger, in making the kind of argument I am making, to revert back to a strong version of the old Sapir-Whorf hypothesis, in which a language, conditioned by the physical environment in which its speakers live, comes to shape the sensory and cognitive faculties of its speakers. Sapir-Whorf was popularized by the myth that Inuits have around one hundred words for snow and therefore perceive finer distinctions in snow than anyone else. In fact, it is the Yupik people who have ninety-nine words for *sea ice*, which turns out to be an incredibly useful resource for making predictions about the weather.[399] This is an epistemic effect, not a sensoricognitive effect. There is scant evidence that linguistic diversity plays any significant role in structuring differences in embodied experience. Sapir-Whorf makes the same error that strong versions of Universal Grammar and generative semantics make, only in reverse.

Certainly we can identify cognitive structures that enable and constrain grammatical structures, and to be sure, grammatical particularities have little impact on those structures. However, grammars are more than just epiphenomena of a given set of cognitive structures. There may not be much give and take between the cognitive and the grammatical, but the relationship between the grammatical and the epistemic is far more dynamic. So although, for instance, episodic memory and the division of thematic roles may belong to universal cognition, the particular expressions of those thematic roles, such as the functional misalignment of the topic and the subject that we occasionally see, are grammatico-epistemic and not universally cognitive. Grammars do not produce sensory experiences but they oblige speakers to reveal certain kinds of information about an experience, and they economize the communication of concepts. Anything can be said in any language, but not everything *must* be said. Often, these obligations are analyzable, as in Kewa (a New Guinean language), in which, when reporting on an event, one is obliged to indicate whether it was personally witnessed or learned from hearsay (an *evidentiality* construction).[400] Occasionally, a speaker is obliged to provide information that has little to do with the knowledge or reality of an event but with one's prior relationship to objects in the event. An example can be found in African American English where, in addition to functioning as a directional adverb or as a preposition, *up* serves as a sort of locative determiner that nevertheless indicates familiarity with the person in the location, as in "I was *up* at Jill's place." But you would be less likely to say "I was up at *that girl* Jill's place," since the attributive phrase *that girl* in this case indicates an unfamiliarity with *Jill*, which contradicts the familiarity indicated by *up*.[401]

Grammars also put constraints on the construction of concepts in particular ways, and they do so without the direct influence of universal cognitive or grammatical structures. For instance, certain kinds of affixes continue to be grammatically productive, such as *–tion, un-, post-,* and *–ness*. Other affixes remain only in whole lexical chunks as sort of morphemic zombies. Take *–th* for example. It is occasionally productive when we want to use a fictive ordinal in a statement like, "This is the *umpteenth* time I've told you to do the dishes!"[402] But in most areas, it is no longer analyzable from the word, as in *health*. English almost never uses the adjective form *hale* anymore unless it is part of the formulaic sequence, *hale and hearty*. Instead, the still productive affix *–y* is added to make *health* an adjective. And every time someone constructs the term *healthiness*, they are adding another nail to *–th*'s coffin. The life and death of affixes shouldn't have much epistemic effect as long as we can, for instance, add *–ness* to any construction where we might have added *–th*. But we're dealing with an emergent system, and there is no principle that applies evenly across this kind of language change. So, in questions of age, you could say that *old* is the unmarked prototype in English. Again, no one asks "How *young* is she?" unless the person's youth is somehow relevant or remarkable. But notice what I've just said: "unless the person's *youth*…" Even though *old* is the unmarked prototype in questions of age, there is no economical way to express the concept of old age or agedness or oldness as there is for *youth*. *Youth* is not grammatically analyzed from *young* as *agedness* and *oldness* are analyzed from *age* and *old*. Aesthetically, *youth* can be paired nicely with other unanalyzed terms such as *beauty* and *hope* in a way that an analyzed term like *oldness* cannot. Of course, I'm leaving out *age* as an unanalyzed term, but as it also has a more generic connotation, it lacks some of the definite thingness that *youth* has (not to mention that *youth* and *age* come out of different lineages, the former being Anglo-Saxon and the latter being Norman French).

The unevenly distributed lives of affixes in a grammar can come around to affect the consistency of any prototype rules that might be in place. For instance, in questions of height (often expressed as *heighth*), the unmarked version is "How *high* is it?" As an unanalyzed concept, *height(h)* pairs with *high*. And *length* pairs with *long*. But there is no *oldth*[403] to pair with "How *old* is she?" As a matter of fact, *-th* never seems to have been affixed to *old* or *eald* in the first place, the preferred forms being *ealdness* or *ealdung*.[404] There is no principled reason why *–ness* should have lived past *–th*, *-lock*, or *–hood* in the abstract nominalization of adjectives, but just because the grammar seems to have made an arbitrary choice, that does not mean that its epistemic effects are negligible.

Finally, although grammars have little impact on sensory experience, they can have a significant effect on the epistemic organization of sensory experience. These effects sometimes work as obligations and constraints. For instance, in Carrier, an endangered language in British Columbia, speakers cannot talk about the handling or motion of objects without communicating tactile information about those objects and about the nature of the motion.[405] Different verb constructions for *give* (me) will be selected for two-dimensional, flexible objects, mushy objects, fluid objects, hay-like objects, and fluffy objects.[406] Furthermore, it must be indicated whether the handler is or is not in control of the object or if the object is acting without an external agent.[407] And in the case of giving, a distinction must be made between the giving of something in exchange for a service (the control verb) and the giving of something as a pure gift (the non-control verb).[408] Carrier has a noun classification system, which consists of stick-like objects, round objects, and things with spatial, areal, or temporal extension; however, there is no fixed classification as there is in Dyirbal. For instance, the description of an object like a rope as being thick will carry the *stick-like* classification, but it will not be marked as such in the description of a rope as being long.[409] And because noun classifiers are far exceeded by object-specific verb classifiers, there is no internal mechanism for analyzing the verb type (mushy, fluffy, etc.) from a fixed set of classified nouns. Carrier speakers, then, must rely upon familiarity and analogy when selecting a verb for a particular interaction with an object. The grammar is therefore structured to be open to new ways of organizing knowledge by analogy in ways that other grammars may not be.

Languages employ a few different strategies for opening themselves up to new terms and concepts. The easiest and most widespread way of doing this is simply by taking on loan words from other languages. As such, English has been a very busy tongue for the past thousand years. It's been both conquered and, more often, conqueror. The only significant grammatical changes English has undergone in its native territory have come by way of contact with the Vikings, which initiated a process of morphosyntactical simplification, as is common in koineization. But it has picked up loan words from just about everywhere, making it by far the largest lexicon in the world. Once a language gets hold of a word, there are a variety of ways in which it can make the word its own. For instance, *robotics* can be derived from the Czech *robota* [labor] and the Hindi-Urdu *shampoo* can become the gerund *shampooing*. Loanwords are also particularly open to the analogous expansion of meaning. Think, for instance, of what English has done with *pundit* (Sanskrit), *shtick* (Yiddish), and *chav* (Anglo-Romani).

Another way of taking on new terms and concepts is calquing.[410] Calquing occurs more often within specific communication genres, such as those of war, technology, sport, and philosophy. Unsurprisingly, English has calqued several terms from German philosophy, such as *worldview* [*Weltanschauung*] and *thought experiment* [*Gedankenexperiment*], though in more recent imports from French philosophy (*jouissance, dispositif*, etc.) English seems to have just kept the loans as they are. Calquing is sometimes ideologically motivated as well. Given the notorious lack of linguistic cosmopolitanism amongst its native speakers, English is surprisingly comfortable taking on loan words as they are. But languages with a national authoritative body are sometimes subject to official interventions into lexical imports. Who could forget the French effort back in 2003 to discard *email* in favor of *courriel* (from *courier electronique*)? Results of such efforts are decidedly mixed.

Certain genres may be equipped with a grammar with a highly analytical structure for the integration of new concepts, as in the case of the phylogenic and cladistic binomial taxonomies in biology. Often, the structures of even highly regularized systems emerge out of analogies. This seems to be the case in particle physics, where the norm is that when a distinguishing property of a newly theorized particle is identified, the property is given a truncated Greek name, followed by the affix *–on*. It begins with the naming of the electron. There is some controversy as to who gets credit for the discovery of the thing we call an electron, and its onomastic story is even murkier. Credit for the name is given to Michael Faraday (unlikely), Pieter Zeeman, J.J. Thompson, and George Jonstone Stoney (most likely). Depending on whom you ask, *electron* comes as a whole package from the Greek (a piece of amber) or as a portmanteau of *electric* + *ion*. What is more certain is that Ernst Rutherford subsequently named the *proton* in similar fashion from the Greek *protos* ("first"). Particles continued to be named in the mode of the first *electron-proton* analogy, including Yukawa's *meson* (originally, the *mesotron*), which comes from *mesos* ("middle") because its mass was in between those of an electron and a proton. This system was extended to classes of particles, such as *nucleons* (particles of the nucleus), *hadrons* (heavy particles), and *leptons* (light particles). Once the *–on* affix was fully regularized, the grammar was freed to deviate from the Greek adjectives. Thus we have *bosons* from Satyendra Nath Bose, *fermions* from Enrico Fermi, and the hypothetical *graviton* from the Latinate *gravity*. The fact that Murray Gell-Mann was able to take the name *quark* from Joyce's *Finnegan's Wake* and make it stick for the particle he and George Zweig theorized means that the grammar of particles is not entirely closed, but the discourse of particle physics remains a striking example of the relationship between analogicity and analyticity in the organization of knowledge.

Perhaps the most interesting way of making new knowledge out of sensuous experiences is onomatopoeia. Besides being really fun to say, onomatopoeia is just a fabulous name for the phenomenon it describes: the poetics of naming. Most onomatopoetic words are already fully regularized into the lexicon, complete with their own morphological derivations. We all know what a *splash* is, and we also know that we can *splash* and be *splashed*, and that furthermore liquids are not the only things that can *splash*. Paint on a canvas and even words on a page can do it too. For a long time, it was thought that onomatopoeia, in conjunction with deixis, was the midwife to language itself. There is indeed something magical about making a meaningful utterance out of nothing but a sonorous imitation of something. If language seems like an abstract, analytical endeavor, onomatopoetic words feel physical, as if they're a real thingy thing conforming to another thing. But as I have argued, conformity is imitation with context, and vice-versa. Anyone who's ever been to a party lifeless enough that the host resorts to a desperate game of charades knows that communicating imitation with a minimum of context is a hard thing to do. The same is true for genuine cases of onomatopoeia. Onomatopoetic utterances are generally embedded within narratives and performed with paralinguistic signals, such as hand gesticulations. For the same reason, onomatopoeia is far more common in comic books and graphic novels than it is in text-only genres.

Poetry is pretty good at using a sort of onomatopoeia (in the form of assonance and consonance) as a way of doubling the sensuous experience of a text's imagery. Coleridge was a master of this, and he was at his best in "Kubla Khan":

> *As if this earth in fast thick pants were breathing,*
> *A mighty fountain momently was forced:*
> *Amid whose swift half-intermitted burst*
> *Huge fragments vaulted like rebounding hail,*
> *[...]*
> *Five miles meandering with a mazy motion [...]*[411]

Coleridge is not inventing new words from imitation, nor is he using recognizable onomatopoetic words. He's making meaning out of what we would otherwise regard as the scraps of words, the candy bar wrappers, the mere and arbitrary sounds we use as a means to get to what we assume words really are: discrete packets of meaning. Coleridge is asking us, momentarily, to do the reverse and discard the candy bar, to open ourselves up to the unintegrated meaning in his language. This is a sensuous experience of the language, but it is not entirely a passive experience. The reader is responsible for acknowledging the effects the language is having on her and to create knowledge from those effects.

Part of what Coleridge has made in "Kubla Khan" was hewn from convention and part of it was taken from intuition. Consider the "Five miles" line. The /m/ is a nasal bilabial (voiced) occlusion. It's a double vibration. Air is forced through the vocal chords and stopped at the lips as sound is redistributed to the nasal cavity. It is well known that when the /m/ is multiplied in many words, it slows down the tempo of the language. And certainly Coleridge was not the first to employ the device. What was less conventionalized, however, was the repetition of dental and labiodental fricatives (*earth, fast, thick, breathing, swift, half, huge, fragments, vaulted*), which suggests something being forced through an aperture. Clearly, this is ejaculation, procreation, creation, and all that. The combination of sonorous and semantic allusion adds to the fullness and the power of the image. The sonorous and semantic provide just enough context for one another for Coleridge to communicate effectively his imitation of an orgasm, whereas one type of allusion alone might not have done it.

The invention of semantic context for a sonorous imitation of something is pure poetry. All the phallic stuff in "Kubla Khan" is maybe a bit on the nose, but still pure poetry. However, as K. David Harrison's research on Tuvan (a Turkic language spoken in southern Siberia, and in parts of Mongolia and China) shows, a grammar too can provide context for sonorous imitation. Tuvans, known for their overtone singing, engage actively in onomatopoetic communication. It's slightly reminiscent of Humpty Dumpty, who insists "When I use a word…it means just what I choose it to mean—neither more nor less." What Alice tried to make Humpty Dumpty understand is that having the power to make words does not mean that you have the power over words. As soon as you start stringing words together, grammar and genre steal that power back from you. But Alice didn't know Tuvan, which is less jealous than other grammars in some respects, for it allows its speakers to invent onomatopoetic words and effectively communicate them with a minimum of paralinguistic or semantic context. It has done so by constructing classes of sounds out of consonant pairs. According to Harrison, "With eight vowels, Tuvan provides many possible combinations, and speakers can use and understand most of these combinations, even if they have never heard them used before."[412] Harrison lists several onomatopoetic words that were observed from a single /š/-/l/ pair construction:

> šülür: sound of a nearly dried up river, or sound of mucous (snot) being forcefully blown out of the nose.
>
> šölür: sound of a bundle of wood falling loudly, or sound of loud slurping.
>
> šalyr: sound of dry leaves or grass rustling.
>
> šolur: sound of water in a babbling brook.
>
> šylyr: sound of rustling (e.g. paper in the wind).
>
> šulur: to chatter or blab.
>
> šilir: something to do with water sounds.[413]

When we put these examples together, a pattern begins to emerge. These all appear to be sounds of uncontrolled movement. But it's unclear whether semantic similarity or phonological similarity is motivating the pattern. Tuvan, like other Turkic languages, exhibits vowel harmony, which means that a vowel in one part of a word will put constraints on the type of vowel that can be located in another part of the word. This is probably useful in language acquisition, and I can't help but wonder if this type of patterning assists in facilitating the regularity of improvised sounds, such as those we see in the Tuvan grammar of onomatopoeia. My guess is that like Dyirbal gender, the Tuvan onomatopoetic grammar is affected by a complex network of both semantic and phonological analogies, which might even include other sensory associations as well.

What the grammars of Dyirbal, Carrier, particle physics, and Tuvan tell us is that the content of knowledge systems is driven by analogy and that they are economized by analytical structures, which themselves emerge largely by from the circulation of analogies. In this way, analyticity can never be considered a real quality of a system. As far as a system goes, analyticity is accidental and relative. In Dyirbal, there is no atomizable quality belonging to each element of a gender category that, as a self-same entity, constitutes the domain of that category. But neither do the elements of a category belong arbitrarily. And neither are the distinctions between the categories themselves arbitrary. The elements and categories relate to each other by a complex system of conceptual, sensuous, and phonological similarities. And yet, despite the complexity of the relations that constitute the categories, they do function analytically and effect epistemic economization, for instance in the classification of the hairy mary grub with other harmful things. Relative to Dyirbal taxonomy, classical binomial taxonomy in biology has a high degree of analyticity. With its descending hierarchy of domains (kingdom, phylum, class, order, family, genus, species), species were classed according to what could be observed as their most general traits, such as eutheric/metatheric gestation and endothermy/ectothermy. More recent phylogenic taxonomies demonstrate an even higher degree of analyticity, often discounting common phenotypical traits in favor of relationships based upon genetic similarity, DNA being considered a more general domain in living creatures. But we needn't see an increase in analyticity as necessarily running parallel to the march of scientific progress. As ecological systems are increasingly understood not just as epiphenomena of climate and geography but as complex assemblages with a broad range of important actors, classification based upon *ecotypes* is becoming prominent. Ecotype classification, in turn, often relies upon folk taxonomies (sometimes coming from endangered languages like some of those we've looked at in this chapter), bearing a lower degree of analyticity.

Chapter 6
The Dynamic Lives of Languages and Genres

> *And when I am formulated, sprawling on a pin,*
> *When I am pinned and wriggling on the wall,*
> *Then how should I begin [...]*
>
> T.S. Eliot

As I argued in the last chapter, it simply won't do to think of reference as being at the heart of language, nor even as being central to language's relationship to knowledge. Everywhere, reference plays a subordinate role to communication and epistemic organization, both of which work through grammar and genre. Correspondingly, the most interesting relationship in language, as with knowledge systems in general, is between analogicity and analyticity. But of course, when reference is at the heart of language, as it has been in the philosophy of language since the early twentieth century, the most interesting and fundamental distinction is between analytic and synthetic propositions. This is true whether the distinction is to be maintained (e.g Carnap) or denied (e.g. Quine). As I discussed in the last chapter, even Quine held on to the dream of moving from known referents to knowable syntheses with his idea of atomizing experience for empirical observation. In stronger versions of what I call *analytic-synthetic reification* (ASR), referents would be analytic by virtue of synonymic necessity. In even stronger versions, the mind itself is considered to be a system of modular domains to which all referents and relational possibilities between referents can be mapped. What is common to all instances of ASR is that even if all possible knowledge is infinite, it is generated from the combination of limited, atomistic, self-same referents. This is a very convenient description of epistemic generation because it contains within it a means of epistemic justification. If you can combine two analyzed referents into a proposition, such as "All bachelors are messy men," all you need to do is check to see if the predicate *are* [...] should be in the *on* or *off* position, since a) there is no included middle in analytical logic (nothing outside of [*all*] *are* and [*all*] *are not*) and b) *are* refers to an absolutely singular mode of existence irrespective of the object that actually exists. Neither assumption about the predicate is internally justified, however. There is no reason, in other words, to assume that $p \neg p$ is necessary and that objects do not share in their own predication.

What's more, ASR fails to describe how knowledge actually emerges. In ASR, objects may or may not be real, but in any case, they are objects of knowledge. There seems to be no room for knowledge objects, since all knowledge is reducible either to relations of synonymy, abstract domains, or the non-being of an act (as is the case for Sellars). Even under such a reductive regime, a *knowing* should at least be an event, if not an object capable of interacting with other objects. And in the more immediate, sociological reality of knowledge generation, we can see that concepts interact with each other differently, depending upon grammatical obligations, cultural traditions, and genres of communication Again, this is not to assert that knowledge can be reduced to all of those things we associate with culture (even those things we associate with culture cannot be reduced to culture), but those things do create organizing entities which in turn play a significant role in the enabling and constraining of new knowledge objects.

Ludwig Wittgenstein famously turned away from his earlier work in the logical analysis of language for a view of language that puts context in front of reference. Wittgenstein's later philosophy, along with J.L. Austin's *speech act* philosophy, formed the cornerstone of what would become the poststructuralist and postmodernist philosophies of language and knowledge. What appealed to thinkers such as Derrida and Lyotard was the notion that the representation of ideas is but a substrate in the overall linguistic function and that language, as it actually works, both structures and performs social functions. And, as it is so deeply woven into the fabrics of social structures, language is never power-neutral. Localized examples of this include the asymmetrical divisions of signs, such as *master/mistress* and *steward/stewardess*. In his *Postmodern Condition*, Lyotard theorized language performativity at more global level, weaving it into a historical analysis of knowledge-making institutions. Lyotard pointed out, for instance, that there was a profound connection between the increasing price tag of doing science and the evolution of truth conditions. Even back in 1979, when Lyotard wrote his *"rapport sur le savoir,"* the nation-state was being eclipsed as the primary client for scientific research. Science, instead, was answering directly to multiple, private clients who had the capital to invest in costly research, provided of course that there would be a calculable return on the investment.[414] And indeed, two years after Lyotard published his report, the United States congress passed the Bayh-Dole Act, allowing even publicly funded universities to retain licensure of intellectual properties and negotiate directly with corporate clients. This broke down a lot of barriers to the flow of capital into research, but it also raised a lot of barriers to knowledge flow between institutions and between researchers, which itself has made research even more costly. One of the effects of this trend, Lyotard argued, was that the project of constructing universal truth conditions in scientific discourse would be abandoned in favor of epistemic performativity.[415] In other words, if knowledge could successfully be turned into capital, then it needed no logical or social justification. His argument about the fragmentation of scientific discourse fed into Lyotard's more famous argument about the dissolution of the *grand narratives* of the nation-state, dialectical materialism, etc. All of this, of course, got washed out into popular culture as the postmodern denial of truth and progress (we're all living in opaque language boxes, etc.).

What's relevant to the epistemology of language is the idea that language, as it actually happens, is fragmented into various *language games* (á la Wittgenstein) which are governed more by conventions than by codified rules, and that those language games structure and are structured by a matrix of ideology and social institutions, and that furthermore any attempt at a metalanguage of truth conditions will invariably be steeped in this matrix. This argument has been summarized and caricatured a million times in the past few decades, and in the interest of brevity, I am no doubt adding to the caricature. It should be clear that, *contra* the postmodernists, I am all for reintroducing metaphysical realism to language and epistemology, but I do not want to discard Lyotard's critique of knowledge production in the process. It is perfectly consistent, in other words, to recognize that discursive conventions play a decisive role in the production of legitimate knowledge (and the exclusion of illegitimate knowledge) while forwarding a metaphysical argument, even if that metaphysical argument is itself caught up in a given set of discursive conventions. We have, in the past, been given precisely two options with regards to language and truth, both of which turn out to be mere means of escape: We could either escape language, rendering its idiosyncrasies (with all the epistemic and poetical possibilities therein) down to analyzable, referential appendages, or we could escape from truth into language. Language, we've been led to believe, is either epiphenomenal of the mind or of the world (whether that be the natural or the social world). But the truth is that language is saturated with objects with realities like those of objects everywhere. And in order to say something about language's relationship to knowledge, we must descend (or ascend) to the level of objects.

Genres

Outside of philosophy itself, the field of composition studies has done more than any other discipline in the academy to take up the challenge that poststructuralist/postmodernist thinking has put to the epistemology of language. The field as we know it has really only been around since the early 1960s, having been accompanied by the influx of students to colleges and universities as a result of the G.I. Bill in the United States. From the late 1970s until quite recently, the dominant school of thought in the field had been what is called *Process Pedagogy*. The Process movement grew out of a discontent with traditional writing pedagogies, which emphasized the identification and correction of error and the imitation of best practices in writing. The result was that students in writing classes were doing a whole lot of proofreading and reading a lot of literature.

Indeed, teaching composition was commonly seen as a sort of purgatory for literature scholars who could not get a literature post after graduate school. Unsurprisingly, women formed the majority of this workforce. Composition was and still very much is a gravy boat for universities, who suck up enormous amounts of surplus value from the largely contingent workers who teach it. Given the dissatisfaction with the pedagogy and the perceived lack of disciplinary legitimacy, composition scholars began to take up methods from psychology and linguistics to create new knowledge about writing in order to (in Kuhnian terms) effect a paradigm that would bring about normal science practices. Instead of gathering anecdotal information from successful writers, scholars of the Process movement went to study what student writers actually do. One of the most important findings to come from this research was that writers discover and develop arguments well into the writing process, rather than as a result of brainstorming and outlining ahead of time. The pedagogical application of this research was then to intervene at various stages of the writing process, to focus on the process instead of the product. With this research program came a sort of generative grammar of writing, in which a simple draft with a few key ideas recurses into a more complex piece of writing. Generative principles were applied even at the sentence level, where students practiced sentence combining, or the embedding of sentences as clauses into other sentences in order to create a more complex thought.

Influenced in part by Lyotard's theory of epistemic production and its relation to Wittgensteinian language games, compositionists have, in the past couple of decades, called into question the ontology of writing. Whereas the Process movement located the ontology of writing in a kind of grammar (which includes and supersedes linguistic grammar), the so-called *Post-Process* movement finds the real being of writing at the level of genre. The idea is that writing is just as much an act of interpretation as it is generation. The interpretation of an audience's needs and expectations has been central to writing pedagogy since the beginning of composition studies; however, the interpretation of and action within the occultic rules of a given language game is a relatively recent emphasis. The practical argument behind genre-centered pedagogy is that you cannot simply bootstrap your way up from a standard freshman composition essay to a lab report, an executive summary, or an academic journal article with a single set of principles. Likewise, there is no universally recognized discourse of truth to draw upon in the production of legitimate knowledge. Making a set of claims and backing them up with evidence in a well-organized fashion is not enough. Legitimate knowledge, according to the Post-Process philosophy, is not only composed but performed within the conventions of a given genre. Performing speech or writing within a genre is an interpretive process and not a formal procedure because even genres with a relatively stable form, such as the scientific research paper, are packed to the gills with conventions and fuzzy boundaries that go far beyond any basic layout of sections and citation rules.

Pedagogical responses to this new disciplinary paradigm are varied. One approach, which fits in rather well with the neoliberal philosophy of higher education (in which the college is a white collar trade school), has students working straight away within a variety of professional genres, with competence being privileged over any explicit critique of institutional power structures in which writing genres are implicated. Other approaches are more critical, attempting to cultivate a sort of metacognitive language with which to reflect upon one's interaction with genres and the institutions with which they are associated.

I've surely betrayed my preference in the above description of the two approaches, but there must be a further subdivision in the critical approach. There is a very good argument to be made for a materialist analysis of genres and their relationship to knowledge production. One of the things Lyotard picked up on all the way back in 1979 was the rapid convergence of capital upon information. The mobility of and capacity for the storage and processing of digital information were growing exponentially, smashing barrier after barrier to the flow of capital. This in combination with the fragmentation and corporatization of knowledge production further dissolved the distinction between information and other commodities like cars or corn. The commoditization of information, of course, has a recursive effect on the development of information technologies. And with the development of information technologies comes new economic sectors, academic disciplines, social networks, forms of entertainment, political organizations, crimes, wars, all of it. All of these things bring with them an explosion in communication genres. New modes of communication create new opportunities to extract value from workers, as in the insistence, in some professions, that one be responsive to e-mail and texts well beyond the hours of the workday. New modes of communication also provide the opportunity to extract information capital directly, as in the conducting of market research from social networking activity and the exploiting of the production of new idioms for advertising material. The genres on which all of this information traverses play an important part both in the disciplining of communicative action and in the innovation of new action. Once again, there is a recursive component in all of this, as those genres will be affected by the material constraints of their media (e.g. textual limits and visual accessibility).

As a way of analyzing the effects of the relationships between capital, information technology, media, and communication genres, a materialist approach makes a lot of sense, and indeed it's a good launching point for theorizing resistance to the kinds of exploitation that accompany these relationships.[416] But if you want to look at how genres themselves move and affect the production and legitimation of new knowledge, you must go down (or up) to the level of objects.

I have already discussed at some length the relationship between analogical movement and analytical structure in grammar, a relationship that can only be understood within an object-oriented framework. The reader will not be surprised, then, when I suggest something similar about genres. But first, a word about the distinction between grammars and genres. I've already used the term *grammar* way more loosely than a lot of linguists would be comfortable with. In addition to speaking about grammar in terms of basic syntactical concerns like predicate-argument structure, I've also extended it to structures like the Tuvan onomatopoetic grammar. Mikhail Bakhtin, whose work in many ways paralleled that of his contemporaries in the West, Wittgenstein and Austin—and who is generally regarded as the founder of modern genre theory—offers a pretty good distinction. Bakhtin draws a line between sentence and grammar on the one hand, and utterance and genre on the other.[417] Whereas the ostensible content of a grammatical sentence and a generic utterance may overlap, they are, Bakhtin argues, different in form. For one, the boundaries are different. The important boundaries for a sentence are not those which mark the beginning and the end of the sentence, but the internal boundaries between phrases and between clauses. This makes good sense when we think about sentence recursion (N.B.: Bakhtin did not discuss this explicitly). Take the following constructions:

> My rabbit gets along fine with dogs. She doesn't care for guinea pigs, however.
> My rabbit, who doesn't care for guinea pigs, gets along fine with dogs.

The two constructions are pretty similar in meaning, though, of course, the first is composed of two sentences and the second is just one sentence with embedding. The main difference is not meaning or context but the location of phrases and then of clauses. Each construction, on the other hand, no matter how it is put together, may constitute a single utterance. The boundaries "of each concrete utterance as a unit of speech communication are determined by a *change of speaking subjects*, that is, a change of speakers."[418] We should not be thinking, however, that utterances exist only when interlocutors are physically present to each other:

> Any utterance—from a short (single word) rejoinder in everyday dialogue to the large novel or scientific treatise—has, so to speak, an absolute beginning and an absolute end: its beginning is preceded by the utterances of the others, and its end is followed by the responsive utterances of others (or, although it may be silent, others' active responsive understanding, or, finally, a responsive action based on this understanding).[419]

Finally, any grammatical construction operating within an utterance is selected for style based upon that dialogic context or genre:

> There is not a single new phenomenon (phonetic, lexical, or grammatical) that can enter the system of language without having traversed the long and complicated path of generic-stylistic testing and modification.[420]

If we buy into Wray's notion of morphosyntactic objects being drawn from formulaic lexical chunks (and I do), then Bakhtin's argument about linguistic emergence is pretty spot on. But just because the emergence of utterances and the selection (and occasional emergence) of grammatical objects is dialogical, that does not mean that there is a sort of "clunk causality"[421] going on. There is no sense in which the chain of utterances realizes itself in contradictions, as in "I said this and so she said that and so I said this and so…" Indeed, Bakhtin is careful to distinguish his dialogical philosophy from the "monologism" of Hegelian dialectics.[422] The response of one utterance to another does not unfold as one *after* another. Utterances do not only affect each other, they are also always-already being affected by genre, which means that the generic effect on a response may affect the utterance being responded to before the response utterance is uttered. Take the storytelling genre in Panare (a Cariban language spoken in southern Venezuela), for instance. The burden of working within generic conventions is not put to the storyteller alone. The listener is expected to interpolate periodically with an "Ummm."[423] This is not simply an affirmation of the listener's attentiveness, but an integral part of the story's rhythm. The form of any utterance within the story is therefore affected by its response before the response joins the utterance chain. We may say then that a genre's effects are distributed rather than ordered, which of course fits in pretty well with Morton's description of a hyperobject. What we can also say is that the utterances do not begin entirely at their beginning. They also begin at their middle, which means that they, like other objects, share in their own predication.

It should once again be emphasized that grammar is not a stable set of principles that form recombinant sentences to accomplish the goal of an utterance. The relationship between grammar and genre is often one of convergence as much as it is one of divergence. As William Salmon argues, the similarities between *construction grammar* and genre may be more than coincidental. Construction grammar deals with grammatical phenomena at the periphery of standard syntactical patterns that generative grammarians might consider innate. A construction grammar, Salmon explains,

> can be considered a bundle of information which limits the potential surface forms of the construction as well as a range of other information, potentially including pragmatic and usage information, semantic and morphological information, prosodic information, functional restrictions, and so on, and

it can range in size and complexity from that of an individual word to a complex syntactic frame.[424]

This is almost a restatement of Bakhtin's definition for an utterance, minus the centrality of interlocution.

There are two go-to tropes that Chomsky employs in almost every public lecture on his linguistic theory. One involves Martians looking down on us earthlings and concluding that we all basically speak the same language. The other is the construction of a syntactically well-ordered sentence that also happens to be nonsensical. The most famous of these is "Colorless green ideas sleep furiously." The idea is that a sentence can make sense grammatically or seem right without any contextual or pragmatic considerations. It is supposed to demonstrate the independence of syntax from semantics, although Chomsky has also claimed, conversely, that semantics may be dependent upon syntax. But according to construction grammar, the opposite can be true. A sentence like "Him be a doctor!?"[425] if not syntactically off, is certainly strange morphologically. And yet it is perfectly sensible if adjacent to "He wants to be a doctor." Furthermore, a sentence may be both morphosyntactically right and wrong, depending upon the semantic contents of its predicate-argument structure:

> Liza sent Stan a book
> *Liza sent storage a book.[426]

Finally, for what it's worth, "Colorless green ideas sleep furiously" has become totally meaningful—and perhaps has even become a lexically chunked sequence—as it has been affected by the genre of the linguistics lecture. The point is that regardless of how exceptional their morphosyntactic structures are, certain constructions may be regularly selected to act in relation to a given genre. There cannot be a stable analytical distinction or a domainal hierarchy between grammatical sentences, utterances, and genres.

Linguistic and Generic Emergence

As objects, grammars and genres change in response to the effects of cultural and physical ecologies, but also to the effects they have upon themselves. I want to suggest then that the principle distinction between grammar and genre is less a matter of formal classification than it is a matter of speed. Deleuze and Guattari argue that "[s]peed and slowness, movement and rest, tardiness and rapidity subordinate not only the forms of structures but also the types of development."[427] Speed increases the number of connections between things and therefore the production of differences and therefore the production of forms. I would argue that relationships of speed must also be enabled by form in the first place and that it is similarities rather than outright differences that emerge, but the basic argument seems to me correct.

The most profound changes in a grammar come as a result of asymmetrical contact between on grammar and another. We can see this in the processes of koineization and creolization,[428] as opposed to the much more gradual and self-animating process of grammaticalization. Koineization and creolization, for instance, are often the products of conquest, enslavement, or cultural-economic hegemony. When there is a common interest between peoples, for instance, in religion or trade, a *lingua franca* may be used, although the particular language that gets selected as the lingua franca is usually the result of past or present asymmetries in political and/or economic power (as in the latinization of western Christendom). Lingua francas sometimes retain much of their morphosyntactic complexity, as in Russian's reign as a lingua franca in the territories stretching from Poland to Mongolia at the height of Soviet power. Other times a lingua franca gets simplified, as in the relatively simple grammar of the once powerful Persian (a lingua franca in Central Asia for the Arabs, the Mongols, and the Turks), which can be contrasted with its much more complex sibling, Dari, which itself continues to serve as a lingua franca in Afghanistan. But morphosyntactic simplification is at its most dramatic during the processes of koineization and creolization. There is an all-too-common assumption that koines and creoles are syntheses of two or more languages, but that's not really the case. They might maintain lexical items or even idiomatic constructions from various languages, but the grammar is single malt, as it were.

English, for instance, underwent koineization with the settlement of Vikings in England, and to this day English retains a whole lot of Norse words, including almost all of its *sk-* words. Remarkably, the

Norse contribution also includes the lexico-morphological *they* (and its derivatives), but beyond that, English did not import grammar from Old Norse so much as it changed in response to the contact itself. In the process of simplifying the language for adult learners, English began shedding elements like noun classes. For example, the dative case was dropped in favor of a separate, one-size-fits-all preposition like *to*. Again, it is important to stress that what happened here was not a synthesis. A lot of cool things came out of Norse immigration to England—as is well documented by the preeminent historians on the matter, Led Zeppelin— but it wasn't a jolly melting pot. The koineized English that emerged came about by the process of anamorphosis. What emerged was both Anglo-Saxon and not. Again, in anamorphosis, objects emerge not as syntheses, but as distortions of contacts with other objects. This distortive emergence is very evident when we compare different instances of creolization. In a synthetic view of creolization, we would expect that the most important factor in the formation of a creole would be the genetic distances between substrate languages and the superstrate language. But the most significant thing about genetic distance is that it plays a role in how quickly a new language emerges. When the languages in contact are close enough to be koineized (e.g. Old Norse and Old English) the process may take place over hundreds of years. In the case of ON and OE, speakers could functionally communicate without being truly bilingual. This only began to shift when Edred recaptured York for the English in 954. When genetic difference is great, however, as between languages like Ewe, Yoruba, Wolof, and English or French, the process is necessarily quicker. After genetic difference, the most important factor is the particular kind of contact substrate speakers have with the superstrate language. As Lumbsden argues, there are more and less "radical" creoles, depending upon the nature of the contact.[429] For instance, Haitian Creole is considered a more radical creole (resembles the superstrate French less) than is Louisiana Creole. This most likely has something to do with the fact that during French domination of the two areas, the African population on Saint Domingue was much larger than the French population, whereas in Louisiana, the number was about equal. Thus, "most of the Africans in [Saint Domingue] had fewer opportunities for personal interactions with native speakers of French than was the case for Africans in Louisiana."[430] Furthermore, because of this limited contact on Saint Domingue, the creole that emerged was much more important in its role as a lingua franca for newly arrived African slaves speaking a variety of mutually unintelligible languages.

Creolization shares similar features with the far slower and more generalized process of grammaticalization, such as phonological reduction. For example, in Crucian (the creole spoken on St. Croix), *You ain't want to go there?* (Do you want to go there?) becomes *You ain waan go deh?* with *want to* being reduced to *waan*.[431] Similarly, in the process of grammaticalization, English has moved from:

> I'm *going to* tell you the truth

to

> I'm *gonna* tell you the truth

to other dialect-specific forms, such as the Western Illinois

> I *mohn* tell you the truth.

In both creolization and grammaticalization, lexical items or chunks may also be reanalyzed for grammatical functions. Tok Pisin (a New Guinean creole), for instance, has taken the English formulaic sequence, *by and by*, transformed it into *bambai*, reduced it to *bai*, and turned it into a tense particle and then an aspect marker (habitual).[432] Certain kinds of *semantic bleaching* are common to the grammaticalization process as well. In many languages, words having to do with desire or intention get grammaticalized to express future tense. In Kalderash Romani future construction, for example, the verb *kam-* (to like) loses its inflection and moves to the front of the phrase:

> *Kamav* te piyav čai. [*I like* drinking tea.]
>
> *Kam* piyav ekh taxtai čai. [I'm *going to* drink a cup of tea.]

Similarly, in English, *will* has gone from the Old English *willa* [to wish/want] to serve as an auxiliary, except when used to describe or express volition.

What we see in examples like Tok Pisin's *bai* or English's *will* is both the anamorphosis of an object and a sort of isolation or closing off of the object. *Kam*, *willa*, and *by and by* created a distortion after repeated contact with constructions in which intension and temporal proximity were expressed. Neither was synthesized with existing future or habitual markers. As these distortions affected other objects *as objects*, the ways in which they affect them (e.g. as an auxiliary affects a verb) become some of the qualities by which they themselves were identifiable as objects. The qualities with which these objects are identified also become boundaries, precluding them from coming into proximity with certain kinds of objects. *Will* is less able to enter into a synthetic relationship with a direct object noun. The only way *I* (my affective capacities as an object are limited too) can wrest the auxiliary *will* from its position within a future construction (outside of its volitionary connotation) is to notice a similarity between, for instance, it and the Kalderash *kam* or between it and something that rhymes with it, like *pill*. Out of this contact comes something new (knowledge or action) that would be impossible inside of the object's analytic-synthetic relations.

We see some of the same anamorphic and isolating processes occurring in generic change. Again, if we follow Bakhtin's notion that genres consist of utterances and that utterances begin where others end, then a *turn* becomes an important component of a genre. The more formalized a genre is, the more formulaic generic turns tend to be. For instance, in American congressional proceedings, *I yield back the balance of my time* is a common turn, and in the courtroom, *Objection, your honor* is well known as an interpolating turn. In various social networking genres, *LOL* [Laugh Out Loud] can function as a turn both at the beginning and at the end of an utterance. *LOL* began in chat rooms as a contextualizing lexical item to indicate either sarcasm or that the previous utterance was funny or pleasing. Other items, such as *ROFL* [Rolling On the Floor Laughing] and *LMAO* [Laughing My Ass Off] were derived from *LOL*. *LOL*, however, has become both genericized and grammaticalized. With respect to its genericization, it functions as a turn, which may begin or end an utterance. And in concert with his larger argument that texting is "fingered speech," McWhorter contends that *LOL* has moved from a lexical item to a lexico-morphological structure, a particle that functions as a tag question, similar to the Japanese *ne* or the *yo* in African-American English.[433] As a matter of genericization, there is nothing extraordinary about a particular lexical item or construction becoming a regular feature of a genre within a couple of decades. But in grammatical time, it's lightning fast!

Genres may preserve certain language conventions long after they have become superannuated in other communication settings, as in the courtroom honorific, *your honor*. But genres may often accelerate linguistic changes, as in the case of *LOL*. Genres tend to move faster than grammars, and linguistic changes often hitch a ride. Those linguistic changes can become more generalized if the genre on which they travel comes into contact with other genres. This can be an uneven process because genres interact with specific communication settings. Amy Devitt, for example, has conducted a study of the decline of Scots-English in various writing genres from the years 1520 to 1659, as Scotland edged closer to its union with England. She looked in particular at the replacement of four morphological forms and one phonological form:

Anglo-English form *replacing*	Scots-English form
present particle inflection *–ing*	*-and*
negative particle *no/not*	*na/nacht*
indefinite article *a* before consonants and *an* before vowels	*ane* before all environments
preterite inflection *–ed*	*-it*
relative pronouns spelled with *wh-*	*quh-*[434]

The replacements were observed in five genre groupings: religious treatises, official correspondences, private records, private correspondences, and private records. The particular forms were replaced unevenly within genre groupings, with the present participle inflection *–and* being replaced by the Anglo-English *–ing* more rapidly than the other forms across genres. But in terms of overall replacement between genres, there was also a significant amount of unevenness, with replacement occurring at a much faster rate in religious treatises than in public records, which had not actually achieved full replacement in any of its forms at 1659.[435]

Of course, writing is not speech. Writing is a more deliberate mode of communication with more conscious selections of stylistic features than in speech. And clearly, varieties of Scots-English continue to differ significantly from those of Anglo-English to this day. However, there is evidence to suggest that the presence of certain kinds of literacy can affect speech in particularly generic speech situations.[436] Furthermore, although writing involves a more conscious selection of stylistic features, stylistic features are also chosen inside of speaking genres, so there is reason to believe that the kind of uneven changes Devitt observes in writing genres would be similarly uneven across a given set of speaking genres within a given frame of time. Devitt finds no explicit ideological motivation amongst individuals for the linguistic conservativism in the public record genres or for the rapid replacement that occurred in the religious treatises.[437] The difference seems to be a matter of contact. The concerns of the Scottish Privy Council became increasingly localized as Scottish and English political structures grew intertwined, whereas with the ascendency of James VI (James I of England) to the English throne there was a concerted effort to bring the Kirk closer to the Anglican Church.

In summary, grammaticalization is a relatively slow process unless it is accompanied by a catastrophic contact event like those associated with creolization. Otherwise, language changes can occur relatively quickly in the non-generalized setting of a genre. In order to become more generalized, a genre in which an innovation has occurred must come into contact with other genres, as chat room genres came into contact with texting genres. But as with my previous argument about koines and creoles, I want to assert that genres themselves do not emerge from the synthesis of existing genres, but rather by distortion and analogy. Genres are classic midlevel objects, existing between (but not reducible to) individual interactions and grammatical constraints on the one hand, and cultural, institutional, and technological contexts on the other.[438] Genres are not synthetic because there is never an identifiable domain by which all features of a genre can be named and reduced to analytical, self-same properties. As Salmon puts it in his comparison of genre to jazz:

> The mental object of the composition cannot surface in a state that is uninterrupted. If it is at play in the world, then it has come to be so through someone's interpretation or rendition of it. As with genre or the formal idiom, we don't have direct access to any abstract form or mental object: even

though it is through this that we can talk about "shared" in the first place.[439]

No particular utterance begins uninterrupted. An utterance itself is an interruption and it is presupposed by the interruption of it. Utterances begin amongst utterances and new genres begin at their middles.

As I have argued, grammars acquire stable, analytical features by the action of a complex, recursive system consisting of several types of analogies. The capacity to build such analytical features increases with neural entrainment, which itself works by repetition of similarity. Genres too may develop analytical features that serve to segment and order generic utterances. These analytical features appear as formal structures, such as typified subsections and turns. However, knowledge of a given set of analytical features of a genre has very little generative power as compared with implicit knowledge of a grammar's analytical features because genres are situation specific. One must discover by interpretation the kind of communicative situation she finds herself in, interpretively select the appropriate genre for the situation, and then interpret the constraints of the genre itself. This triple interpretation process itself varies in its degree of analyticity. The situation of a workplace accident will likely be accompanied by a well ordered procedure and a standard form, though even within these structures, the employee will find herself guessing at how to narrate the particulars of the incident, feeling perhaps obliged to eliminate inconsistencies among multiple accounts and assigning some sort of blame for what happened. In order to do this, the employee must make decisions such as what kind of narrative agency she should use in the report. In order to enact these decisions, she may make analogies from existing reports or from the language of the accident report form itself. More often, the interpretive triplet of a communicative situation has far less analyticity, however, than when one is asked to write a message on a sympathy card for someone she barely knows or when she finds herself communicating on an unfamiliar medium. Here, the reliance on analogy is much greater. And again, because the analytical features of any genre do not have a lot of generative power, one cannot simply synthesize those features from other genres in order to communicate within the new genre. There's got to be something gestalty about communicating within genres, and within new genres in particular. In making analogies between what Devitt calls an *antecedent genre*[440] and a new genre, antecedent genres must be taken as the whole, midlevel objects they are. That's the only way anything is available in an analogy. And the greater amount of analogicity required to invent and to communicate inside of a genre, the more distortion there will be, and the more quickly changes and, eventually, new genres will emerge.

Chapter 7
Form and Knowledge

Both grammar and genre affect the production and organization of knowledge. They emerge at different speeds as complex systems of analogies that assemble more or less stable analytical structures. New sentences and utterances appear to be generated through the synthesis of analytic structures, but such syntheses are not in fact at the beginning of language and communication. Fields of enquiry too appear to be set up to synthesize new knowledge from known, analytical structures that constitute epistemic domains whose only exterior is the field of knowable facts that correspond to reality. But this does nothing to explain the emergence of new objects around which fields of enquiry are created. New objects radical enough to initiate a new field of enquiry and new methodologies may, as Thomas Kuhn argued,[441] come out of anomalies in existing procedures of epistemic production. They may also originate in radical analogies, as in Yukawa's meson physics or in Felix Haussdorff's imagining of fractional spatial dimensions by analogy with arithmetical dimensions (giving rise to Mandelbrot's fractal objects).[442] Or they may by shaped by negative analogy, the effects of a nonlocal, excluded object like Foucault's madness. In either case, new objects of enquiry do not come into a field of enquiry by the same synthetic methods used to make knowledge about objects that are already given to the field.

Concepts and Domains

In Nietzsche's critique of language and knowledge, he gives us the concept *leaf* as an example of the way in which knowledge comes at the expense of discarding the singularities of objects within the conceptual domain. This, according to Nietzsche, leads us to forget that the concept *leaf* did not actually come before the multiple experiences of leaves.[443] Not only does this forgetting cause our knowledge of things to be "drained of its sensuous force,"[444] but it also means that out knowledge of things (by way of concepts) is subjected to human power relations before we can even speak of our experiences of things. The truth of something, therefore, always resides in a domain that humans have synthesized, always excluding the truth of the experience of the thing:

> If I make up the definition of a mammal, and then, after inspecting a camel, declare "look, a mammal," I have indeed brought a truth to light in this way, but it is a truth of limited value. This is to say, it is a thoroughly anthropomorphic truth which contains not a single point which would be "true in itself" or really and universally valid apart from man.[445]

That we forget this and assume that there is a true correspondence between the domains we have synthesized and what is common and self-same to the things we place inside those domains is, for Nietzsche, a scandal. The drive to create such universalizing concepts is an inescapable part of human nature, Nietzsche argues, so the only remedy for the forgetting and anthropomorphizing is to continually produce new metaphors and transferences so as to constantly threaten our own universalizing tendencies with irregularity and instability. That, of course, would be the job of art.

It is true that the domainization of knowledge always involves a subtraction of being, just as the metaphysics of representation does. The analyzed properties of a thing synthesized into a domain must be self-same in order to be iterable, in order for a domain to house $n+1$ individuals. A domain with only one individual is no domain at all because if there were a 1:1 correspondence between the domain and the individual member, then the individual would presumably be identical to the domain, which would mean that the domain would lose its being as an abstraction and would therefore no longer be able to be put into play with other domains in an analytical system. We have already seen Badiou's solution to this problem, which is to include the Ø with each denumerable individual. Since Ø can never be self-same, no individual is truly 1:1 in and of itself, which means that each individual is also a domain. Domains, then, are no longer subtracted from being.

Otherwise, in order to bring a domain into its proper $n+1$ existence, the singular beings of things have got to be subtracted from the synthesis of their self-same properties. Multiple cows' udders must be subtracted in the concept domain *udder*, and human breasts and cows' udders must be subtracted in the concept domain *mammary gland* so that there are only repeated, self-same instances of the analytical concept of the domain. But this subtraction of being is not a gross subtraction of knowledge. A stable system of domains is a sort of dynamic equilibrium. If a new thing enters a field of enquiry—say, Nietzsche's camel—its own being will be discarded in favor of its analyzable properties which will be assumed to be shared amongst all camels. Let's say those properties of the camel are endothermy, mammary glands, and humps. The predicates of *endothermy* and *mammary glands* are not altered within the domain *mammal*, but the concept *hump* forces a decision on the domain *mammal*. *Hump* cannot be a synthesizable predicate for *mammal* because not all mammals have humps, so either *hump* must become a subdomain of *mammal* or *mammal* must become a subdomain of something else. Either decision will immediately result in new knowledge, but the stability of the analytical system constituting the domain *mammal* was a necessary precondition for the event of the decision to emerge.

Synthetic thinking is always potentially productive in this way so long as it excludes lateral movement between domains (the kind that can be seen in some analogies). The exclusion of lateral movement between domains is also its weakness, for it discourages the imagining of new kinds of objects in a cosmology. Thus, in Yukawa's case, the force holding together the atomic nuclei was assumed to match the properties of an electron-neutrino exchange pair, as it was known that a neutron could decay (beta decay) into a proton, an electron, and a neutrino. The only new thing that could be imagined in the synthetic approach was a new combination of existing, self-same properties. Obviously, it was an intractable problem until Yukawa imagined a lateral movement, a distortion of the idea of the photon, out of which emerged the idea of the meson. Of course, Yukawa's meson became part of a hierarchical domain of force carrier particles, but it contributed to the instability of the existing analytical system, an instability that allowd for the proliferation of new particles.

Included Exclusions

In synthetic thinking, new knowledge is created in one of two ways. Most commonly, existing analytical properties are synthesized into a new domain. This is the rational construction of knowledge. But the impetus might be empirical as well. Here, new knowledge is forced upward from a newly observed object or a mathematical or logical anomaly to the furthest domain that will be affected. Think of camels and mammals. The idea here is that the primary domain with which a field of enquiry is concerned is always given until something in the world changes that. Rational synthesis, in turn is pressed into service to solve the problems of the empirical. This gives rise to a historical sense of rationality in which our knowledge is in continuous convergence with the world as it really is. Synthetic thinking is therefore tied to progressive incrementalism. This view was challenged in different ways by Kuhn and Foucault, who argued that epistemic movement begins at the level of discourse and not in the relationship between epistemic domains and real particulars (although Kuhn allowed that a real anomaly could be the impetus for discursive change).

Discursive change, for Foucault, begins with an included exclusion, such as *madness*, which interacts with various normative institutions (family, work, religious communities, etc.) in different ways and at different times. Those things that register as deviances within those normative institutions coalesce into a single object around which a field of enquiry takes shape (*pace* Foucault: "discourse"). Thus, the primary domain with which a field concerns itself is neither given nor discovered as an object in the world. It is distributed across multiple "surfaces of appearance" before coalescing into a natural object about which empirical knowledge can be produced. In the nineteenth century, according to Foucault, the excluded object (madness) was included in various fields thusly:

> art with its own normativity, sexuality (its deviations in relation to customary prohibitions become for the first time an object of observation, description and analysis for psychiatric discourse), penality (whereas in previous periods madness was carefully distinguished from criminal conduct and was regarded as an excuse, criminality itself becomes—and subsequent to the celebrated "homicidal monomanias"—a form of deviance more or less related to madness). In these fields of initial differentiation, in the distances, the discontinuities, and the thresholds that appear with it, psychiatric discourse finds a way of limiting its domain, of defining what it is talking about, of giving it the status of an object—and therefore of making it manifest, namable, and describable.[446]

For Foucault, the ways in which an exclusion is distributed across discourses itself constitutes a particular regime of knowledge, one that could not simply be assigned to a period following a theoretical sea change or a massive overhaul in modes of production or political regime. Thus, a positively defined epistemic period, such as 'the quantum age' (in which we are sometimes said to be living currently) would not be sufficient to explain the real motivations and truth conditions of the period's knowledge practices.

The range of topics and historical settings that Foucault addressed in the span of his "archeological" period (from 1963's *Birth of the Clinic* to 1975's *Discipline and Punish*) was truly staggering. And yet, he admitted that in choosing to focus on madness and psychiatry, he was actually setting the bar low. He believed the application of the same methods to other sciences, such as physics or organic chemistry would be "excessively complicated,"[447] though *The Order of Things* seemed to have been a gesture in this direction. But we can at least speculate on the effects of the distribution of included exclusions in other knowledge-making practices. It seems to me that particular kinds of metaphysics are also included as exclusions across knowledge-making practices, though they never constitute a specific object of study in the way madness does for Foucault. We're used to thinking of a metaphysics as positively shaping areas of scientific enquiry. We can think, for instance, of Aristotle's metaphysics of species and genus, and its effects on biology right up to the Darwinian revolution. There is no doubt too that Newton's physics was not only positively shaped by the metaphysics of corpuscularianism, but even by his own unconventional theology as well. But as much as, for example, corpuscularianism can be defined positively, it is also a negative metaphysics. Corpuscularianism replaces the matter-form pair with a matter-force pair, and as such it involves the denial of the Aristotelian version of substance, specifically the geocentric view of gravity in which identical elements within objects are attracted to their natural place. We can therefore say that the apocryphal story of the apple falling from the tree was all about excluding the apple itself.

Likewise, we can see another included metaphysical exclusion in knowledge-making practices up to the current moment, across disciplines. What is excluded from physics to biology to economics is *design*. Evangelical atheists like Richard Dawkins and Sam Harris would obviously like us to believe that this is all about the replacement of superstition of the divine with reason, but the truth is that outside of debates about science education, God has very little to do with it at this point. Not every evolutionary biologist is an atheist, and there are certainly a lot of God-fearing economists who must exclude design in their fields of enquiry in order for those fields to be epistemically productive. It is not the designer who must be excluded, but also any organizational structure that could in any way be analogized to the logic of either a divine or a human designer. We can think of the exclusion of design as a manifestation of post-theism or posthumanism, but as a matter of fact, the function of this exclusion is both to preserve the autonomous otherness of nature and to maintain science as an autonomous, universalizing discourse, to free it from history even as its discoveries are empowered to make history.

In liberal economics, the absence of design delimited both descriptive and prescriptive knowledge, although this was not a total exclusion of design, since the order of the market was linked to a moral order which was manifested in transcendent reason. But as Foucault argues, the liberal trajectory is one that moves from justice to truth, with the market as the ground on which veridical principles are established:

> In other words, it is the natural mechanism of the market and the formation of natural prices that enables us to falsify

and verify governmental practice when, on the basis of those elements, we examine what government does, the measures it takes, and the rules it imposes. In this sense, in as much as it enables production, need, supply, demand, value and prices, etcetera, to be linked together through exchange, the market constitutes a site of veridiction, I mean a site of verification-falsification for governmental practice.[448]

Government is thus designed and succeeds/fails according to a separate, autonomous entity against which the design can be tested. In regimes of neoliberalism, however, government is to be fully integrated into the market by means of deregulation and privatization. The market is no longer an independent measuring stick for governmental design: the government should *be* the market and the market is its own design (i.e. order without design). It's a chiasmus worthy of a bad Yakov Smirnoff joke, really.

Neoliberal governance is a very visible example of the exclusion of design being integrated into the techniques of design. But we can see this too in technologies of artificial intelligence and in the designing of other tools. For one, the exclusion of design is closing the gap between neural science and cognitive science. Humanities-minded types are often scandalized by the claims of contemporary neurophilosophers who see the inevitable reduction of subjective experience to physical processes. But these sorts of claims are far from new, and I suspect that we'll always find ways of talking about consciousness, qualia, intuition, etc. as being phenomenal, despite any advances in neuroscience and artificial intelligence. What is more significant is the replacement of the modular epistemology of the mind with a nodular understanding. This is visible in the shift in metaphors about the mind, from *language* to *computer* to metaphors of complex systems, such as the *connectdome*.

The understanding of the mind as *language* was part of the early-to-mid twentieth century convergence of psychology, anthropology, and linguistics that would subsequently ride by the handle *structuralism*. Here, the dyad of the sign and the negative identity of the signifier became the epistemic prototype in the human sciences. And language, after all, was supposed to be uniquely and intrinsically human. Language in its formal, ideal state (the kind by which mathematics had hoped to establish its own consistency and truth conditions) was the starting point for modern digital computers. In a Turing machine, each symbol possesses a discrete, negative value, which represents a given state of an operation. The machine moves according to algorithmic *if/then* rules matching the binary values of the symbols (1, 0). The states of an operation can themselves be assigned discrete, binary values, which means that the operations of one machine can themselves become encoded as a program of another machine in a recursive fashion.[449] The forms of the algorithmic instructions of such programs and the relationships between input and output can be described in terms of *syntax* and *semantics*. And not long after the dawn of the digital age, the mind (along with its linguistic capacities) was being described as a computer, complete with discrete units or modules and separate functions for memory and processing. Thus, digital processing was informed by a formal understanding of language, and then digital processing was folded back into the epistemology of language, moving *language* as the organizing metaphor for the mind to the *computer* as the organizing metaphor for the mind.

With the functional and symbolic union of the computer and the mind, possibilities for artificial intelligence and language translation programs emerged. But the computer as an object of human design is beginning to prove inadequate to the task. The mind, as it turns out, is not a collection of independently ruled modules but a complex system of nodular connections forming networks of unevenly distributed sizes and strengths. It appears as well that there is no firm exclusion of information processing from memory retrieval, as there is in the digital computer. The emergent designs of an ant bridge or a weather system are beginning to look like better models and metaphors for the mind than the computer. Just as language was folded into the computer model of the mind, it looks like any advances in AI will involve the folding of the mind-as-complex-system into computational machines.

The Return of Design

Some of the leading figures in the Intelligent Design movement are not actually biologists, but are, like William Demski, mathematicians. Probability has been the most potent weapon in ID's arsenal in its battle with Darwinism. There is a massive asymmetry between the quantity of phenotypic traits that actually exist in life and the number of possible combinations of amino acids that, in turn, form proteins. By undesigned, random mutation alone, the chances that an organism would develop any particular protein, let alone a beneficial one, are astounding. You don't have to be a young earther to see that life simply has not been around long enough for evolution to be a completely random process. People in the ID movement did not invent this problem for Darwinian evolution, but they have certainly made it socially relevant enough to prompt scientific investigation that is necessarily restricted to a non-ID solution. Once again, we see that an included exclusion can be epistemically productive.

The solution that seems to be surfacing involves a certain kind of design, although this one is the emergent, self-similar design of a complex system. First of all, we need to call into question our received distinctions between randomness, probability, and design. As Andreas Wagner points out, randomness is thought of as being the *equiprobability* of a given set of outcomes for an event.[450] Probability is the ascertainable non-equiprobability of outcomes, and design is a predictable relationship between input and output based upon constraints that have been imposed from outside the system. While genetic inheritance is a probable event, genetic mutation has been seen as a random event. Furthermore, a mutation event coupled with the chances that the mutation will affect the survival and reproductive chances of an organism may be seen as a double-random event. Wagner, however, argues that even mutation events are at least affected by context and probability:

> For example, some [nucleotide] bases are methylated, which influences their propensity to mutate; so does the active replication of DNA, which favors certain kinds of point mutations over others; and the DNA strand ("top" or "bottom") of the double-stranded DNA helix in which a base occurs also influences the kind of changes that this base can undergo […] The list could go on and on.[451]

Thus, randomness—

> as a deviation from a prior expectation—is a property not just of a natural phenomenon but also of our knowledge about this phenomenon. As our knowledge increases, this expectation may change. Nonrandomness is a moving target. Whether

> we call mutations in genotypes random may depend on our knowledge about genotypes and the mechanisms behind their change.[452]

We see here a major departure from the Enlightenment narrative of rationality, which begins from the assumption that a natural phenomenon is designed as a whole but that as our knowledge about it increases, the phenomenon is described as mechanically ordered (according to laws of interaction) or as a random process. Thus, existing design or architecture is to be seen as mere sensuous impression or even superstition, whereas descriptions of mechanical order and randomness are products of rational investigation which produce knowledge that corresponds more closely with reality as it is. But could it be that randomness is every bit as much of a sensuous quality as is design?

The difference in the conceptions of design between those in the ID movement and those, like Wagner, in evolutionary developmental biology (or "evo-devo") is that in the former the work of an external designer is apparent, and in the latter design is inherent in the form of the system. Perhaps with a long enough view, the two needn't be mutually exclusive, but the evo-devo description certainly does not need an external designer. I would argue, however, that what *is* presupposed in the evo-devo description is the reality of similarity. Wagner imagines a Borgesian library that contains every possible combination of letters. The vast majority of these combinations would appear as gibberish, but also present would be all the novels ever written, all novels that could ever be written, as well as all ideas that have or could have ever been uttered. Under conditions of total randomness, the time it would take to get from one book to, say, *War and Peace* would be immeasurably vast.[453] But, at least in terms of biological evolution, there exist networks of similar genetic configurations and similar phenotypes that allow for either rapid, small substitutions or for dramatic innovations. Phenotypes are self-similar, so "one can step from one genotype to its neighbor, to the neighbor's neighbor, and so on without ever changing a phenotype."[454] In the reverse, a genotype network can also be self-similar with respect to the different phenotypes it affects, so

> the neighborhood of any two genotypes on the same genotype network […] contains very different novel phenotypes. This

means that even if two genotypes differ only modestly, their neighborhoods do not contain the same phenotypes.[455]

Thus, as opposed to an analytic-synthetic system where discrete genotypical configurations (randomly assembled) synthesize discrete phenotypes, we have a messier analog system in which change can be rapid and continuous but in which there is less disparity between noise and information (i.e. between functional configurations and those we have previously thought of a junk or gibberish). As in Deleuzean metaphysics, change is entered into a state of asymmetry. But contrary to that metaphysics, there is not a 1:1 identity between the strata of coding and expression in genes, and between genotype and phenotype.[456]

The Return of Form

As I have argued, the modeling of the mind onto computational systems or robotics will most likely have to depart from the idea that a digital computer itself is an adequate model of the mind. For one, information processing and information retrieval are not discrete processes in the mind as they are in a digital computer. Second, as Hofstadter and Sander argue, the mind's most basic cognitive innovations do not come from categorical synthesis but rather from "slippage," which is an analogical phenomenon.[457] In other words, new categories are not created to subsume and differentiate new data; instead, categories are constantly engaged in playful imitation of one another. To this end, Hofstadter and Mitchell have developed the *Copycat* program which, like the Turing machine, began as a theoretical object.[458] Copycat works to model analogical slippage and to minimize the gap between cognition and perception, which is perhaps the biggest single obstacle to AI. One of the principles of Copycat is that intelligence need not be a spatially or principally localized phenomenon. Not only does this mean that AI needn't be modeled from the mind-as-computer but it needn't be modeled on the human mind at all.

The strongest competition to the human mind for an AI model comes from a most unlikely creature: the octopus. Biologists have been marveling at octopus intelligence for a long time now. Octopi are remarkably intelligent and inventive by any standard in the animal kingdom, which is all the more remarkable because, for one, they have a very short lifespan (a maximum of around five years), and for another, their neural system is highly distributed. When we think of an intelligent machine, we tend to visualize some sort of android or cyborg, or else we think of a massively intelligent central processing unit that has crossed the so-called "singularity" event horizon. Perhaps Watson, the mighty scourge of *Jeopardy!* champions, is the best nonfictional approximation. But in order to minimize the gaps between processing and retrieval, as well as those between cognition and perception, an octopus-like droid may offer the shortest distance, since for octopi, interpretation and response to an environment does not require synthesized messages to be sent to and returned from a central processor. Instead, distributed neural networks interpret and adapt to a particular situation in similar ways.

But the octopus's cognitive structure is not the only thing about it that intrigues engineers. The astounding jointless dexterity of the octopus's arms has also become an important model for robotics research, particularly as it applies to elastofluidic movement in which conforming to an environment and meaningfully acting within it are folding into one another.[459] Indeed, it may be the very elastofluidity of octopus kinesiology that holds the key to the close relationship between perception and cognition in its intelligence. Hydrostat robotics like the kind modeled on octopus kinesiology is part of a growing interest in monoform machine design: that is, machines that are not assembled from multiple parts. In traditional polyform machinery, the strength and functionality of a machine is located in the interaction of its parts, whereas in monoforms, strength and function are distributed nonlocally, thus making their affective power as objects more apparent.[460] There is a temptation to think about monoform machinery with the same futuristic, utopian enthusiasm that the geodesic dome was met with in the 1960s (think Epcot Center and hippy Volkswagen vans), but monoform design is converging on the rise of the 3-D printer, which—time will tell—may have some impact on the Fordist and Post-Fordist models of production, modes that have defined social organization for the past century. The owl of Minerva flies at dusk, etc., etc., and I'll speculate no further on this, except to say that our received notions of materiality—from Marx to Deleuze—have been crucially informed by the metaphysics and sociology of assembly, both of which complemented the centrality of analytic-synthetic thinking inherited from the Enlightenment. We take things to be animated, useful, or meaningful either because they have been assembled for a purpose or because they have been lifted out of the plenum to be entered into an assembly. When we look for origins, we look for synthesis. This is true for physical objects synthesized from particles of matter; it is true for epistemic objects synthesized as extensions of given spatial and temporal domains, and it is true for economies synthesized from interlocking human interests at the market. Sovereignty, once mythologized as a semi-autochthonous power vested in orphaned wolf-children, swords in stones, and dynastic blood, now emerges in the nation-state as a representative body synthesized from many political bodies. The only alternative to synthesis, it would seem, is emergence *ex nihilo*. Forms and their objects have been rendered epiphenomenal of their assembled materials. This makes sense in an era of polyform production because the dialectic of labor and value attached itself to the material of a product at each stage of its assembly, and so it was through material that the extraction of surplus value could most usefully be traced. Just as Slavoj Žižek does his parallax thing and calls himself a *Christian atheist*, it would be useful to begin thinking along the lines of a *Marxian amaterialism* in which the concepts of commodity, labor, time, and value could be posed about the production of form in an economy of unassembled production (which includes 3-D copying and information reproduction as well as affective labor).

Chapter 8
Marxian Amaterialism

Actually, it's not the matter that we must be "a-" about in our *amaterialism*; it is the mechanics of materialism. Marx's earlier arguments with the Young Hegelians rested on this complaint: the Young Hegelians, by merely secularizing the religious terms of the Old Hegelians (e.g. turning *Spirit* into *Man*), had failed to rationalize Hegel's system. In other words, the YHs were doomed to repeat the folly of the OHs so long as their secularized concepts merely stood on their own, without additional grounding. The YHs, argued Marx, were still tethered to the spirit of the Hegel they didn't like. As for this entity called *Man*, Marx could care less if you wanted to distinguish it from other forms of life by its consciousness or by its opposable thumbs or whatever else. (I'm paraphrasing, but Marx does dismiss this *Man* with a detectable and rather pleasing snarkiness.) The important thing about *Man* is as follows:

> They themselves begin to distinguish themselves from animals as soon as they begin to *produce* their own means of subsistence, a step which is conditioned by their physical organization. By producing their means of subsistence, men are indirectly producing their actual material life.[461]

In other words, it is in the production of the means of production when the bare materiality of living existence becomes joined to social existence. Social relations, at this point, are also material relations, and thus the life of social life (i.e. history) is material as well. The life of social life, therefore, is not presupposed by a subject, be it transcendental or radically multiple.[462] What we see here is not just the materiality of the life of social life, but the emergence of a new object *Man* by way of a formal transformation. It is the form of this object that becomes of interest for the material analysis of its relations. That's pretty spot-on, and it's not where the problem lies.

The problem lies at Hegel's own doorstep. Hegel had the same problem that the YHs had. He tried to consign mechanics to science and to the realm of appearances, purging it from the philosophical realm of the true. But just as the YH secularization of Hegel was cosmetic, Hegel's consignment of mechanics was, at best, incomplete. As I've discussed, the modern mechanical project, which began with corpuscularianism, was about replacing the form-matter pair with the force-matter pair. The point of doing this was to eliminate epistemic opacity, to simplify God's creation, to move knowledge away from the occult and towards the public. But the protestant ethos of simplicity and accessibility, it could be argued, was a vanishing mediator. The effect of the mechanical turn would be to oppose the unity of appearance to the real processes beneath it. Again, as Latour so eloquently describes it, the role of science (the mechanical science we have inherited) is to seek out the truth beyond the unified appearance which is present in our immediate relations with things. It is the very opposition between immediate presence and the contradiction-powered movement underneath that Hegel preserved in his dialectics, meaning that his rejection of mechanics was more or less superficial—probably the only thing superficial about Hegel, but it's a big one.

Materiality for mechanical science is not much different in its mode of existence from the more general Hegelian mode of being. We're used to thinking about science as being all about what can and cannot be observed. The eye of the subject is the star of the show, but it has a number of proxies, such as microscopes, sonograms, spectrometers, etc. Mathematical models, too, may serve as proxies. Materiality, it would seem, is all that may enter into a relationship with the eye or its proxies. Those things like ghosts and gods are excluded from that relationship, and are therefore immaterial, and are therefore-therefore not real. But that's not really it, is it? Materiality is not about the relationship between the observing subject (and its proxies) and the observable object, but about the unity of the observable object and the processes that effect that unity of appearance. As long as the oppositional relationship between appearance and process holds, we have materiality. Materialism and its scientific partners give the impression of progress because there is always a void to be chased after, just beyond the unity of appearance—the void that sutures appearance to process. Materialism is thus always projected into the future. So actually, ghosts shouldn't be such a problem for materialism. As long as we can imagine some process opposing itself to the appearance (e.g. the interaction of ectoparticles or some such thing), ghosts can be perfectly material. Gods or God, on the other hand, might have a more difficult time of it, particularly if we think of a god like that of Aquinas or even just the *eyeh asher eyeh* god of the burning bush, because such a god is simple existence, pure act. Mechanical and fully materialist science may value epistemic transparency (the Occam's Razor principle and all that), but it abhors simple things.

This is why the subject too is doomed in a materialist regime. The subject is not doomed because it is unobservable, but because it is simple. Thus, while psychoanalysis attempts to demystify the subject, self, mind, etc., it is simultaneously engaged in preserving the subject by eliminating its simplicity, by opposing its appearance to its processes. The mind need not be located in a particular, observable physical space in order for the oppositional relationship to hold, and therefore in order for the mental subject to be a material entity. And yet, even as the mental subject seems knowable and real by virtue of its analyticity, its analytical components and their movements too face the problem of simplicity. What, for instance, are the experiences of the Lacanian Imaginary? Surely, they too are divided between appearance and process. Deleuze and Guattari recognized this very problem in materialist psychoanalysis, and so they reversed the trajectory so that instead of looking beyond the unity of appearance for the void that sutures unity to process, they rejected the category of the negative altogether. For example, instead of positing a void on which the imaginary whole of woman/mother/etc. is predicated, the whole itself was a site of positive production. The simple unity of appearance was, therefore, not a necessary part of reality, and hence the interest in the schizophrenic subject. This was a brilliant maneuver, and it saves the materialist subject, but as I discussed earlier with regards to Harman's question, it leaves us with objects that do not endure beyond the interactions by which they emerged.

In an object-oriented framework, the simplicity of a thing poses no problem at all. Again, as Harman states, an object is "*less* than the sum of its parts."[463] The real object is withdrawn from its interactions with others so that it is capable of enduring beyond those interactions. I have argued that it does so by means of self-similarity so that even as its real qualities come and go, affect and are affected, the real object is similar to itself throughout. Similarity, I have argued, is an emergent phenomenon, not based in existing laws or prototypes. If similarity emerged out of separate, abstract and preexisting prototypes, we would then have to conclude that time was a self-same container, rather than a property of objects themselves. And it looks like that is not at all the case.

Knowledge is knowledge-objects that interact and organize by means of similarity. And here I join Hofstadter and Sander in their assertion that analogy is "the core of cognition."[464] There is thus no need for a metaphysics of equivocity to account for the relationship between knowing and being. As Latour rightly points out, however, traditional materialist epistemology demands just this sort of equivocity:

> Under the rubric of "matter," two totally different types of movement had been conflated: first, the way we move knowledge forward in order to access things that are far away or otherwise inaccessible; and, second, the way things move to keep themselves in existence. We can identify matter with one or the other, but not with both without leading to absurdity. Of course, we might marvel at the miracle of a "correspondence," between geometrization of the ways we know and the geometrization of the things that are known, but this is because we commit, wittingly or unwittingly, a little sleight of hand and explain this spurious correspondence by the fact that the "primary qualities" of objects known are themselves geometrical. That is easy to do when all other qualities—those that will become the 'secondary qualities'—have been carefully eliminated, one after the other.[465]

That's from Latour's short piece, "Can We Get Our Materialism Back, Please?" What Latour is describing in the passage above is the "idealist materialism"[466] that has long fancied itself as the only materialism in town. In order to ensure the possibility of knowledge, the secondary qualities of appearance must be opposed to the primary qualities of reality. Those qualities are real insofar as they correspond to abstract geometrical prototypes that exist outside of those qualities. In order for those abstract geometrical prototypes to exist "indefinitely in a timeless, unchanging realm…"[467] we again have to assume that time is a container rather than something of things themselves.

The Reassertion of the Material and Its Limits

But let's get back to Marx. In that same article, Latour argues that "Marx's own definition of material explanation [is] infinitely more subtle than what his successors made of it."[468] That's true, but it was also perhaps simpler than what was made of it. We know that after Marx's death, Engels took great pains to limit the overextension of dialectical materialism. He sets the boundaries as follows:

> According to the materialist conception of history, the *ultimately* determining element in history is the production and reproduction of real life. More than this neither Marx nor I have ever asserted.[469]

He goes on to argue that, in fact, the economics of production and reproduction cannot explain all of history:

> Without making oneself ridiculous it would be a difficult thing to explain in terms of economics the existence of every small state in Germany, past and present, or the origin of the High German consonant shifts, which widened the geographical wall of partition, formed by the mountains from the Sudetic range to the Taunus, to the extent of a regular fissure across all Germany.[470]

What we see is that Marx did not begin his analysis of value at material as such, but rather at particular *forms* of material interaction. There were, in fact, forms of production which Marx did not allow into the scope of his material analysis, sometimes to the consternation of postmodern Marxists. Here is in a footnote to *Grundrisse* (Marx is always best in his footnotes):

> The piano maker reproduces *capital*; the pianist only exchanges his labour for revenue. But doesn't the pianist produce music and satisfy our musical ear, does he not even to a certain extent produce the latter? He does indeed: his labour produces something; but that does not make it *productive labour* in the *economic sense*; no more than the labour of the madman who produces delusions is productive. *Labor becomes productive only by producing its own opposite.* Other economists therefore allow the so-called unproductive worker to be productive indirectly. For example, the pianist stimulates production; partly by giving a more decisive, lively tone to our individuality, and also in the ordinary sense of awakening a new need for the satisfaction of which additional energy becomes expended in direct material production. This already admits that only such labour is productive as produces capital; hence that labour which does not do this, regardless of how *useful* it may be—it may just as well be harmful—is not productive for capitalization, is hence unproductive labour.[471]

Actually, Marx is being a bit clever here, even ambiguous. It seems as though he's dismissing the productive potential of the pianist's labor by its very nature, perhaps because the piano is a thing assembled from material elements with labor objectified within it at its stages of production. But in fact, Marx is only imagining—for polemical purposes—that the social relationship between pianist and paying audience exists in a vacuum. That is, if there were an owner of the recital hall extracting value from the pianist's labor, then that labor would be productive, at least from the perspective of the recital hall owner. And so conceivably, even consumption itself, if entered into a similar social relationship—say, the consumption of conspicuously branded clothing—would be productive as well. This is not a new argument. In fact, it has been one of the central tenets of Marxist theory for half a century now.

The reaction to this kind of postmodern Marxism, with its emphasis on the production of the sign, has been to reassert the centrality of the material. This is completely understandable, because we seem to have gone from a place where productive consumption is admissible to the story of capital to a place where it has become central to the story. The production and consumption of the virtual, it would seem, precedes even material production. This makes for a new proletariat of Gucci bag owners. (Shall we stand in proud solidarity with *Comrade* Kardashian?) Material production has not gone away, but rather has been redistributed and obscured from the cities that house most of our pomo Marxist thinkers. It is against such a cultural-geographical veil that those who wish to reassert the primacy of the material stake their arguments.

When we talk about information as commodity, it is all too easy to set adrift its ties to the hardware produced in inhumane conditions, the metals mined from territories controlled by warlords and sycophantic governments, and the energy taken from countless generations of organic life. But of course, analyzing an information commodity back to metal and fossilized organic matter misses the point entirely. Marx is not concerned with bases and origins but with moments and movements. There is no place for atomism in Marxist philosophy, and access to the materiality of an object by no means opens up an absolute epistemic window into that object. The internal movement that appears as a unified phenomenon within a moment works by the suspension of subjectivity, just as it did for Hegel. Epistemic access, then, begins with the suspension of the phenomenon and the appearance of its relations. We find capital thusly:

> On the one side, the objectivity in which it exists has to be worked on, i.e. consumed by labour; on the other side, the mere subjectivity of labour as a mere form has to be suspended, and labour has to be objectified in the material of capital.[472]

Two things. One, we see that material is not necessarily a given. The kind of material Marx is talking about—which seems to differ from *raw material* (defined by Marx as "formless matter")—emerges out of the relations between labor and capital. This is socialized matter, which cannot be understood by any other material that might be considered more basic. Socialized matter occupies a relative rather than an absolute position. Second, and likewise, we see that subjectivity is a relative position, and that consumption is merely the asymmetrical relation between subject and object, which is why a consuming subject in one relationship can be the value-augmenting object in another. It seems to me, then, that if we discard something like the *Absolute Spirit* of Hegel, as his secularizers have done, there is no reason why the subject should maintain a unique and absolute position between absolute negativity and absolute materiality. Neither the subject nor the material occupy absolute positions.

But of course, I've left something out. I've been referring to socialized material, whose materiality is relative to the form of its relations. Can the same be said about so-called "raw" or "formless" material? Here, nature and history constitute each other's limits. Raw material by itself is that which has not joined socialized material in its relation with labor (form) within the subjective "*material* moment."[473] The material moment is a subject insofar as it constitutes the activity of labor changing (consuming) material.[474] Thus, in order for raw material to cross the chasm between nature and history, its natural formlessness must be negated by the form of labor, this negation being the activity from which the being of the historical moment emerges. This is pure Hegel, of course. But once the absolute difference—the chasm between nature and history—has been crossed, material becomes self-similar. That is to say the materiality of objects between separate moments of the production process is neither self-same nor absolutely different:

> Cotton which becomes cotton yarn, or cotton yarn which becomes cloth, or cloth which becomes the material for printing and dyeing, exist for labour only as available cotton, yarn, cloth. They themselves do not enter any process as products of labor, as objectified labour, but only as material existences with certain natural properties.[475]

Two more things. Marx calls the properties of these cottony things "natural," which we can assume are non-historical properties; yet we cannot assume that the cottony properties are the *same* between moments of the production process—cotton yarn and cotton cloth possess *similar* properties. Secondly, can we really assume that the raw material cotton is itself non-historical, given that cotton is a cultivated plant? Same rules apply, of course. There would still be a chasm between uncultivated cotton and cultivated cotton. But in order for an uncultivated plant to enter into a formal relationship with labor, to join in the material moment (a being with its potential to become cultivated), the uncultivated plant would have already had to have entered into a formal relationship with some kind of labor, though without the potential to become cultivated. Its noticed properties would have made it useful for some activity. This puts the real chasm not between the cultivated plant and the uncultivated plant, but between the uncultivated plant in the first moment and the pre-cultivated plant in the second moment. Both the uncultivated and the pre-cultivated plant enter into a relationship with labor, and the materiality of these material objects wouldn't seem to be different (they are both non-cultivated cotton plants), so the separation between the plants in moments 1 and 2 lies in their affects on potentially laboring humans, which is an objective thing and not a material one.

I hope I am not missing the point by subjecting a universal argument with a particular illustration (cottony things) to a particular argument (the cultivation of cotton). But Marx stakes his system on the primary distinction between the "abstract materialism"[476] of natural scientists—who, according to Marx, erroneously try to reduce social realties to bare material interactions—and *historical* materialism, in which material is joined to the social in the production of the means of production (in which raw material is further joined to socialized material instruments and is retroactively formed by historical subjectivity, producing social reality). What Marx considers the ontological distinction (ontologized by the production of the historical subject) between objects of natural material and objects of historical material is a relationship of similarity, and their respectively *proper* relationships with labor are part of the objects themselves, not of the presence or absence of a historical subject.

The Subject and Its Limits

Still, we might say that the nature of the relationships between objects of historical material and labor only emerge with the emergence of a historical mode of production, whose own subject is the class that controls the means of production. So finally, then, what is the nature of the limits of the being of this subject by which we might determine its substance? The easy answer is that the subject is limited by matter and that, correspondingly, the subject is matter in process. This is the kernel of the psychoanalytic subject. Here, the subject emerges in the suspension of the material body or, elsewhere, of the material aggregate (the *Real*), leaving matter in the absence of that suspension (i.e. death). But at least in the case of the historical subject, its limits in the material are more indirect, if not tenuous. Consider the capitalist as historical subject. The capitalist stands in relation to the product (or objectified labor), which is itself a relationship of raw material and the instrument of labor, put into motion by the activity of labor. By entering into this process, labor is itself materialized and formed into a material object. So, our limits here are the raw material, labor-as-material-object, and the instrument of labor. The instrument of labor, as Marx says, is itself a product of similar provenance to other objects, and thus its limits are the limits of the product. So, the real limits are raw material and labor. And thus, the limit of the capitalist subject would appear to be located in one of three events: 1) the emergence of labor-as-subject by means of revolt; 2) the failure of labor power, or 3) an ecological catastrophe that disrupts both the appropriation of raw material and the material body of labor.

The first limit was the project of leftist politics in the early twentieth century, and while the project still exists, it does not seem to be the threat to capital that it once was. The second limit was, in a way, taken up by the Marxism of Louis Althusser and his successors. Althusser begins with the question, "What [...] is *the reproduction of the conditions of production?*"[477] In other words, the reproduction of the *means* of production is one thing, but it is necessarily preceded by the reproduction of labor power. Althusser's argument is that labor power is reproduced not according to a biological minimum, but according to a "historical minimum."[478] This historical minimum is produced, maintained, and altered by ideology. Ideology itself is guaranteed by educational, religious, and cultural institutions, all of which are mediated by language. Thus labor power, ideology, and language are inextricably bound, and so it is through the limits of ideological institutions and language that the limit of labor power is to be found.

The third, ecological limit, which seems to be the project of twenty-first century leftist politics, is, in some ways, a return to the first limit (labor in revolt). The project of the second limit (labor power) could promise little more than a diffuse awareness that would, at best, effect a gradual reform of language and ideological institutions and would, at worst, trap us in an endlessly recursive production of meta-identity (the postmodern dystopia). The ecological limit, while not exactly a revolution in and of itself, is at least seen as being catastrophic, a real event. But one must be suspicious of such messianic anticipation. If the twentieth century taught us anything, it is that such anticipation can be pregnant with fascism, or something like it. Besides, if we are to believe Marx, capitalism is endlessly inventive, and even as it seems to hurl itself towards its own material limits, it continues to adapt. And so, even if material is capital's substance and limit, that does not mean we can make any claims about epistemic access to that limit.

The problem of accessing the substantial limit of the capitalist subject is central to Hardt and Negri's project of the *multitude*. As such, they reject both the Kantian project of *transcendental critique*[479] and the necessity of the negative in the Hegelian subject. What this means is that, first of all, there is no way to theorize a final limit of capitalism into which a single-minded revolutionary subject can intervene because, as they point out, capitalism is "in its essence a *productive* system,"[480] producing through its crises not just more commodities but *new kinds* of commodities and new consumer identities for those commodities. This happens not just through the appropriation and exploitation of those things we might think of as "natural" resources, but also through the appropriation and exploitation of *common* resources: things like linguistic formations and heirloom crop strains, which may or may not be invisible and may or may not escape our consciousnesses, but which are nonetheless affecting us and each other (think again of Graham Harman's example of the floor beneath us). Capitalism is productive in that it produces visibility of those common resources as commodities. Hardt and Negri's project, then, is not the negation of that kind of production *per se*, but the "biopolitical"[481] production of new commons as political bodies, with the multitude (rather than "the people") as the subject of the commons. Here, subjectivity emerges from experience rather than critique.

One of the things a project like Hardt and Negri's recognizes in its negation of negation is that catastrophes do not bring about absolute and uniform change to the world. Something like an ecological catastrophe would not be an absolute reduction in resources which the powerful would simply hold on to and distribute according to their interests. Catastrophes are productive. One need look no further than the proliferation of financial products in the wake of the West's manufacturing crisis or in the capitalization of relief resources after Hurricane Katrina[482] for evidence. And although it runs counter to Hardt and Negri's univocal ontology, this is why it is advantageous to think of things like global warming as objects (*pace* Morton) which effect their own temporal pull rather than occurring within absolute catastrophic time.

As a historico-political subject, the multitude is leaderless and without a stable identity that might be represented by a leader or a party. Like Deleuze and Guattari before them, Hardt and Negri reject the metaphysics of representation, which they necessarily tie to identity.[483] They've been criticized for looking for hope in such a subject. There is, on one hand, the traditional leftist notion that people are blinded to their own interests by ideology and so need a coherent program to counter the dominant ideology. And then there is the Hobbesian-flavored reductionist notion that humans are inescapably *natural* beings, and that without a cultural infrastructure to oppose and subdue the natural, there is no guarantee that the multitude will advance towards a more humane future. Hardt and Negri counter that nature itself is by no means fixed, and that there is no ontological gulf between nature and culture in the first place.

Instead of doing away with nature altogether, as Harman and Morton have done, Hardt and Negri vitalize it:

> The claim that nature is subject to mutation is closely related to the philosophical proposition of a constituent ontology—the notion, that is, that being is subject to a process of becoming dictated by social action and practices.[484]

Here, as with Latour, the "social" exceeds the boundaries of human culture. Again, in Latour the social relationship is one in which there is no 1:1 ratio of cause to effect. I hold to that idea of the social as well. Nevertheless, we mustn't conflate the asymmetry of causes and effects with an equiprobability of effects. Mutation is undirected, but at the level of form, it is attracted; it is constituted by similarity rather than sameness or absolute difference. Within truly social relationships, like those in mutation, identity exists though without representation.

In fact, the lumping together of representation and identity is precisely where materialism and idealism find common cause. This is the partnership that Latour takes to task. It's the "sleight of hand"[485] that takes the geometrical qualities of things as the essence of the things themselves. Representation is about being able to name the essential limits of a thing, the idea that things are not really what they are. It is identity in subtraction. In both materialism and idealism, identity is always subtracted from being, and so either identity is not real or the thing is not real. But when objects are primary, identity is present and sensuous. The identity of the whole object is *evoked* by the form of its parts in contact with other objects. Identity is present in each contact and similar in all contacts. It is important to understand identity this way because it forces us to rethink the relationship between an identifiable whole and its parts, as well as the relationships between wholes. In the mechanical ontologies of materialism and idealism, a whole thing is composed of a number of parts working together. Since those parts ultimately have no parts themselves, they are self-same. The identifiable whole is composed only of those parts and is absolutely different from anything with different parts. If, in a mechanical ontology, you accept that *kinds* of things are real, it is only because each individual in the kind is composed of the same parts. And this is what allows mass production and commodification to sustain one another.

Commodification only works under the illusion that things made of the same things are essentially the same. The relationship between parts and the whole individual is repeated in the relationship between whole individuals and the abstract commodity. And the relation between individuals and commodity is once again repeated in the relationship between commodities and money. Here, money begins to look like the source of value and, eventually, of identity. This becomes all the more the case under the regime of financial capitalism, where money buys and sells itself in the form of synthetic securities (e.g. debt bundling). If money can create itself as a commodity, then it can create anything as a commodity, including all of those visible and invisible things of the commons.

This is why I'm not so sanguine about escaping monetary reduction by means of material reduction. But if we consider identity as the evocation of the form of the whole from its parts and the evocation of the real object from its whole form, we escape such reductions. There, we get a different understanding of novelty. Hardt and Negri want us to understand reality as being unfixed, as being in a constant state of social production and creativity. This is the production of the commons that capital is always trying to fix and abstract into monetary identity. They provide the constant movement of mutation as an illustration of the unceasing creativity of social production and as a model for escaping fixity. But again, as we are beginning to see in evolutionary developmental biology, novel forms can emerge from very similar groupings of genotypic elements, and similar forms can emerge from radically different genotypic groupings. Animal flight, for instance, has emerged several different times, and each appearance cannot be reduced to the expression of the same genotypic grouping inherited by all animals. We can see this too in the development of human technologies like writing, which was created at least three times, independently, and under quite different conditions. This, I would argue, is the way to look at the new: the emergence of difference from the similar, and the emergence of the similar from difference. The *same* is to be found in neither direction. This view of novelty escapes the same-different dialectic that results on one end with atomism and the illusion of epistemic transparence (always to the exclusion of new kinds of things), and on the other end with the illusory abstraction of individuals as self-same commodities to be represented by market value or as a *people* to be represented by the will of a sovereign.

Objects of the Commons

I have been talking about objects in this book, but if you'd rather think about something like the multitude as a political subject or an event instead of a Mortonian *hyperobject* (as I would prefer), that's fine. At any rate, I agree with Hardt and Negri that the political challenge of our day is the production and recovery of the commons, and that it is a task for an extra-public thing like the multitude. But what can be said about the commons? Again, much of the commons is composed of those objects which we rely upon in our day-to-day existence but of which we are rarely conscious. Objects of the commons are often appropriated directly in the production of capital, as in, for instance, the exploitation of knowledge about local plant life or in more banal instances such as the appropriation of a new idiom for commercial advertising. The commons may generate capital too without any deliberate appropriation by what are known as *positive externalities*.[486] The generative quality of positive externalities is very often a matter of aesthetics. A familiar example of this is when artists begin moving into a low-rent neighborhood and effect a certain vibe that becomes attractive to new residents and developers, thus driving up profits for real estate owners. More broadly,

> The common appears at both ends of immaterial production, as presupposition and result. Our common knowledge is the foundation of all new production of knowledge; linguistic community is the basis of all linguistic innovation; our existing affective relationships ground all production of affects; and our common social image bank makes possible the creation of new images.[487]

Things like linguistic communities, social image banks, and common knowledge cannot be atomized into self-same cognitive modules or grammatical rules. But neither are they amorphous soups, occasionally spewing out something new at random. These commons are composed of objects with forms that interact and create new objects.

The production of the new in knowledge communities, linguistic communities, and social image banks is mediated by genres. Again, a genre is an object *par excellence*, since it cannot be reduced to a stable set of self-same rules or actors; it affects each utterance or sign as a whole. New genres emerge as wholes when the form of one genre is analogized into the utterances of another context (an asymmetrical contact). Genres mediate the production of new utterances and signs precisely because they are resistant to analysis. They are networks of *typified* actions,[488] not codified actions. Because genres are not the repetition of the same, utterances and signs produced in generic action only function (e.g. hit their rhetorical marks) aesthetically. There is, for instance, no 1:1 rubric for determining whether or not the utterances of a wedding toast or a letter of resignation were genre-appropriate; the toast or the letter is felt as a whole to be either appropriate or inappropriate. It is true that in many work situations, such as the fast food line, employers do attempt to codify genre by making workers go off of a script: "Welcome to McSo-and-So's. Will this be dine-in or carryout?" This sort of thing alienates the worker from her labor just as much (if not more) than performing a single task on a conveyer belt all day. The difference between the fast food line and the production line, however, is that when a consumer buys a pair of trainers that have been produced on a line, she is likely to identify with those trainers. (The color, the style, the logo...say something about her.) The fast food customer, on the other hand, might herself feel alienated by the interaction, as if she herself has been made to be a cog in the machine (though it is the worker who usually gets blamed for the lack of "service"). The customer is shielded a little bit more from the alienation in a sit-down restaurant because there the genre of taking orders works towards the production of new utterances with the rhetorical goal of making the customer feel special, just like that new pair of trainers does. Here, again, genre-appropriateness is felt, not analyzed. The restaurant may have training manuals that direct customer interaction, but anybody who's ever waited tables for a living knows that the order-taking genre is internalized by shadowing experienced wait staff and learning about responding to customer types over a cigarette shared in the employee bathroom.

And here's the point. In the realm of immaterial production, the capitalist cannot fully supply the means of production. In the service industry, for instance, the capitalist owns the walls, tables, and cash registers, but she cannot supply communication genres. Those are objects of the commons, and the capitalist can only exploit them. She cannot own them. Perhaps such objects can serve as the limits of capitalist power and denaturalize property altogether.

The political identification of such objects of the commons is no pie-in-the-sky dream. Knowledge of local plant life from speakers of marginal and endangered languages has generated in excess of 85 billion dollars in revenue for pharmaceutical companies,[489] much of which has been appropriated without compensation. Such knowledge does not simply exist in the relationship between an identifying term and its predicates, but within the entire grammatical network of a language. And in order to appropriate knowledge about a local ecosystem, a grammar must be recorded and documented so that any one chunk of local knowledge can be understand and turned into capital. Thus, intervention in the theft of knowledge must be made at the level of documentation. This is exactly what The Living Tongues Institute for Endangered Languages is doing. First, a language is recorded and documented so that it does not pass out of existence, and with the hope that younger members of the community can learn it should the last speakers pass away. Second, the rights to the language itself and the knowledge contained therein are owned by the community, with individual contributors retaining the right to "limit or restrict access to their intellectual property as they see fit..."[490]

The linguists and other volunteers in this project hardly fit the description of dangerous political radicals, but there is the seed of something very dangerous in the project. In Modernity, linguistic identity politics was one of the most powerful weapons in the nationalist's arsenal. It is difficult to imagine, for instance, Irish Fenianism or Zionism being as successful as they were in the twentieth century without the pathos of shared linguistic identities. The political goals of *an Athbheochan Ghaelach* [the Gaelic Renaissance] and the construction of Modern Hebrew reflected very modern political concerns: the decolonization of the Irish mind and, for the Jews, the nationalization of a group in diaspora whose identity had been religious but which was increasingly becoming racialized. Likewise, the goals of the contemporary language preservation movement reflect the contemporary political landscape. Areas of the world most affected by environmental destruction and global warming can be mapped with remarkable accuracy onto so-called "language hotspots,"[491] areas of immense linguistic diversity and language endangerment. Rapid environmental and economic destruction results in population movements, particularly amongst young people, who often cut ties to their linguistic communities as they seek employment and educational opportunities elsewhere. Secondly, this is an age of unprecedented power for multinational agriculture and pharmaceutical companies who have the means to turn local knowledge into billions in profits. The language preservation movement is a small but important point of resistance to the power imbalance created by global capitalism and exacerbated by global warming.

Language preservation is not a perfect model, however. After all, the very institution of intellectual property, such as it is, is a key mechanism in the neoliberal governance of knowledge, wherein knowledge created in public institutions can be bought and sold by private interests. Furthermore, although assigning speakers property rights to the languages they helped document is a brilliant innovation, the same could not be done for other objects of the commons (e.g. genres) even if it were desirable to do so. Nonetheless, the very idea of such objects of the commons *as* objects with their own capacities to affect bodies, knowledge, and capital is truly dangerous. It is a dangerous idea because it is impossible even to imagine breaking down by analysis an object like a genre and knowing it, owning it, reproducing it, and commodifying it any more than one can imagine doing all of that to the internet or to global warming.

You might imagine that conceiving of things like grammars, genres, the internet, and global warming as objects is a sort of epistemic or rhetorical borrowing of objectness from other things like baseballs, mountains, and mesons. But the borrowing must go the other way. Genres, global warming, and even grammars are never fully codifiable, can never be reproduced as exactly the same because they have no self-same identity to be accessed. They are instead typified. We understand them by their forms, just as they affect other objects with form. It is only when we find our old idea of objects standing on its head that we can reverse the logic of mechanical mass production that continues to naturalize private wealth and the monetization of life, even in a regime of production that is antithetical to that very logic.

Conclusion
Know. Fish. Happy.

You might remember from this book's introduction that Hideki Yukawa liked to draw the characters, *Know*, *Fish*, and *Happy* in lieu of signing autographs, and that those characters come from Zhuangzi's parable of the happy fishes. And by way of a conclusion, I would like to return to that parable. When Huizi pointed out that Zhuanzi's knowledge of the fishes was limited by Zhuangzi's own subjectivity, Zhuangzi countered that Huizi's subjectivity too must exclude his own knowledge of the limits of Zhuangzi's subjectivity. Cast in Greek dialectical terms, we can say that Huizi begins with the following enthymeme:

> Zhuangzi is not a fish.
> (Therefore) Zhuangzi cannot know if a fish is happy.

The excluded major premise which makes Huizi's argument an enthymeme would be:

> A non-fish cannot know if a fish is happy.

In his response, Zhuangzi essentially turns the enthymeme into a full syllogism and extends it:

> Huizi is not Zhuangzi.
> A non-Zhuangzi cannot know what Zhuangzi knows.
> (Therefore) Huizi cannot know what Zhuangzi knows.
> (Therefore) Huizi cannot know what Zhuangzi knows about the fishes.

The parable in no way anticipates Kantian finitude, but it does have something to say about the debates over formal logic that were raging just as Yukawa was beginning his career as a physicist. Huizi speaks for logic, though in order to do so, he must speak enthymematically, leaving the major premise of his argument to intuition. Huizi cannot speak logic and speak *for* logic in the same instance. Logic needs a medium through which to speak, and that medium is the withdrawn premise of the enthymeme, which belongs to the intuition. Huizi must begin his argument for logic with an appeal to intuition, which is the very same appeal Zhuangzi made in his initial statement about the fishes being happy. Yukawa's point in relaying this parable again and again was that all knowledge, falsifiable or speculative, must pass through the doors of intuition. Since for Yukawa intuition was the product of aesthetic experiences (analogy chief among them), he believed that we must not see the narrative of scientific progress as an ongoing detachment of public reason from private aesthetic experience. (As a working physicist, his concerns about the internalization of such a narrative were practical as much philosophical.)

In contemporary terms, Yukawa might be seen as a scientist who was against scientism. But in truth, I don't really know what *scientism* is supposed to mean, and it's a word I tend to avoid. I suspect the term is leveled most often as a complaint against a certain sociological attitude, the notion that questions posed in all fields (including politics) can be answered by empirical science, and that, therefore, all fields *should* be answerable to empirical science. So, perhaps what we're dealing with here is the old, technocratic instrumentalism wrapped up in a slightly more inspiring package. Or maybe *scientism* describes a stance on metaphysics. Certainly, the idea that everything is matter can be integrated easily into sociological scientism. But, then again, materialism is a big tent, housing many critics of sociological scientism as well, so we cannot really say that scientism has a metaphysics all to its own. If Yukawa was anti-scientism, his complaints were certainly leveled at some of those sociological tendencies in science, but his complaints register most of all with the epistemological tendencies of what we might call "scientism."

If there is a particular epistemology attached to scientism, it is probably positivism. *Positivism*, like *scientism*, has become a pejorative term in many circles. We tend to think of it as an unreflective, rather conservative stance towards knowledge. We too easily forget that it is actually a very powerful means of validating knowledge and that—at least in its twentieth century incarnation—it is also deeply rooted in anti-totalitarian politics. The problem is that positivism treats epistemic validity and epistemic motivation[492] as two sides of the same coin. In other words, if valid knowledge is accessible by way of logical consistency, and if we can gain access to a logically consistent meta-discourse of logical consistency, then our very access to that meta-discourse is enough to motivate the production of new and valid knowledge. The same goes for the wider phenomenon of correlationism, of which positivism can be considered a part. Correlationism posits a kind of equivocal reality in which there exists both a primary division and a mutual dependence between subject and object. For instance, knowledge of causality in the world of objects can be obtained only by correlating events and attaching categories to those correlations. Since the subject relates to the world of objects through categorization, it is the categorization of objects inside of correlated events that provides the knowing subject's *raison d'être*. So again, there is no distinction between the recognized limits of valid knowledge and the motivation for producing new knowledge. It seems to me that Wilfrid Sellars, more than any other twentieth century philosopher, recognized the need to address epistemic validity and epistemic motivation as separate matters, and that's why I agree with those on the rationalist side of Speculative Realism that Sellars is long overdue for a renaissance in popularity. Sellars, as discussed in Chapter 4, believed that epistemic motivation resides with deontic modality in language. Deontic modality gives knowledge a normative dimension, and it is that normative dimension which separates knowledge claims from mere transmissions of information. It's an inspired move, but one of my goals in this book has been to look for something more universal than that, and I believe I have found it in the realm of aesthetic experience.

Again, Yukawa had hoped to reattach aesthetic experience and reason by placing analogy at the center of thought. And this is where my own project picked up. But in order to reattach aesthetics and reason, we must think our way around the well-entrenched notions that reality is primarily matter and that thought is primarily synthetic. In both cases, we need to think in terms of objects. The problem, however, is that the modern mode of thinking about objects usually begins with synthesis itself.

Modern ideas on synthesis and objects begin with the relationship between time and repetition, and here we can start with Hume. As discussed in Chapter 4, Hume thought that resemblance was an important part of the journey from concrete to abstract thought. But for Hume, resemblance was the repetition of self-same qualities in different moments, and our understanding of predicative objects begins as a contracted repetition of those self-same qualities. Our understanding of time is itself a repetition of that process—only here, it is the repetition of objects that is contracted into time. Having been awoken from his dogmatic slumber by Hume, Kant nevertheless puts time (and space) in the realm of *a priori* knowledge, meaning that it is necessary to have an intuition of time and space before having an understanding of objects. The idea is that if objects have a relational identity to time and space, then the subject, for whom the identity is relational, can have concepts for those objects that are different from the objects themselves. It is thus the subject, with its *a priori* understanding of time and space, that synthesizes concepts from those relations. In both Hume and Kant, knowledge of objects is a synthesis of properties from self-same and given domains. Though it would be a huge mistake to call Hume and Kant (but especially Kant) materialists, their philosophies share the same basic logic of synthesis which is inherent in materialism—that is, that knowledge of objects is derived from properties or domains that are more fundamental than the objects themselves.

Phenomenology represents a significant departure from synthetic thought, and we can see this most clearly in Heidegger and Merleau-Ponty, both of whom privilege unintentional and embodied relationships with objects. But it is Deleuze and his brand of materialism to which I've so often returned in this book. His philosophy is where we see the most creative articulation of the relationship between knowledge and emergence, and he articulates the relationship both by rejecting analogy and doubling down on synthesis. For my own thinking, Deleuze is the proverbial delicious and spicy curry that you always agree with, but which never seems to agree with you. So, it is in distinction to Deleuze that I can best rearticulate my own argument on knowledge and emergence.

The main project of Deleuze's *Difference and Repetition* in particular is to ground thought in difference without the need to provide additional grounding for difference itself. Deleuze points out that since Aristotle, difference and otherness have been distinct from one another, with difference always needing a third term to put the first two terms in relative communion.[493] The difference in the two terms is underwritten by the repetition of the third term. Difference, therefore, could never be difference for itself because it exists only in relation to something else. Deleuze sees the same problem in the Kantian subject, to whom space and time are given. In Kant, difference is always a difference relative to spatial and temporal extension, and thus space and time play the role of the third term. In order to get beyond the third term in this case, Deluze dissolves the Kantian subject. Instead of having a subject who actively synthesizes concepts in relation to the self-same domains of space and time, he posits the subject as a *passive synthesis*.[494] The Kantian subject, argues Deleuze, is passive only insofar as it receives intuition of the temporal, and so Kant has not pushed passivity or synthesis far enough. Time too is a synthetic product: "Time is constituted only in the originary synthesis which operates on the repetition of instants."[495] Furthermore, "Time is subjective, but in relation to the subjectivity of the passive subject."[496] The "originary synthesis" to which Deleuze is referring is an extension of the Humean idea of contraction. The repetition of different instants is contracted into the past, but that contraction is always in the present. The contraction of repeated past instants constitutes a particular, just as the contraction of qualities constitutes a particular object for Hume. The contracted presentation of the past then opens up an anticipation of the general, which is the future. Again, this comports with the idea that the contracted presentation of a particular object opens up an anticipation of a general domain for the object (a category) in repetition. The important thing to bear in mind here is that the contraction of past instants onto the present is a passive act; it is not done by a subject that knows itself as a subject. We are not yet dealing with memories of the past or predictions about the future since memory and prediction, according to Deleuze, are reflexive phenomena which exist in relation to a subject that sees itself as existing in serial time. In other words, memory and prediction belong to the realm of representation, which is a product of active synthesis. It is only when memories are synthesized according to the domain of serial time that the subject can imagine future instants as being analogous or similar to memorial representations. So again, the argument is that similarity is never similarity for itself, but always for another domain (time, genus, law, etc.).

I agree with Deleuze that serial time is not a given domain for the subject. Indeed, serial time is not a cultural universal, and seriality itself (which includes counting) does not even seem to be a linguistic universal. For example, as Everett observes in the Pirahã language (where counting is absent), time is an extension of other categories such as fire and tide.[497] And such categories do not exist as concrete representations of categories inside of a more general and abstract domain of time. In his brilliant and nuanced brand of materialism, Deleuze is looking for something more fundamental than (and exterior to) the category. And he needs something exterior even to an ur-category, such as time. He finds it in the repetition of particular instants, which are added together (synthesized) onto the present. The present is a perfect medium for such an "originary synthesis" because it is where representation bottoms out. As soon as a present is representable, it is already a particular added onto another present, so it is never representable as itself. The present belongs to an infinite recursion, a pure repetition that makes the addition (synthesis) of particulars possible.[498] The difference between contracted particular instants from present to present produces a general relationship between contracted particulars, and that general relationship is serial time. As a series, time is both a multiplicity and a category, a synthesis and an empty domain. And this synthetic understanding of time is to serve as Deleuze's model for all categories, the idea being that categories are never given as empty domains, void of internal differentiation.

I once again hold with Deleuze that categories (and, I would add, genres) are never given as empty domains. But I would also argue that categories are not born of synthetic series of particulars either. Synthesis always comes after similarity. Synthesis occurs when we impose the structure of predication onto thought, and then onto reality. One of the trickiest objections to the preceding statements comes out of the idea of the *concrete universal*. Deleuze actually picked the idea out of the Hegelian lexicon, but concrete universals are also familiar to prototype theory in psychology. The idea is that when you're asked to think of a general category, you will not help but think of a concrete or particular stand-in for that category. For example, you won't be able to think the concept *dog* without bringing to mind the image of a particular dog, perhaps a tubby black lab standing in profile with its tongue hanging out. There is no formal category for which this dog is a particular instance, but instead all other objects to which the category *dog* is applied exist in a series, with your black lab in the center of that series. In Deleuzean synthesis, your image of the particular black lab becomes the category *dog* because of its intensity, because it is really multiple instants that have undergone a great amount of repetition for you. It is the image of that dog in its intensity that makes it different from the image of that dog as such. But let's go back to the distinction I took from Longinus (Chapter 4) concerning the amplified and the sublime. There, I associated familiarity with amplification (the repetition of the same) and fame with sublimity (repetition by imitation). In terms of Deleuzean synthesis, we might say that the particular image of the black lab becomes the category *dog* because it is most familiar, because it has been amplified to a certain level of intensity. But I would argue that the image of the black lab, as the category *dog*, is famous as well. It is not simply that the repetition of the same image becomes different in its intensity; the repeated images, all and sundry, are repeated in different contexts, each context interacting with the image-object in its own way. At each instance the image of the black lab comes to mind, or at each instance it is deployed as the category *dog*, the image does not present itself as a collection of the same, finite qualities, such as black, tubby, tongue-hanging-out, etc. Some qualities are withdrawn and some are present. Some are foregrounded and some are backgrounded. In other words, the image of the dog is never present as a synthesis of analyzable parts. Each instance in which the image presents itself is an aesthetic experience, even as it is being deployed as the category *dog*. At each instance, the image is a translation of the image in other instances. The category *dog* is an object, and it is an object in repetition, but it is a repetition of similarity. It is a self-similar being like all enduring objects. It is not its intensive familiarity that brings forth its identity, but its fame. It is only after such an object is identified that we parse out its qualities and synthesize them from a system of predicate domains, such as fur, four legs, etc.

My argument in this book has been that similarity emerges wherever there is translation (which is also imitation and conformation) amongst objects, and that causality itself works by translation rather than by mechanical synthesis. It is in accord with this basic metaphysical stance that I have placed the relationship between knowledge and emergence. Knowledge, or that which can be thought privately and publicly, works through the production of categories. The production of categories is mediated across the public-private divide by the production of grammars and genres. And analogy is the medium on which categories, grammars, and genres are produced. Categories, grammars, and genres are, in turn, what make representation possible.

It is understandably difficult to swallow the argument that analogy precedes representation for a couple of reasons. For one, as I pointed out in Chapter 3, the historical understanding of analogy in the West begins with proportion. Such an understanding presupposes the intuition of mathematical categories, such as seriality and geometric form. Those categories serve as domains in which all can be represented. The irony here, of course, is that the category *analogy* has been analogically extended so far beyond proportion so as to be virtually unrecognizable to the original concept. Second—and this is the more difficult part—we tend to see analogy as a voluntary judgment, something that an active subject does to its intended objects. But those analogies that we represent *as* analogies are, in fact, the very rare exception to the swarms of analogies affecting us at every moment. Hofstadter and Sander put it beautifully:

> Like fish swimming in a medium of which they are unaware but that allows them to dart nimbly from one spot to another in the vast briny depths, we human beings float, without being aware of it, in a sea of tiny, medium-sized, and large analogies, running the gamut from dull to dazzling. And as it is the case for fish, it's only thanks to this omnipresent, unfelt medium that we can dart nimbly from one spot to another in the vast ocean of ideas.[499]

To that I would only add that the medium is not so much unfelt as unrepresented. It is thanks to this ocean that we can do something as mundane as turning on a water faucet. As we turn the handle, our experience translates other experiences of faucets, just as our hand translates the ergonomically designed faucet handle to its own form. Analogies, therefore, are not representations of similarity but *acts* of similarity, just as translating one's hand to a faucet handle is an act of similarity. In the end, there is no separating aesthetics and reason, just as there is no separating aesthetics and causality. So, if the dialectics of reason fail us, perhaps we should try the ergonomics of reason on for size.

Endnotes

1. Hideki Yukawa, *Tabibito*, trans. Laurie Brown and R. Yoshida. Singapore: World Scientific, 1982. Page 68.
2. Yukawa, *Tabibito*, 64.
3. Frank Close, *The Infinity Puzzle: Quantum Field Theory and the Hunt for an Orderly Universe*. New York: Basic Books, 2011, Page 30.
4. Close, *The Infinity Puzzle*, 29.
5. Quoted in Close, *The Infinity Puzzle*, 73.
6. Hideki Yukawa, *Creativity and Intuition: A Physicist Looks at East and West*, trans. John Bester. Tokyo: Kodansha International, 1973, Page 107.
7. Laurie Brown and Helmut Rechenberg, *The Origin of the Concept of Nuclear Forces*. Bristol, UK: Institute of Physics, 1996. Page 102.
8. Quoted in Brown and Rechenberg, *The Origin of the Concept of Nuclear Forces*, 102.
9. Brown and Rechenberg, *The Origin of the Concept of Nuclear Forces*, 20-21.
10. Brown and Rechenberg, *The Origin of the Concept of Nuclear Forces*, 31.
11. Yukawa, *Creativity and Intuition*, 159.
12. Brown and Rechenberg, *The Origin of the Concept of Nuclear Forces*, 105.
13. Close, *The Infinity Puzzle*, 185.
14. Yukawa, *Creativity and Intuition*, 160.
15. Jim Al-Khalili, *Quantum: A Guide for the Perplexed*. London: Weidenfeld and Nicholson, 2004, Page 170.
16. Brown and Rechenberg, *The Origin of the Concept of Nuclear Forces*, 112.
17. Yukawa, *Tabibito*, 40.
18. Yukawa put Taoism in diametric opposition to Confucianism, of which he was no fan at all. According to Yukawa, Taoism was a philosophy of being in the world, whereas Confucianism emphasized the possibility of control over the world by reason and will, a position he consistently rejected in his own philosophy.

19. Takehiko Takabayashi, "Some Characteristic Aspects of Early Elementary Particle Theory in Japan," in Laurie Brown and Lillian Hoddeson (Eds.), *The Birth of Particle Physics*. Cambridge, UK: Cambridge University Press, 1983, Page 296.

20. Satio Hayakawa, "The Development of Meson Physics in Japan," in Brown and Hoddeson (Eds.), *The Birth of Particle Physics*, 93-94.

21. Laurie Brown and Lillian Hoddeson, "The Birth of Elementary Particle Physics: 1930-1950," in Brown and Hoddeson (Eds.), *The Birth of Particle Physics*, 25.

22. Hideki Yukawa, "Zhuangzi: The Happy Fish," ed. Victor M. Mair, *Experimental Essays on Zhuangzi*. St. Petersburg, FL: Three Pines Press. Pages 59-60.

23. Yukawa, "Zhuangzi: The Happy Fish," 60.

24. Yukawa offers the proton as an example of the inadequacy of such atomistic thinking: "[M]eson theory tells us [a neutron] will become a proton upon the addition of a positively charged π-meson, and the reverse is also true. However, it would be wrong to conclude from this that the proton is a composite particle consisting simply of a neutron and a positively charged π-meson." Yukawa, *Creativity and Intuition*, 171.

25. Graham Harman, *The Quadruple Object*. Winchester, UK: Zero Books, 2011. Page 5.

26. Martin Jay, *Downcast Eyes: The Denigration of Vision in Twentieth Century French Thought*. Berkley, CA: University of California Press, 1994. Page 588

27. Bruno Latour, *On the Modern Cult of the Factish Gods*. Durham, NC: Duke University Press, 2010. Page 114.

28. And in the Cartesian legacy, which extends all the way down to Chomsky's Generative Grammar, there is hardly a difference between mathematical and grammatical logic.

29. "Herbert Spencer's principle of evolution never freed itself from the vice of mechanical explanation. The future and the past could all be calculated from the present. All is given." quoted. in Herbert Wildon Carr, *Henri Bergson: The Philosophy of Change*. Charleston, NC: Nabu Press, 2010. Page 76.

30. Quoted in Melanie Mitchell, *Complexity: A Guided Tour*. Oxford: Oxford University Press, 2009. Page 106.

31. Mitchell, *Complexity*, 106.

32. Adrian Bejan and J. Peder Zane, *Design in Nature: How the Constructal Law Governs Evolution in Biology, Physics, Technology and Social Organization*. New York: Doubleday, 2012).

33. Karl Marx, *The German Ideology*, available at <https://marxists.org/archive/marx/1845/germanideology>, accessed October 2, 2013.

34. He really sticks it to the French: "When they begin to think, they speak German, being sure that they could not make it with their own language." Martin Heidegger, *The Question Concerning Technology: Philosophy of Technology*, trans. and ed. Robert Schaff and Val Dusek (Malden, MA: Blackwell, 2003), 44. It's hard to tell how serious Heidegger is being, but since humor didn't seem to be his strong suit, we'll take him at his word.

35. Mitchell, *Complexity*, 52.

36. Bruno Latour, *Pandora's Hope: Essays on the Reality of Science Studies*. Cambridge, MA: Harvard University Press, 1999. Pages 212-213.

37. Mark C. Taylor, *The Moment of Complexity: Emerging Network Culture*. Chicago: University of Chicago Press, 2001. Page 203.

38. Actor-Network-Theory (ANT), a key concept in philosophies of complexity, is most closely associated with Latour. Here, actors know no boundaries between subject and object. However, where interactions between human and non-human actors are concerned, Latour prefers Alfred North Whitehead's term *propositions*. In Latour's words, "What distinguishes propositions from one another is not a *single* vertical abyss between words and the world but the *many* differences between them, without anyone knowing *in advance* if these differences are big or small, provisional or definitive, reducible or irreducible." *Pandora's Hope*, 141.

39. J. Engelmann et al., "Neurobiology: Hydrodynamic Stimuli and the Fish Lateral Line," *Nature* 408 (2 Nov 2000): 51.

40. I'm going to be referring to this a few more times, so here's a brief explanation. Very simply, supersymmetry refers to the possibility that there is a matter particle that exists as a partner with a force-carrier counterpart (bosons), and a force-carrier particle that exists as a partner with a matter particle (fermions). Each superpartner should have a half-unit spin difference from the spin of its partner. Fermions carry a whole-unit spin and bosons carry a half-unit spin, so the reality of one partner is approximately 180° from the reality other partner. One of the least exotic (but most important) implications of the supersymmetric principle is that at short enough distances (i.e. high enough energy levels), the different strengths of electromagnetic interactions, weak nuclear interactions, and strong nuclear interactions converge, thus implying that they all share, at a more fundamental level, the same force. Among other things, the superpartners are thought to balance out the energy levels (i.e. mass) of the bosons (W+, W-, and Z bosons) that carry the weak nuclear force by drawing mass out of the Higgs field, which is where the W and Z bosons also draw their mass. This deposit and withdrawal activity at the bank of the Higgs field is why the Higgs boson turns out to be less massive than expected, and why the weak nuclear interactions are observed to operate at such a larger scale of strength than gravitational interactions do. If the W and Z bosons became as massive as the current Standard Model allows, their exchange range would be smaller, and the intensity of gravity, which gets stronger at shorter distance ranges (unlike the strong and weak nuclear forces), would approach that of the weak force. Therefore, just as we have seen in philosophies of complexity, maintaining internal differences in the scale of interactions within a system protects the ontological unity of the system itself. On the other side of the coin, in order to maintain the distinctive quality of weak nuclear interactions (so as to hide the ontological unity of all force interactions), the actors that carry out those interactions must exist at a distinctive quantity of distance.

41. At the time of this writing, the supersymmetric partners that would regulate the energy of the Higgs field (and therefore maintain the enormous disparity between the strengths of the weak nuclear force and gravity), have not yet been detected. However, the history of particle physics has tended towards the unification of fundamental forces. From 1873 to 1967, magnetic interaction, electrical interaction, and weak nuclear interaction were coupled and re-coupled under the same *electroweak* force. The inability of the Large Hadron Collider (LHC) to detect supersymmetric particles at its current energy range capability would suggest that if the particles do exist, they are far too massive to exist in a symmetrical relationship

with their partners. But it may turn out that instead of being more massive than was originally calculated, the supersymmetric partners are illusive because they are unstable and ephemeral, like Yukawa's π-meson. See Natalie Wolchover, "As Supersymmetry Fails, Physicists Seek New Ideas," *Quanta Magazine* (20 Nov. 2012), available at https://www.quantamagazine.org/20121120-as-supersymmetry-fails-tests-physicists-seek-new-ideas, accessed November 10, 2013.

42. To be precise, *correlationism* is Quentin Meillassoux's term for the Kantian doctrine of finitude, in which the mind of the subject cannot be thought apart from the world it confronts, and vice versa. Meillassoux is one of the four original participants of the 2007 conference at Goldsmiths College, University of London that gave rise to the name "Speculative Realism," a heading which also included Graham Harman, Ray Brassier, and Ian Hamilton Grant. See Levi Bryant, Nick Srnicek, and Graham Harman, "Towards a Speculative Philosophy," in *The Speculative Turn: Continental Materialism and Realism*, Levi Bryant, Nick Srnicek, and Graham Harman (Eds.) Melbourne: re.press, 2011. Page 3.

43. Graham Harman, "Response to Shaviro," in Bryant et al. (Eds.), *The Speculative Turn*, 294.

44. Gilles Deleuze and Félix Guattari, *A Thousand Plateaus: Capitalism and Schizophrenia*, trans. Brian Massumi. Minneapolis: University of Minnesota Press, 1987. Page 236.

45. Lev Tolstoy, *Voina i Mir* [War and Peace] v. 3-4, (Moscow: Biblioteka Shkolnika, 1960), 284.

46. Tolstoy's unconventional brand of idealism in combination with the remarkably materialist image of the *swarm life* makes him an unexpected emissary between Schopenhauer and Deleuze.

47. Tolstoy, *Voina i Mir* [War and Peace] v. 3-4, Page 8.

48. Tolstoy, *Voina i Mir* [War and Peace] v. 3-4, 85.

49. Bruno Latour, *Reassembling the Social: An Introduction to Actor-Network Theory*. Oxford: Oxford University Press, 2005. Page 54.

50. Latour, *Reassembling the Social*, 54.

51. Tolstoy, *Voina i Mir* [War and Peace] v. 3-4, 85.

52. Latour, *Reassembling the Social*, 53.

53. Latour, *Reassembling the Social*, 71.

54. Latour, *Pandora's Hope*, 153.

55. Latour, *Pandora's Hope*, 153.

56. Latour, *Pandora's Hope*, 153.

57. Gilles Deleuze and Claire Parnet, *Dialogues*, trans. Hugh Tomlinson and Barbara Habberjam. New York: Columbia University Press, 1977. Page 134.

58. Gilles Deleuze, *Difference and Repetition*, trans. Paul Patton. New York: Columbia University Press, 1995. Page 223.

59. Deleuze, *Difference and Repetition*, 172-173.

60. Brian Massumi, *Parables for the Virtual: Movement, Affect, Sensation*. Durham, NC: Duke University Press, 2002. Page 218.

61. Deleuze and Parnet, *Dialogues*, 7.
62. Deleuze and Guattari, *A Thousand Plateaus*, 238.
63. Deleuze and Guattari, *A Thousand Plateaus*, 399.
64. Baruch Spinoza, *Ethics*, ed. and trans. G.H.R. Parkinson. Oxford: Oxford University Press, 2000. Page 76.
65. Deleuze and Guattari, *A Thousand Plateaus*, 215. Emphasis added.
66. Deleuze and Guattari, *A Thousand Plateaus*, 253.
67. Deleuze and Parnet, *Dialogues*, 103.
68. Lucy Kimbell and Graham Harman, "The Object Strikes Back: An interview with Graham Harman," *Design and Culture* 5.1 (2013), 104.
69. To explain n-fold symmetry, Close offers the snowflake as a simple illustration. A snowflake has a 6-fold symmetry means that it must be rotated 60° in order for its symmetry to become apparent. Frank Close, *The Infinity Puzzle: Quantum Field Theory and the Hunt for an Orderly Universe*. New York: Basic Books, 2011. Pages 130-131.
70. Deleuze, *Difference and Repetition*, 21.
71. Please note well that the addition or restoration of symmetry at the quantum level is the mechanism that gives rise to the fundamental forces (or at least to those excluding gravity, since the putative agent of that force, the graviton, has not yet been found). What the relationship between Deleuzean "speed" and the scales of strength amongst the different forces might be unclear. What is known is that the strong force arises out of the restoration of a three-part symmetry (the restoration of three different 'colors' of quarks), and the much weaker electro-magnetic force arises out of the restoration of a one-part symmetry, which is the balance of charge. See Roger Jones, *Physics for the Rest of Us: Ten Basic Ideas of 20th Century Physics*. New York: Fall River Press, 2011. Pages 256-257)
72. Deleuze, *Difference and Repetition*, 255.
73. Gilles Deleuze and Felix Guattari, *Anti-Oedipus: Capitalism and Schizophrenia*, trans. Robert Hurley, Mark Seem, and Helen R. Lane. Minneapolis: University of Minnesota Press, 1983. Page 26.
74. Deleuze and Guattari, *Anti-Oedipus*, 25.
75. From Russell's Antinomy. If we treat a set-of-things as a thing-in-itself (as Cantor's set theory requires us to do), then for the most part, the things-in-the-set and the set-of-those-things-itself are fundamentally different entities. The set-of-things is predicated upon the things-in-the-set, and so the predication itself forces an ontological rift between the two entities. There is a symmetry, a moment of identification between those two entities. Much more on this later.
76. Kaons are a type of meson that decays into either two or three pions (π-mesons). It appears that antikaons flip over to being kaons at a slightly greater rate than kaons flip to antikaons. See Frank Close, *Lucifer's Legacy: The Meaning of Asymmetry*. Mineola, NY: Dover Publications, 2013. Kindle edition, Chapter 12.
77. Rodgers W. Redding, *Exploring Physics: Concepts and Applications*. Belmont, CA: Wadsworth, 1984. Pages 433-434.

78. See Amanda Gefter, *Trespassing on Einstein's Lawn: A Father, A Daughter, the Meaning of Nothing, and the Beginning of Everything*. New York: Bantam Books, 2014.

79. Structural realism is arguably the dominant current in the philosophy of science today, and it comes in two flavors: epistemic and ontic (the latter also known as OSR). Epistemic structural realism, in its current incarnation, begins with the work of John Worrall in the late 1980s. Worrall and other ESRs are concerned primarily with the history of science, and in particular with those epistemic structures that persist despite revolutions in scientific theory. OSR, whose major proponents include Steven French and James Ladyman, is concerned with what claims can actually be made about reality despite ongoing changes to particular pictures of physical reality.

80. Steven French and James Ladyman, "Remodelling Structural Realism: Quantum Physics and the Metaphysics of Structure," *Synthese* 136: 2003, 43.

81. French and Ladyman, "Remodeling Structural Realism," 43.

82. These are further speciated into symmetry groups. From there, it all depends upon whether you individuate members of these groups as members of a set or as pure binary relations.

83. Credit for joining laws of conservation with continuous symmetry goes to the unsung hero of 20th century mathematics/physics, Emmy Noether, in what is known as *Noether's Theorem*. See Kenneth W. Ford, *101 Quantum Questions: What You Need to Know about the World You Can't See*. Cambridge, MA: Harvard University Press, 2011. Pages 171-172.

84. Measuring the possible states of these different classes of particle is done with either Bose-Einstein statistics (for bosons) or Fermi-Dirac statistics (for fermions). Their principle difference comes out of Pauli Exclusion, which again means that no two fermions of the same type can occupy the same energy state.

85. Christian Wüthrich, "The Structure of Causal Sets," *Journal for the General Philosophy of Science*, 43 (2012): 225.

86. Hermann Weyl, *Symmetry*. Princeton, NJ: Princeton University Press: 198. Page 41.

87. Alain Badiou, *Number and Numbers*, trans. Robin Mackay. Cambridge, UK: Polity Press, 2008. Page 18.

88. Which is a little bit different from the Deleuzean repetition of pure difference.

89. Badiou, *Number and Numbers*, 32.

90. Note that set = system. The brand had not yet been crystallized as 'set' at this point.

91. Richard Dedekind, *Essays on the Theory of Numbers*, trans. Wooster Woodruff Beman. Chicago: Open Court Press, 1924. Page 63.

92. Dedekind, *Essays on the Theory of Numbers*, 64.

93. Badiou, *Number and Numbers*, 54.

94. Again, in complexity theory, self-similarity is a term related to the dynamics of scale. It refers, for instance, to how a super-system can emerge from a number of sub-systems that function as near copies of one another at different scales.

95. Deleuze, *Difference and Repetition*, 20.

96. E.H. Gombrich, *Art and Illusion: A Study in the Psychology of Pictorial Representation*. Princeton, NJ: Princeton University Press, 1960. Page 129.

97. Etymological throwaway: contrary to appearances, *Identity* does not share a root with *Idea*, and does not, therefore, share a root with *Separate*. Both *Idea* and *Separate* come from the Proto-Indo-European *weid-*, which is "to see" (as does the Greek *eidos*, which Husserl uses to talk about the real qualities of things, and which becomes a crucial part of Harman's Object-Oriented Ontology). *Identity*, on the other hand, comes out of the lexicalization of a demonstrative pronoun. This is slightly disappointing since *Identity*, as it is used, tends to close that circle between *Idea* and *Separate*.

98. Graham Harman, *The Quadruple Object*, 26-27.

99. Harman, *The Quadruple Object*, 28.

100. Aristotle, *Metaphysica*, trans W.A. Ross. Oxford: Clarendon Press, 1908 Line 1043a.

101. Thomas Aquinas, *The Soul (De Anima)*, trans. John Patrick Rowan. St. Louis: B. Herder Book Co., 1949. Page 12.

102. Aristotle, *Metaphysica*, 1032a.

103. Thomas Aquinas, "Commentary, *V* Metaphysics, lect. 2," edited and translated by Thomas Gilby, in *St. Thomas Aquinas: Philosophical Texts*. Durham, NC: Labyrinth Press, 1982. Page 46.

104. Ergonomics is a fascinating topic because it blurs the boundary between science and aesthetics in an unexpected way. Being a discipline for engineers, it might be called a science of aesthetics, but because ergonomics also includes machine interface design, it is a key part of accessing information in the first place. So, it could rightly be called an aesthetics of science as well. Ergonomics calls attention to a sort of primitive phenomenology that antecedes entry into particular knowledge systems. Consider skeumorphism, which is a central element in interface design. The most common examples of skeumorphism are the "Save" button (shaped as a 3½ inch floppy disk that is no longer used for saving data) and the file folder icon (shaped as a manila folder that is now rarely used for storing documents). The idea is that someone coming to the interface for the first time would need analytical knowledge of the entire interface in order to interact with it effectively. It is expected that the user will make multiple analogical points of entry instead of learning the whole interface as an ordered system of domains. Thus, before an asymmetrical material interaction can take place (e.g. storing altered content by passing and stopping electric current through transistors and capacitors), there must be an interaction between similar forms, such as the form of a memory of a floppy disk and the image-form of a floppy disk on the interface of the program. Asymmetrical material movement is initiated by the emergence of two similar sensual objects. This is not so far off from Deleuze's idea of the *double capture* of affects, except that in the OOO account of things, the sensual object is capable and enduring beyond its emergence. This makes all the difference in the world, because in addition to the continuous production of pure difference that you do indeed get from asymmetrical material interaction, you also maintain a formal cause of that interaction that need not be explained away by an amorphous force, such as *desire*, which is all used up in the interaction itself.

105. Timothy Morton, *Realist Magic: Objects, Ontology, and Causality*. Ann Arbor, MI: Open Humanities Press, 2013. Page 113.

106. The sheet, of course, was originally meant to be the funereal shroud. The shroud represented a barrier to existence in death, which itself was unknowable (and thus scary) but sensible to the living.

107. Harman takes this term from the English ghost writer M.R. James, and makes it function to describe his mapping of the different ways an object relates to itself. See Harman, *The Quadruple Object*, 124.

108. Harman, *The Quadruple Object*, 91.

109. One set A can contain all the subsets of another set B, including set B. But of course, B cannot have itself as a member. See David Foster Wallace, *Everything and More: A Compact History of Infinity*, introduction by Neal Stephenson. New York: W.W. Norton, 2010. Page 274.

110. "I term *void* of a situation this suture to its being. Moreover, I state that every structured presentation unpresents 'its' void, in the mode of this non-one which is merely the subtractive face of the count." Alain Badiou, *Being and Event*, trans. Oliver Feltham. New York: Continuum, 2005). Page 55.

111. Graham Harman, "Tristan Garcia and the Thing-in-Itself," *Parrhesia*, 16 (2013), 32.

112. A possibly grave objection: dinette sets and chairs are fine, but what about horrific acts of destruction, such Hiroshima or the slow death from a typhus outbreak on a Trans-Atlantic slave ship? This is where it's easy to sound callous. Surely, to make the claim about the chair and dinette set one must have the courage to replace those objects with victims of such events. It is more easily justified than stated.

113. Harman, *The Quadruple Object*, 117

114. Badiou, *Being and Event*, 67.

115. Badiou, *Being and Event*, 69.

116. Indeed, in written Russian, the elided "to be" construction is often positively represented with an em dash, as in *Moskva—gorod* [Moscow *is* a city].

117. Badiou, *Being and Event*, 10.

118. Alain Badiou, "Infinity and Set Theory: How to Begin with the Void," lecture at the European Graduate School in 2011. Available at http://www.egs.edu/faculty/alain-badiou/articles/infinity-and-set-theory, accessed 20 June, 2014.

119. It must be noted that Badiou has already criticized Heidegger in this particular position as having been seduced by a "poetic ontology." See Badiou, *Being and Event*, 9-10.

120. In R.M. Dixon, "Copula Clauses in Australian Languages: A Typological Perspective," *Anthropological Linguistics* 44.1 (Spring, 2002): 22.

121. Dixon, "Copula Clauses in Australian Languages," 21.

122. "*j ung tói* 'a table' (a flatty of table)." John McWhorter, *What Language Is: (And What It Isn't and What It Could Be)*. New York: Gotham Books, 2011. Page 32.

123. Graham Harman, "Concerning Stephen Hawking's Claim that Philosophy is Dead," *Filozofski vestnik* n. 2 (2012): 20.

124. *Harvey*, directed by Harry Koster (1950; Universal City, CA: Universal Studios, 2001), DVD.

125. To be clear, when Badiou talks about mathematical predication and being, he is not doing so in a physicalist language (see Badiou, *Being and Event*, 7). Similarly, on the other side of the issue, Morton asserts that "quantum theory and relativity are valid physical theories to the extent that they are object oriented." The point is that neither philosophical approach to predication depends on physics to make its case. See Morton, *Realist Magic*, 30.

126. Harman, *The Quadruple Object*, 38.

127. Nota bene: "completely" has been used very deliberately instead of "fully" or "totally." We cannot say that objects are ever fully present to themselves or to other objects, but as I have argued, they can be complete for others. Completeness is an aesthetic impression and/or judgment.

128. Morton, *Realist Magic*, 113.

129. Morton, *Realist Magic*, 111-112.

130. Morton, *Realist Magic*, 120.

131. Morton, *Realist Magic*, 120.

132. Morton, *Realist Magic*, 121.

133. To be clear, non-local entanglement is far from established dogma in physics. The prospect of non-locality probably has philosophers and pop-science folks licking their chops more than it has physicists. Free will and the metaphysics of information are two tasty morsels that will likely fall on philosophers' plates if a loophole-free test of non-locality is ever successfully performed. The idea is that nothing in the universe is faster than the speed of light, and therefore information cannot travel faster than the speed of light. If, however, particles such as photons are caught influencing each other at a time and a distance faster than another photon could mediate between them, we would have to seriously rethink the nature of information itself. The possible alternatives range from a cosmic conspiracy against free will (in which the photons *and* the experimenters were destined to act together in a certain way) to the idea that causality is not only non-local but non-linear in the way we understand time. The latter explanation seems to be what Morton is endorsing.

134. Timothy Morton, *Hyperobjects: Philosophy and Ecology after the End of the World*. Minneapolis: University of Minnesota Press, 2014, Kindle edition, the chapter entitled "Phasing."

135. Morton, *Hyperobjects*, the chapter entitled "Phasing."

136. Morton, *Hyperobjects*, the chapter entitled "Phasing."

137. "Internet," of course, is short for "Internetwork." So, the root of the word (*network*) is an endocentric compound that is affixed by *inter-*, which means "between" or "among." The almost polysynthetic structure of the word is a good match for the thing's own ontological ambiguity.

138. Badiou, *Number and Numbers*, 106.

139. Bob Dylan, "Ballad of a Thin Man," *Highway 61 Revisited* (Columbia Records, 1965).

140. Badiou, *Being and Event*, 180.

141. Badiou, *Being and Event*, 202.

142. Badiou, *Being and Event*, 203.

143. Well, there is the Danelaw, whose linguistic and onomastic legacy endures to this day. And it's true that divergent political and religious allegiances in the North periodically threatened English unity, most notably resulting in two major harryings (i.e. massacres), one under William I and another under Elizabeth I.

144. The Vendée had long been a thorn in the side of French unity, particularly as it was a Huguenot stronghold in the 16th century. Indeed, even before Paris dispatched Republican soldiers to deal with the Vendean uprising in 1793, the Vendeans were known as a *race maudite*. The argument as to whether or not the massacres of the Vendeans constituted a *genocide* in the modern sense has been a subject of bitter dispute amongst historians of the Revolution since the 1980s. See D.M.G. Sutherland, *The French Revolution and Empire: The Quest for a Civic Order* Malden, MA: Blackwell, 2003. Page 223.

145. Benedict Anderson, *Imagined Communities: Reflections on the Origin and Spread of Nationalism*. London: Verso, 1983. Page 80.

146. Anderson, *Imagined Communities*, 7.

147. C.L.R. James, *The Black Jacobins: Toussaint L'Ouverture and the San Domingo Revolution*. New York: Random House, 1963. Pages 71-76.

148. Thomas O. Ott, *The Haitian Revolution: 1789-1804*. Knoxville, TN: University of Tennessee Press, 1973. Page 9.

149. Ott, *The Haitian Revolution: 1789-1804*, 11.

150. Long form: *gens de couleur libres*.

151. James, *The Black Jacobins*, 38.

152. James, *The Black Jacobins*, 46.

153. I take this language from Franklin W. Knight, who gives singular credit for the elevation of human rights over civil rights, particularly with regards to anti-colonial struggles, to the Haitian Revolution. "The Haitian Revolution and the Notion of Human Rights," *The Journal of The Historical Society*, v. 3 (2005), 394.

154. In Theresa Levitt, *The Shadow of Enlightenment: Optical and Political Transparency in France 1789-1848*, Oxford: Oxford University Press, 2009. Page 177.

155. Granted, it was hardly a heroic gesture at this point. The British had long since proven that the exploitation of feudal labor (particularly in India) was far more profitable than slavery.

156. The struggle for the rights of women, I would argue, occupies a unique place in all of this. The movement of women's suffrage in the West was by and large a phenomenon of modern nationalism. However, beginning in the latter part of the 20th century, women's rights took on a universal universalist flavor, particularly with the emergence of black feminism and the LGBTQ movement.

157. James, *The Black Jacobins*, 20-21.

158. Toussaint L'Ouverture, "A Refutation of Some Assertions in a Speech Pronounced in the Corps Législatif...by Viénot Vaublanc," edited and translated by Laurent Dubois and John D. Garrigus, *The Slave Revolution in the Caribbean*

1789-1804: A Brief History with Documents. Boston: Bedford/St. Martins, 2006. Page 149.

159. National Convention Deputy Cambolous opened the proceedings with the following sentiment: "Since 1789, a great transformation remained incomplete; the nobilities of the sword and the Church were eliminated, but an aristocracy of skin still ruled; it has just breathed its last. Equality is established..." The National Convention, "The Abolition of Slavery: February 4, 1794," edited and translated by Dubois and Garrigus, *The Slave Revolution in the Caribbean 1794-1804*, 129.

160. The National Convention, "The Abolition of Slavery: February 4, 1794," edited and translated by Dubois and Garrigus, *The Slave Revolution in the Caribbean 1794-1804*, 131.

161. Latour, *On the Modern Cult of the Factish Gods*, 107.

162. Latour, *On the Modern Cult of the Factish Gods*, 110.

163. Latour, *On the Modern Cult of the Factish Gods*, 112.

164. *Abjection* is a key part of the experience. The term is obviously of enormous significance to psychoanalytic theory, and as such, it brings with it a wealth of nuances and diverse applications, but what's important to this discussion is that *abjection* describes a state in which one's familiar sense of subjectivity flees, in which one is left as an object of a situation.

165. Jean-Jacques Dessalines, "The Haitian Declaration of Independence," edited and translated by Dubois and Garrigus, *The Slave Revolution in the Caribbean 1794-1804*, 189.

166. Dessalines, "The Haitian Declaration of Independence," 190.

167. It is best not to leave the claim about asymmetrical contact with the legacy-object without annotation. So, the legacy of a person is self-similar both in that it endures as an object and in that it takes as qualities similar (even if contradictory) biographical facts of the person, connections made during the person's lifetime, and general impressions of that person. The legacy's contact with others is clearly going to be asymmetrical, considering that it may come into contact with a mother, a co-worker, a well-worn chair, or perhaps even an unborn descendent of the deceased.

168. Peter R. Anstey, *The Philosophy of Robert Boyle*. New York: Routledge, 2000. Page 118.

169. Boyle was careful not to attribute the thesis that he was arguing against either to Aristotle or to his Greek commentators: "I say *modern* Aristotelians, because divers of the *ancient*, especially Greek, commentators of Aristotle seem to have understood their master's doctrine of forms much otherwise and less incongruously than his Latin followers, the schoolmen, and others have since done." Robert Boyle, "The Origin of Forms and Qualities According to the Corpuscular Philosophy," edited by M.A. Stewart, *Selected Philosophical Papers of Robert Boyle*. Manchester: Manchester University Press, 1979. Page 53.

170. Robert Boyle, "About the Excellency and Grounds of the Mechanical Hypothesis," edited by M.A. Stewart, *Selected Philosophical Papers of Robert Boyle*, 140.

171. Steven Shapin and Simon Schaffer, *Leviathan and the Air-Pump: Hobbes, Boyle, and the Experimental Life*. Princeton, NJ: Princeton University Press, 1985. Page 69.

172. As Shapin and Schaffer argue, the existence of the vacuum is also a key component of Boyle's theological debate with Thomas Hobbes. Hobbes was a plenist who believed in a corporeal God, whereas Boyle argued for a transcendent, non-corporeal God who must have created the material universe out of nothing. See Shapin and Schaffer, *Leviathan and the Air-Pump*, 205-206.

173. Shapin and Schaffer, *Leviathan and the Air-Pump*, 46.

174. Robert Boyle, "The Origin of Forms and Qualities According to Corpuscular Philosophy," edited by M.A. Stewart, *Selected Philosophical Papers of Robert Boyle*. Manchester: Manchester University Press, 1979. Page 6.

175. Boyle, "The Origin of Forms and Qualities According to Corpuscular Philosophy," 5.

176. Boyle, "The Origin of Forms and Qualities According to Corpuscular Philosophy," 8.

177. The Spanish Empire, for instance, would not have come close to achieving the reach and shelf-life it did had it not been for Bartholemé de Medina's mercury and salt brine extraction process for silver ore, which he developed in the late 16th century, just as the Spanish had taken possession of the enormous Potosí mine in what is now Bolivia. The invention of this process was about as close as Europeans had ever come to making alchemy work.

178. Shapin and Schaffer, *Leviathan and the Air-Pump*, 57, footnote 66.

179. Shapin and Schaffer, *Leviathan and the Air-Pump*, 57.

180. Shapin and Schaffer, *Leviathan and the Air-Pump*, 56.

181. Shapin and Schaffer, *Leviathan and the Air-Pump*, 60.

182. *Jurassic Park*, directed by Steven Spielberg (1993; Universal City, CA: Universal Studios, 2012), DVD.

183. I take the terms *epistemic opacity* and *epistemic transparency* from Till Grüne-Yanoff and Paul Weirich, "The Philosophy and Epistemology of Simulation: A Review," *Simulation and Gaming*, 41 (1), 2010: 25.

184. See Dawkins's illustrated book for kids, *The Magic of Reality: How We Know What's Really True*. New York: Free Press, 2012.

185. Taylor, *The Moment of Complexity*,

186. Michael Hardt and Antonio Negri, *Empire*. Cambridge, MA: Harvard University Press, 2000.

187. Werner Heisenberg, *Physics and Philosophy: The Revolution in Modern Science*. New York: HarperPerennial, 1958. Page 123.

188. Heisenberg, *Physics and Philosophy*, 123.

189. That is not to say that a material investigation of the ant bridge would extend no further than the individual ant, but that in order to do so, new matter-forms would need to be established. However, in an emergent system such as an ant bridge, the material processes underlying the form of the individual ant would be insufficient for building a description about the material processes underlying the

form of the ant bridge. The ant bridge system is not merely a multiplication of the material processes underneath its material actors.

190. Please note that in Harman's own Object-Oriented Ontology, forms are to be considered real objects. In my own scheme, form and matter designate the modes in which objects and qualities relate to one another, as in:

Matter		Form
Real Qualities	for	Real Object
Sensual Qualities	for	Sensual Object

191. Harman, *The Quadruple Object*, 50.

192. James R. Hurford, *The Origin of Meaning: Language in the Light of Evolution.* Oxford: Oxford University Press, 2007. Page 91.

193. When the subitizing range for an individual reaches n+1, either counting or estimating kick in. My guesses of "six" were most likely estimating, which is a different mechanism from either counting or subitizing.

194. Hurford, *The Origin of Meaning*, 91-92.

195. Counting is an analytical practice, but its analyticity varies from culture to culture. Even with different base numbers (e.g. the Celtic vegisimal system or the Babylonian sexagesimal system), we're very used to thinking of counting systems as being abstract and self-referential. However, certain systems, like that of Foe speakers in Papua New Guinea possess a lower degree of analyticity. Foe has a base-37 system, with all thirty-seven numbers corresponding to upper-body parts ("Foe" Living Tongues). Furthermore, as Everett (2012) reports, the Pirahã of Brazil have no counting system at all, but instead have terms for comparative quantity. Thus, counting itself may be a case of linguistic opulence.

196. Lana M. Trick, "More than superstition: Differential effects of featural heterogeneity and change on subitizing and counting," *Perception & Psychophysics*, 70.5 (2008): 745.

197. Trick, "More than superstition," 743.

198. Trick, "More than superstition," 759.

199. Simultanagnosia is a neurological disorder in which sufferers are unable to integrate constituent objects into a larger scene. Hurford, *The Origin of Meaning*, 107.

200. Stanislas Dehaene and Laurent Cohen, "Dissociable mechanisms of subitizing and counting: Neuropsychological evidence from simultagnosic patients," *Journal of Psychology: Human Perception and Performance*, 20 (1994): 958.

201. Dehaene and Cohen, "Dissociable mechanisms of subitizing and counting," 971.

202. Trick, "More than superstition," 759.

203. Number is both a quality and is subject to intellectual speculation rather than sensuous intuition, as the research on subitizing suggests. Number is therefore an RQ, even if the count is just one. Numbers are both real and withdrawn. We know this from the doomed quest to axiomatize the relationships between numbers in the 20th century. We also know this from the immense variability of numerical systems across cultures. Similarly, we know that the color *blue* is real, but whether a thing is this blue or that one is individually or culturally contingent. Even a spectral analysis of a blue is not blue itself.

204. You needn't smell a shoe. In fact, it's probably better if you don't.

205. Anderson, *Imagined Communities*, 15-16.

206. Kallawaya is a critically endangered language spoken by shamans in Bolivia. See *The Linguists!*, directed by Seth Kramer, Daniel A. Miller, and Jeremy Newberger (Garrison, NY: Ironbound Films, 2008), DVD.

207. Foucault is not given enough credit for his prose, particularly in his "archeological" phase. It is true that his rock star personality comes through most clearly in his interviews and lectures, but there are some truly sparkling moments in his books. I confess that I haven't attempted a French reading of *Les mots et les choses*, so credit must also go to the translators at Pantheon. That said, the second chapter of *The Order of Things* ("The Prose of the World"), from which I am quoting here, is some of the most beautiful prose I've read in philosophy, though it's often overshadowed by the first "Las Meninas" chapter. More's the pity. As a weaving together of another world, it's a positively Tolkienian effort.

208. Michel Foucault, *The Order of Things: An Archeology of the Human Sciences* (New York: Pantheon, 1970), 17.

209. Foucault, *The Order of Things*, 27.

210. Foucault, *The Order of Things*, 30.

211. Mitchell, *Complexity*, 260-261.

212. Mitchell, *Complexity*, 260.

213. Mitchell, *Complexity*, 262-266.

214. Veronique Green, "Geoffrey West Finds the Physical Laws Embedded in Human Cities," *Discover* 28 Sept. 2012, available at <http://discovermagazine.com/2012/oct/21-geoffrey-west-finds-physical-laws-in-cities>, accessed August 9, 2014.

215. Mitchell, *Complexity*, 294.

216. Laurie L. Patton, "Introduction," *The Bhagavad Gita*, translated by Laurie L. Patton. London: Penguin Books, 2008. Page xvii.

217. Martin Heidegger, *Aristotle's* Metaphysics Θ 1-3: On the Essence and Actuality of Force, translated by Walter Brogan and Peter Warnek. Bloomington, IN: Indiana University Press, 1995. Pages 2-3.

218. Heidegger, *Aristotle's* Metaphysics Θ 1-3, 3.

219. Battista Mondin, *The Principle of Analogy in Protestant and Catholic Theology*. The Hague: Martinus Nijhoff, 1963. Page 1.

220. Mondin, *The Principle of Analogy in Protestant and Catholic Theology*, 1.

221. Perseus Collection, Greek and Roman Materials, "Romans 12.6," *The New Testament (Greek)*, available at http://www.perseus.tufts.edu/hopper/collection?collection=Perseus%3Acollection%3AGreco-Roman. Accessed September 1, 2014.

222. Perseus Collection, Greek and Roman Materials "Romans 12.6," *Latin Vulgate*, available at http://www.perseus.tufts.edu/hopper/collection?collection=Perseus%3Acollection%3AGreco-Roman, accessed Sep. 1, 2014.

223. Romans 12:6 (*King James Bible*).

224. C.L. Wilibald Grimm, "ἀναλογία," *Greek-English Lexicon of the New Testament*, translated and and edited by Joseph Henry Thayer. Grand Rapids, MI: Zondervan Publishing House, 1962. Page 39.

225. Aristotle, *Metaphysica*, translated and edited by W.D. Ross. Oxford: Clarendon Press, 1908. Line 1018a.

226. Aristotle, *Metaphysica*, 1018a.

227. Aristotle, *Parts of Animals*, translated by A.L. Peck. Cambridge, MA: Harvard University Press, 1961). Line 644a.

228. Aristotle, *Parts of Animals*, 645b.

229. Aristotle, *Parts of Animals*, 645b.

230. Aristotle, *Metaphysica*, 1003a-1003b.

231. πρὸς ἕν = "related to one"

232. Thomas Aquinas, *Philosophical Texts*, translated and edited by Thomas Gilby. Durham, NC: Labyrinth Press, 1982. Page 93.

233. Aquinas, *Philosophical Texts*, 93.

234. Aquinas, *Philosophical Texts*, 93.

235. Kant recognized that an analogy is not necessarily a path to knowledge about the target analogue, and therefore that the analogy does not necessarily subject both analogues to conceptual understanding. For Kant, analogy "does not signify [...] an imperfect similarity of two things, but a perfect similarity of relations between two quite dissimilar things." Thus, a concept can be attributed to the relationship between what humans and God possess (e.g. love) without any understanding of what God's love really is. Within the analogy, however, the love of humans and the love of God have disappeared into a concept. See *Prolegomena to Any Future Metaphysics*, translated and edited by Gary Hatfield. Cambridge, UK: Cambridge University Press, 1997. Page 111.

236. Steve A. Long, *Analogia Entis: On the Analogy of Being, Metaphysics, and the Act of Faith*. Notre Dame, IN: University of Notre Dame Press, 2011.

237. Long, *Analogia Entis*, 2.

238. See Alain Badiou, *Deleuze: The Clamor of Being*, translated by Louise Burchill. Minneapolis: University of Minnesota Press, 199). Having published the book after Deleuze's death, Badiou nonetheless treats Deleuze's arguments without any caricature or simplification whatsoever. The introduction is particularly heart-warming, as Badiou shows how an enduring friendship can emerge out of even the most rigorous debate.

239. Ralph McInerny, *Aquinas and Analogy*. Washington, DC: Catholic University of America Press, 1996. Page 6.

240. Thomas Aquinas, *The Disputed Questions of Truth v. I*, translated by Robert Mulligan Chicago: Henery Regency Co.,1952. Pages 110-111.

241. Long, *Analogia Entis*, 6.

242. The cultural history of infinitesimals is an absolutely fascinating topic on its own. See Amir Alexander, *Infinitesimal: How a Dangerous Mathematical Theory Shaped the Modern World*. New York: Scientific American/Farrar, Straus, and Giroux, 2014.

243. Aquinas, *The Disputed Questions of Truth v. I*, 112.

244. Aquinas, *The Disputed Questions of Truth v. I*, 113.

245. The operative phrase here is "attributed to." There is no evidence that Aquinas himself ever used the term *analogia entis*. And indeed the very fact that Aquinas put greater distance between God and creature than between non-being and creature suggests that the notion of some serial-analogical chain existing between the being of God and the beings of creatures would have been anathema to Aquinas.

246. David Hume, *A Treatise on Human Nature*, edited by David Fate Norton and Mary J. Norton. Oxford: Oxford University Press, 2000. Page 23.

247. Hume, *A Treatise on Human Nature*, 26.

248. Hume, *A Treatise on Human Nature*, 29.

249. Hume, *A Treatise on Human Nature*, 7.

250. Hume, *A Treatise on Human Nature*, 8.

251. Hume, *A Treatise on Human Nature*, 9.

252. Hume, *A Treatise on Human Nature*, 8.

253. Hume, *A Treatise on Human Nature*, 15.

254. *Negentropy* is a portmanteau of *negative entropy*. It's a sort of double-negative. If entropy is the dissipation of information in the accretion of noise, negentropy is a "dissipation of dissipation" of that noise, which turns out to be new information. See Mark C. Taylor, *The Moment of Complexity*, 121.

255. Hume, *A Treatise on Human Nature*, 170.

256. W.V. Quine, *Ontological Relativity and Other Essays*. New York: Columbia University Press, 1969. Page 121.

257. Nelson Goodman, *Problems and Projects*. Indianapolis, IN: Bobbs-Merrill Company, 1972. Page 446.

258. Quine, *Ontological Relativity and Other Essays*, 75.

259. Quine, *Ontological Relativity and Other Essays*, 75.

260. Quine, *Ontological Relativity and Other Essays*, 90.

261. Eric A. Havelock, *The Literate Revolution in Greece and Its Cultural Consequences*. Princeton, NJ: Princeton University Press, 1982. Page 64.

262. Havelock, *The Literate Revolution in Greece and Its Cultural Consequences*, 48.

263. Havelock, *The Literate Revolution in Greece and Its Cultural Consequences*, 81-82.

264. Havelock, *The Literate Revolution in Greece and Its Cultural Consequences*, 99.

265. Morris Halle, "The Strategy of Phonemics," *Word* 10, 1954: 197-198.

266. Though Quine often prefers the softer term "kinds."

267. Nelson Goodman and W.V. Quine, "Steps Toward a Constructive Nominalism," in *Problems and Projects*, Nelson Goodman. Indianapolis: Bobs-Merrill Co., 1972. Page 173.

268. Goodman, *Problems and Projects*, 156.

269. Goodman, *Problems and Projects*, 69-75.

270. Goodman, *Problems and Projects*, 69.

271. Goodman, *Problems and Projects*, 70.

272. Goodman, *Problems and Projects*, 27.
273. Goodman, *Problems and Projects*, 29.
274. Goodman, *Problems and Projects*, 157.
275. Goodman, "Seven Strictures on Similarity," in *Problems and Projects*, 440.
276. Wilfrid Sellars, "Being and Being Known," *Science Perception and Reality*. Austin, TX: Ridgeview Publishing Digital, 1991. Kindle edition, paragraph 16.
277. Sellars, "Being and Being Known," paragraph 16.
278. Sellars, "Being and Being Known," paragraph 17.
279. Sellars, "Being and Being Known," paragraph 42.
280. Melanie Mitchell, *Complexity: A Guided Tour*. New York: Oxford University Press, 2009. Page 63.
281. Ray Brassier, "Concepts and Objects," in Levi Bryant et al. (Eds.), *The Speculative Turn*, page 49.
282. Brassier, "Concepts and Objects," 51.
283. Wilfrid Sellars, "American Critical Realism and British Theories of Sense Perception," in *Neglected Alternatives*, edited W. Preston Warren. Lewisburg, PA: Bucknell University Press, 1973. Page 72.
284. Sellars, "American Critical Realism and British Theories of Sense Perception," 71.
285. Sellars, "American Critical Realism and British Theories of Sense Perception," 72.
286. Sellars, "Empiricism and the Philosophy of the Mind," *Science, Perception, and Reality*, paragraph 1.
287. Sellars, "The Language of Theories," *Science Perception and Reality*, paragraph 11.
288. Sellars, *Empiricism and the Philosophy of the Mind*, paragraph 94.
289. William de Vries, *Wilfrid Sellars*. Durham, UK: Acumen, 2005. Page 28.
290. Wilfrid Sellars, "Behaviorism, Language, and Meaning," *Pacific Philosophical Quarterly* 61 (1980), paragraph 101, available at http://ditext.com.sellars/blm.html, accessed on April 7, 2015.
291. Sellars, "Behaviorism, Language, and Meaning," paragraph 61.
292. Sellars, "Behaviorism, Language, and Meaning," paragraph 102.
293. Sellars, "Behaviorism, Language, and Meaning," paragraph 103.
294. Sellars, "Empiricism and the Philosophy of the Mind," paragraph 105.
295. Sellars, "Empiricism and the Philosophy of the Mind," paragraph 105.
296. Sellars, "Empiricism and the Philosophy of the Mind," paragraph 106.
297. Sellars, "Some Reflections on Language Games," *Science, Perception and Reality*, paragraph 3.
298. Sellars, "Some Reflections on Language Games," paragraph 17.
299. de Vries, *Wilfrid Sellars*, 43.

300. WH- questions are constructions that use the interrogative form of the following lexical items in English: *who, what, when, where, why* and *how.*
301. Please take note of the asterisk in front of sentence *2b*. In standard linguistic notation, asterisks are placed in front of words, phrases, or sentences that would be interpreted as being ungrammatical by native speakers of the language in which the construction appears. This is a device I will be using elsewhere in the book as well.
302. in Michael Tomasello, "Beyond Formalities: The Case of Language Acquisition," *The Linguistic Review* 22 (2005), 190.
303. Tomasello, "Beyond Formalities," 191.
304. Sellars, "Empiricism and the Philosophy of the Mind," paragraph 105.
305. Sellars, "Empiricism and the Philosophy of the Mind," paragraph 106.
306. de Vries, *Wilfrid Sellars*, 45.
307. Timothy Morton, *Realist Magic*, 124.
308. Douglas Hofstadter and Emmanuel Sander, *Surfaces and Essences: Analogy as the Fuel and Fire of Thinking*. New York: Basic Books, 2013. Page 186.
309. Hofstadter and Sander, *Surfaces and Essences*, 204-209.
310. Childhood nostalgia rather than genuine appreciation of Oasis's art has long been the explanation given for fondness for the band.
311. Timothy Morton, blog post at *Ecology without Nature*, November 6, 2010, http://ecologywithoutnature.blogspot.com/2010/11/anything-you-can-do-i-can-do-meta.html
312. Neither the immigrants nor the cruise buffet being, according to Ruth, "on fleek."
313. Naomi Shihab Nye, "Famous," available at http://www.poets.org/poetsorg/poem/famous, accessed October 4, 2014.
314. Don DeLillo, *White Noise*. New York: Penguin Books, 1999.
315. Although I have used Bowie's peculiar locution to practice my phonetic transcription: /ðæ / /w z/ / h i:/ / k zm k/ /d æv/
316. Longinus, "from *On the Sublime*," translated by D.A. Russell and edited Patricia Bizzell and Bruce Herzberg, *The Rhetorical Tradition: Readings from Classical Times to the Present* 2nd edition. Boston: Bedford/St. Martin's, 2001. Page 354.
317. Longinus "from *On the Sublime*," 354.
318. Longinus "from *On the Sublime*," 355.
319. Gilles Deleuze, *Difference and Repetition*, translated by Paul Patton. New York: Columbia University Press, 1995. Page 33.
320. Gilles Deleuze and Félix Guattari, *A Thousand Plateaus: Capitalism and Schizophrenia*, translated by Brian Massumi. Minneapolis: University of Minnesota Press, 1987). Pages 234-235.
321. Deleuze and Guattari, *A Thousand Plateaus*, 236.
322. Deleuze and Guattari, *A Thousand Plateaus*, 236.
323. Deleuze and Guattari, *A Thousand Plateaus*, 12.

324. George A. Kennedy, *A New History of Classical Rhetoric*. Princeton, NJ: Princeton University Press, 1994. Page 19.

325. Quintilian, "from *Institutes of Oratory*," translated by John Selby Watson, *The Rhetorical Tradition*, 401.

326. Giambattista Vico, *New Science*, translated by David Marsh. New York: Penguin Books, 1999. Page 369.

327. Gilles Deleuze, *Difference and Repetition*, 38.

328. Gilles Deleuze, *Difference and Repetition*, 38.

329. "'Tis a strange place this Limbo!—not a Place/Yet name it so—..." Samuel Taylor Coleridge, *Selected Poems*, edited by Richard Holmes. New York: Penguin Books, 1996. Page 214.

330. Deleuze and Guattari, *Thousand Plateaus*, 10.

331. Deleuze and Guattari, *Thousand Plateaus*, 10.

332. Deleuze and Guattari, *Thousand Plateaus*, 10.

333. Deleuze and Guattari, *Thousand Plateaus*, 10.

334. Deleuze and Guattari, *Thousand Plateaus*, 53.

335. This is where Deleuzean metaphysics and Foucauldian philosophy find a common purpose. We see in Foucault (most clearly in *Discipline and Punish*) that institutional practices were not just representative of institutional structures; rather, institutional structures were technological *expressions* of practices that were transferrable between different types of institutions.

336. Deleuze and Guattari, *Thousand Plateaus*, 59.

337. Deleuze and Guattari, *Thousand Plateaus*, 59.

338. Deleuze and Guattari, *Thousand Plateaus*, 59.

339. National Human Genome Research Institute, "Chromosomes," available at http://www.genome.gov/26524120, accessed October 13, 2014.

340. Granted, this asymmetry between genetic and morphological diversity has been exploited by young earth proponents of Intelligent Design. Be apprised that the author's purposes for the present engagement with Deleuze and Guattari correspond in no way with the young earth lot in their refutations of Darwinism.

341. Melanie Mitchell, *Complexity: A Guided Tour*. Oxford: Oxford University Press, 2009. Page 279.

342. Nelson Goodman, *Problems and Projects*. Indianapolis, IN: Bobbs-Merrill Company, 1972. Page 440.

343. James R. Hurford, *The Origins of Meaning*. Oxford: Oxford University Press, 2007. Page 97.

344. Hurford, *The Origins of Meaning*, 97.

345. in Hurford, *The Orgins of Meaning*, 55.

346. Noam Chomsky, "Of Minds and Language," *Biolinguistics* 1 (2007): 24.

347. Steven Pinker and Paul Bloom, "Natural Language and Natural Selection," *Behavioral and Brain Sciences* 13 (1990): 707-784.

348. Derek Bickerton, "How Protolanguage Became Language," in *The Evolutionary Emergence of Language: Social Function and the Origins of Linguistic Form*, edited by Chris Knight, Michael Studdert-Kennedy, and James R. Hurford. Cambridge, UK: Cambridge University Press, 2000. Page 266.

349. Bickerton, "How Protolanguage Became Language," 267.

350. Hurford, *The Origin of Meaning*, 73.

351. Bickerton, "How Protolanguage Became Language," 269.

352. Simply put, *arguments* complete a predicate with respect to its distinction from the grammatical subject.

353. Bickerton, "How Protolanguage Became Language," 269.

354. a = Argument; p = Predicate

355. Bickerton, "How Protolanguage Became Language," 269-270.

356. Daniel Everett, "Cultural Constraints on Grammar and Cognition in Pirahã: Another Look at the Design Features of Human Language," *Current Anthropology* 46.4 (2005): 621-646.

357. Syntagmatic redundancy is the grammatical repetition of information. It includes mechanisms as simple as noun-verb agreement and as complicated as the repetition of grammatical gender information in noun phrases. When adults are obliged to adopt another language in significant numbers—say, on a slave plantation—the result is often the elimination of some syntagmatic redundancies. See: Peter Trudgill, *Sociolinguistic Typology: Social Determinants of Linguistic Complexity*. Oxford: Oxford University Press, 2011.

358. James R. Hurford, *Language in the Light of Evolution, Vol 2: The Origins of Grammar*. Oxford: Oxford University Press, 2011. Page 649.

359. This, by the way, is why school proscriptions on the so-called passive voice are counterproductive and silly.

360. Hurford, *Language in the Light of Evolution, Vol 2*, 651.

361. Alison Wray, *Formulaic Language: Pushing the Boundaries*. Oxford: Oxford University Press, 2002. Page 13.

362. Alison Wray, "Holistic Utterances in Protolanguage: The Link from Primates to Humans," in *The Evolutionary Emergence of Language*, Chris Knight et al. (Eds.). Cambridge, UK: Cambridge University Press, 2000. Page 285.

363. Wray, "Holistic Utterances in Protolanguage," 287.

364. Wray, "Holistic Utterances in Protolanguage," 289.

365. Wray, "Holistic Utterances in Protolanguage," 289.

366. Wray, "Holistic Utterances in Protolanguage," 294.

367. Wray, "Holistic Utterances in Protolanguage," 297.

368. Derek Bickerton, "Language Evolution: A Brief Guide for Linguists," *Lingua* 17 (2007): 517.

369. Bickerton, "Language Evolution," 517.

370. Gerald Knowles, "Variable Strategies in Intonation," in *Intonation, Accent and Rhythm: Studies in Discourse Phonology*, edited by Dafydd Gibbon and Helmut Richter. Berlin: Walter de Gruyter, 1984. Page 229

371. Roger K. R. Thompson and Joël Fagot, "Generalized Relational Matching by Guinea Baboons (*Papio papio*) in Two by Two-Item Analogy Problems," *Psychological Science* (20 Sept. 2011).

372. Roger K.R. Thompson and David L. Oden, "Categorical Perception and Conceptual Judgement by Non-Human Primates: The Paleological Monkey and the Analogical Ape," *Cognitive Science* 24.3 (July-Sept. 2000).

373. George Orwell, "Politics and the English Language," in *Why I Write*. New York: Penguin Books, 2004. Page 106.

374. Chaim Perelman and Lucie Olbrechts-Tyca, *The New Rhetoric: A Treatise on Argumentation*. (outh Bend, IN: University of Notre Dame Press, 1991. Page 402.

375. George Lakoff, *Women, Fire, and Dangerous Things: What Categories Reveal about the Mind*. Chicago: University of Chicago Press, 1987. Page xv.

376. This is known as the *head-first/head-last* distinction. Head-first languages are more common than head-last languages. English is a head-first language, and the largest head-last language is Japanese.

377. Taken from: John McWhorter, "Understanding Linguistics: The Science of Language," *The Great Courses*, available at http://www.thegreatcourses.com, accessed October 10, 2014.

378. Lakoff, *Women, Fire, and Dangerous Things*, 462.

379. Lakoff, *Women, Fire, and Dangerous Things*, 469.

380. Lakoff, *Women, Fire, and Dangerous Things*, 470.

381. George Lakoff and Mark Johnson, *Philosophy in the Flesh: The Embodied Mind and Its Challenge to Western Thought*. New York: Basic Books, 1999. Page 27.

382. Lakoff and Johnson, *Philosophy in the Flesh*, 27.

383. Lakoff, *Women, Fire, and Dangerous Things*, 60.

384. Lakoff and Johnson, *Philosophy in the Flesh*, 51-52.

385. Steven Pinker, *Words and Rules: The Ingredients of Language*. New York: Basic Books, 1999. Page 191.

386. Lakoff, *Women, Fire, and Dangerous Things*, 62.

387. Lakoff, *Women, Fire, and Dangerous Things*, 62.

388. Emma Morris, "How 'holp' became 'helped'," *Nature*, 10 Oct. 2007: 152.

389. Keith Plaster and Maria Polinsky, "Women are not Dangerous Things: Gender and Categorization," *Harvard Working Papers in Linguistics*, 2007, available at http://scholar.harvard.edu/mpolinsky/files/Dyirbal.pdf, accessed November 18, 2014.

390. Robert M.W. Dixon, *The Dyirbal Language of North Queensland*. Cambridge, UK: Cambridge University Press, 1972. Page 307.

391. Lakoff, *Women, Fire, and Dangerous Things*, 94.

392. Lakoff, *Women, Fire, and Dangerous Things*, 94-95.

393. Lakoff, *Women, Fire, and Dangerous Things*, 99.

394. Lakoff, *Women, Fire, and Dangerous Things*, 99.

395. Some examples from unrelated languages include Vlax Romani's *piy-* (to smoke and drink) and Manambu's *kuh-* (to smoke, drink, and eat).

396. Lakoff, *Women, Fire, and Dangerous Things*, 94.

397. Lakoff, *Women, Fire, and Dangerous Things*, 100.

398. Plaster and Polinksy, "Women are not Dangerous Things," 16-17.

399. K. David Harrison, *The Last Speakers: The Quest to Save the World's Most Endangered Languages*. Washington, DC: The National Geographical Society, 2010. Page 10.

400. Lila San Roque and Robyn Loughnane, "The New Guinea Highlands Evidentiality Area," *Linguistic Typology* 16.1 (April 2012): 114.

401. John McWhorter, *What Language Is*, 128-130.

402. Being the most significant number of my own childhood, I was continually puzzled by its absence in mathematics textbooks at school.

403. John McWhorter, *What Language Is: (And What It Isn't And What It Could Be)*. New York: Gotham Books, 2011. Page 80.

404. Ashley Crandell Amos, "Old English Words for Old," in *Aging and the Aged in Medieval Europe*, edited by Michael Sheehan. Toronto: Pontifical Institute of Mediaeval Europe, 1990. Pages 100-101.

405. K. David Harrison, *When Languages Die: The Extinction and the Erosion of the World's Languages and the Erosion of Human Knowledge*. Oxford: Oxford University Press, 2007. Page 217; William S. Poser, "Noun Classification in Carrier," (2004), available at http://billposer.org/Papers/nclass.pdf, accessed November 11 2014.

406. Poser, "Noun Classification in Carrier," 10.

407. Poser, "Noun Classification in Carrier," 12.

408. Which gives new meaning to T.S. Eliot's upanishadic *Da, Datta, Damyata* (Give, Sympathize, Control).

409. Poser, "Noun Classification in Carrier," 5.

410. A calque is a word or a phrase borrowed from one language into another; however, instead of borrowing the exact words from the donor language, the borrowing language does a word-for-word translation into its own language. Therefore, calques often stick out like sore thumbs, syntax-wise.

411. Samuel Taylor Coleridge, *Selected Poems*, edited by Richard Holmes. London: Penguin Books, 1994. Pages 230-231.

412. Harrison, *When Languages Die*, 214.

413. Harrison, *When Languages Die*, 215.

414. Jean-Francois Lyotard, *The Postmodern Condition: A Report on Knowledge*, translated by Brian Massumi. Minneapolis, University of Minnesota Press, 1984. Pages 4-5.

415. Lyotard, *The Postmodern Condition*, 43-45.

416. Philosophical works inspired by the Italian Autonomist movement have been particularly effective in this vein. Hardt and Negri's "Empire" trilogy is excellent and the most famous of these works. But for my money, Paolo Virno's short 2004 book, *A Grammar of the Multitude: For an Analysis of Contemporary Forms of Life* is the best single work in this philosophical current.

417. Mikhail Bakhtin, *Speech Genres and Other Late Essays,* translated by Vern W. McGee and edited Michael Holquist and Caryl Emerson. Austin, TX: University of Texas Press, 1986. Page 70.

418. Bakhtin, *Speech Genres and Other Late Essays*, 71.

419. Bakhtin, *Speech Genres and Other Late Essays*, 71.

420. Bakhtin, *Speech Genres and Other Late Essays*, 65.

421. Timothy Morton, *Realist Magic*, 69.

422. Bakhtin, *Speech Genres and Other Late Essays*, 92.

423. Thomas E. Payne, *Describing Morphosyntax: A Field Guide for Linguists.* Cambridge, UK: Cambridge University Press, 1997. Pages 357-358.

424. William N. Salmon, "Formal Idioms and Action: Toward a Grammar of Genres," *Language & Communication*, 30 (2010): 215.

425. Salmon, "Formal Idioms and Action," 215.

426. Salmon, "Formal Idioms and Action," 215.

427. Gilles Deleuze and Felix Guattari, *A Thousand Plateaus*, 255.

428. Please be apprised that *koines, creoles, pidgins,* and *lingua francas* are not at all the same thing. Koines develop out of contact between adult speakers of two or more languages that are at least somewhat mutually intelligible, as Old English and Old Norse were. Creoles involve a target superstrate language and a number of substrate languages which are mutually unintelligible. The same is true for a pidgin except that a pidgin is never learned as a first language. A lingua franca is a common language adopted for political, economic and/or religious purposes that retains most of its complexity and distinctive features and which may or not also continue as a first language for a group of people.

429. John S. Lumsden, "Language Acquisition and Creolization," in *Language Creation and Language Change: Creolization, Diachrony, and Development,* edited by Michel DeGraff. Cambridge, MA: MIT Press, 1999. Page 134.

430. Lumsden, "Language Acquisition and Creolization," 134.

431. Robin Stern, *Say It in Crucian! A Complete Guide to Today's Crucian for Speakers of Standard English.* Christiansted, United States Virgin Islands: Antilles Press, 2008. Page 35.

432. Lumsden, "Language Acquisition and Creolization," 150.

433. John McWhorter, "Txtng is killing language. JK!!!" *TED*, available at http://www.ted.com/talks/john_mcwhorter_txtng_is_killing_language_jk/transcript?language=en, accessed November 11, 2014.

434. Amy Devitt, *Writing Genres,*. Carbondale, IL: Southern Illinois University Press, 2008. Page 125.

435. Devitt, *Writing Genres*, 128.

436. Shirley Brice Heath, "Protean Shapes in Literacy Events: Ever-Shifting Oral and Literate Traditions," *Literacy: A Critical Sourcebook*, edited by Ellen Cushman et al. Boston: Bedford/St. Martin's, 2001. Pages 443-466.

437. Devitt, *Writing Genres*, 131-132.

438. Devitt, *Writing Genres*, 30.

439. Salmon, "Formal Idioms and Action," 217.

440. Devitt, *Writing Genres*, 92.

441. Thomas Kuhn, *The Structure of Scientific Revolutions* 3rd edition. Chicago: University of Chicago Press, 1996.

442. Douglas Hofstadter and Emmanuel Sander, *Surfaces and Essences*, 444..

443. Friedrich Nietzsche, "On Truth and Lies in a Nonmoral Sense," translated by Daniel Breazeale, in *The Rhetorical Tradition*, 1174.

444. Nietzsche, "On Truth and Lies in a Nonmoral Sense," 1174.

445. Nietzsche, "On Truth and Lies in a Nonmoral Sense," 1175.

446. Michel Foucault, *The Archeology of Knowledge and The Discourse on Knowledge*, translated by A.M. Sheridan Smith. New York: Pantheon Books, 1972. Page 41.

447. Michel Foucault, "Truth and Power," in *The Essential Foucault: Selections from the Essential Works of Foucault, 1954-1984*, edited by Paul Rabinow and Nikolas Rose, New York: The New Press, 1994. Page 300.

448. Michel Foucault, *The Birth of Biopolitics: Lectures at the Collège de France, 1978-1979*, translated by Graham Burchell and edited by Michel Senellart. New York: Palgrave MacMillan, 2008. Page 32.

449. Melanie Mitchell, *Complexity: A Guided Tour*, 64-65.

450. Andreas Wagner, "The Role of Randomness in Darwinian Evolution," *Philosophy of Science* 79 (January 2012), 98.

451. Wagner, "The Role of Randomness in Darwinian Evolution," 101.

452. Wagner, "The Role of Randomness in Darwinian Evolution," 102.

453. Andreas Wagner, Interview by World Science Festival Staff, *World Science Festival* (30 Sep 2014), available at http://www.worldsciencefestival.com/2014/09/smart-reads-andreas-wagners-arrival-fittest/, accessed December 2, 2014.

454. Wagner, "The Role of Randomness in Darwinian Evolution," 109.

455. Wagner, "The Role of Randomness in Darwinian Evolution," 109.

456. Wagner merely offers the library of everything as an illustrative example, but I wonder if this understanding of innovation in biological evolution could, at the very least, be loosely applied to innovation in the evolution of language. Perhaps instead of beginning with self-same modular principles, there are self-similar networks of grammatical objects that have emerged from similar repetitions of whole semantic chunks and that have taken on similarly useful functions in communicative situations.

457. Hofstadter and Sander, *Surfaces and Essences*, 143-144.

458. Douglas Hofstadter and Melanie Mitchell, "The Copycat Project: A Model of Mental Fluidity and Analogy-Making," available at http://www.nbu.bg/cogs/personal/kokinov/COG501/copycat1.pdf, accessed November 11, 2014.

459. Sridhar Kota, "Shape-Shifting Things to Come," *Scientific American* 310.5 (May 2014): 65.

460. Kota, "Shape-Shifting Things to Come," 60.

461. Karl Marx, "The German Ideology: I," in *The Marx-Engels Reader* 2nd edition, edited by Robert C. Tucker. New York: W.W. Norton & Co., 1978. Page 150.

462. This is the weakness of psychoanalytic philosophy. It presupposes a subject as its object of analysis without admitting that it is at least also an object with a particular form. Marx, on the other hand, doesn't care to touch on the subject without noticing something about its form as an object.

463. Graham Harman, "Concerning Stephen Hawking's Claim that Philosophy is Dead," *Filozofski vestnik* n. 2 (2012): 20.

464. Douglas Hofstadter and Emmanuel Sander, *Surfaces and Essences*, 3.

465. Bruno Latour, "Can We Get Our Materialism Back, Please?" *Isis* 98 (2007): 139.

466. Latour, "Can We Get Our Materialism Back, Please?" 139.

467. Latour, "Can We Get Our Materialism Back, Please?" 139.

468. Latour, "Can We Get Our Materialism Back, Please?" 138.

469. Friedrich Engels, "Letter to Joseph Block," in *The Marx-Engels Reader* 2nd edition, edited by Robert C. Tucker, 760.

470. Engels, "Letter to Joseph Block," 760.

471. Karl Marx, *Grundrisse*, translated by Martin Nicolaus. London: Penguin Books, 1973. Pages 305-306.

472. Marx, *Grundrisse*, 298.

473. Marx, *Grundrisse*, 302.

474. Marx, *Grundrisse*, 300.

475. Marx, *Grundrisse*, 302.

476. Karl Marx, *Capital: Volume I*, translated by Ben Fowkes. London: Penguin Books, 1976. Pages 493-494.

477. Louis Althusser, "Ideology and Ideological State Apparatuses: Notes Towards an Investigation," translated by Ben Brewster, accessed on February 2, 2015. https://www.marxists.org/reference/archive/althusser/1970/ideology.htm

478. Althusser, "Ideology and Ideological State Apparatuses."

479. Michael Hardt and Antonio Negri, *Commonwealth*. Cambridge, MA: The Belknap Press of Harvard University, 2009. Page 30.

480. Hardt and Negri, *Commonwealth*, 139.

481. Hardt and Negri, *Commonwealth*, 132.

482. See Naomi Klein, *The Shock Doctrine: The Rise of Disaster Capitalism*. New York: Picador, 2008.

483. Hardt and Negri, *Empire*, 84-85.

484. Hardt and Negri, *Commonwealth*, 171.

485. Latour, "Can We Get Our Materialism Back, Please?" 139.

486. Michael Hardt and Antonio Negri, *Multitude: War and Democracy in the Age of Empire*. New York: Penguin Books, 2004. Page 147.

487. Hardt and Negri, *Multitude*, 148.

488. Carolyn R. Miller, "Genre as Social Action," *Quarterly Journal of Speech* 70 (1984): 151.

489. K. David Harrison, *When Languages Die*, 15.

490. Living Tongues Institute for Endangered Languages, "Ethics," available at http://www.livingtongues.org/aboutus.html, accessed January 28, 2015.

491. Living Tongues Institute for Endangered Languages, "Language Hotspots," available at http://www.livingtongues.org/hotspots.html, accessed on January 28, 2015.

492. Caution: I'm not simply using *motivation* as a way of describing one's interests in doing something. I'm instead using the term in a way similar to how it is employed in the field of generative semantics. In generative semantics *motivation* replaces *prediction*, which is employed in generative grammar. Whereas in generative grammar, the existence of one syntactic structure can be used to predict the existence of another, *motivation* in generative semantics refers to how certain concepts can be linked to other concepts or to grammatical categories by metaphorical or metonymical relationships. Thus, *motivation* addresses both the why and the how of linguistic productivity. My use of *motivation* here addresses the why and the how of epistemic productivity more broadly.

493. Deleuze, *Difference and Repetition*, 30.

494. Deleuze, *Difference and Repetition*, 71.

495. Deleuze, *Difference and Repetition*, 70.

496. Deleuze, *Difference and Repetition*, 71.

497. Daniel Everett, "Cultural Constraints on Grammar and Cognition in Pirahã:," 631.

498. Please remember that addition is to be distinguished from recursion.

499. Hofstadter and Sander, *Surfaces and Essences*, 137.

www.ingramcontent.com/pod-product-compliance
Lightning Source LLC
Chambersburg PA
CBHW051040160426
43193CB00010B/1016